The German Peasants' War and Anabaptist
Community of Goods

McGILL-QUEEN'S STUDIES IN THE HISTORY
OF RELIGION
G.A. Rawlyk, Editor

Volumes in this series have been supported by the
Jackman Foundation of Toronto.

The German Peasants' War and Anabaptist Community of Goods

JAMES M. STAYER

McGill-Queen's University Press
Montreal & Kingston • London • Buffalo

© McGill-Queen's University Press 1991
ISBN 0-7735-0842-2

Legal deposit second quarter 1991
Bibliothèque nationale du Québec

McGill-Queen's Studies in the History of Religion 6
ISSN 1181-7445

Printed in Canada on acid-free paper

This book has been published with the help of a
grant from the Canadian Federation for the Humanities, using funds provided by the Social Sciences and
Humanities Research Council of Canada.

Canadian Cataloguing in Publication Data

Stayer, James M
    The German Peasants' War and the Anabaptist
    community of goods

    (McGill-Queen's studies in the history of religion; 6)
    Includes bibliographical references and index.
    ISBN 0-7735-0842-2

    1. Anabaptists – History – 16th century. 2. Peasants'
    War, 1524-1525. I. Title. II. Series.

    BR855.S83 1991   284'.3'09031   C90-090577-8

This book was typeset by Typo Litho composition inc.
in 10/12 Palatino.

To my father, Raymond R. Stayer

Contents

Acknowledgments

This study began when Professor Hans-Jürgen Goertz of Hamburg University asked me to contribute an essay on Anabaptist community of goods to his collection of short studies of religious communism from the Reformation to the present. My essay was published in German as "Neue Modelle eines gemeinsamen Lebens. Gütergemeinschaft im Täufertum" in Goertz's book *Alles gehört allen. Das Experiment Gütergemeinschaft vom 16. Jahrhundert bis heute* (Munich: C.H. Beck 1984). In the course of writing this piece I came to the realization that community of goods was of much broader significance for Anabaptism, the Reformation and the Peasants' War than had previously been recognized. The topic deserved a book, not just an essay.

Thanks are due to the Social Sciences and Humanities Research Council of Canada for the leave fellowship which supported my research during a 1982–83 sabbatical and for the grant which made possible further work on the topic in the summers of 1986 and 1987. The resources of the Hamburg Universitätsbibliothek, the Zurich Zentralbibliothek, the Hamburg Theological Seminar, the Heidelberg Theological Seminar, the Institute for Swiss Reformation History, Zurich, the Conrad Grebel College Library, Waterloo, Ontario, and, above all, the Mennonite Historical Library, Goshen, Indiana, have been generously at my disposal at different stages of the project. I am grateful to Professor Hans Hillerbrand of Southern Methodist University, the International Research and Exchanges Board (IREX), Princeton, New Jersey, and the Ministerium für Hoch- und Fachschulwesen of the German Democratic Republic for including me in the colloquy on "Radical Currents in the Reformation" in East Berlin and St. Louis in the summer and fall of 1986. As the outcome of that colloquy chapter 6 of my present study was published by *Sixteenth Century Journal Publishers* in Professor Hillerbrand's book *Radical Tendencies in the Reformation: Divergent Perspectives*. An early version of chapter 3 was published in 1988 in the *Mennonite Quarterly Review*. Thanks are due to both publishers for their permission to use these chapters here.

Hans-Jürgen Goertz of Hamburg and John Oyer of Goshen have been most generous with their hospitality and intellectual stimulation, as has Werner Packull of Kitchener-Waterloo, Ontario, whose thorough empirical work is substantially rewriting the narrative of Moravian Anabaptism. Werner Packull has made the most important contribution to the present structure of the book. My series-editor and colleague, George Rawlyk, has been a source of constant support in bringing the manuscript to publication. He and my other colleagues Catherine Brown and Klaus Hansen and my students Geoffrey Dipple, Sonia Riddoch, Laura Gingerich, Teresa Basinski, James Corum, Suzanna Chavez, Victor Thiessen and Barry Mack have all read the manuscript. I thank them for the "honest praise" that authors crave and especially for the candid criticism that authors need. As a pre-computer person who produces primitive handwritten manuscripts, I have been in the hands of the person who produced the typescript from the word processor. It has been a piece of great good luck to have the services of such a pleasant, competent and intelligent secretary as Sharon Judd. All these debts are gratefully acknowledged and I beg indulgence for the ones I have ungratefully overlooked.

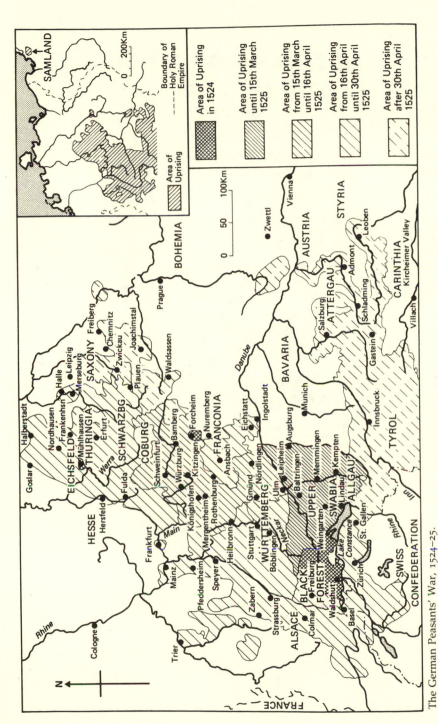

The German Peasants' War, 1524–25.
From *The German Peasant War of 1525 – New Viewpoints* by Bob Scribner
and Gerhard Benecke, reproduced by kind permission of Unwin
Hyman Ltd.

The Twelve Articles of the Peasants, 1525.
Title woodcut from *Buch der Reformation*.
Eine Auswahl zeitgenössischer Zeugnisse (1476–1555),
adapted by Detlef Plöse and Günter Vogler from the edition
of Karl Kaulfuss-Dietsch (Berlin: Union Verlag 1989), 359.
Made available by Hans-Jürgen Goertz.

On the New Transformation of a Christian Life, 1527.
Full t.p., *Hans Hergot und die Flugschrift*
"Von der Newen Wandlung Eynes Christlichen Lebens!,"
facsimile edition, Max Steinmetz
(Leipzig: VEB Fachbuchhandlung 1977), 69.
Made available by Hans-Jürgen Goertz.

An die versamlung gemayner Pawer-
schafft/so in Hochteütscher Nation/vnd vil ande
rer ort/mit empörung vñ aufftrür entstande. ꝛc.
oß jr empörung billicher oder vnpillicher ge
stalt geschehe/ vnd was sie der Oberkait
schuldig oder nicht schuldig seind. ꝛc.
gegründet auß der heyligen Göt-
lichen geschrifft/ von Oberlen-
dischen mitbrüdern gütter
maynung außgangen
vnd Beschriben. ꝛc.

Hie ist des Glückradts stund vnd zeyt
Gott wayst wer der oberist bleybt.

Hie pawrßman
güt Christen.

Hie Romanisten
vnd Sophisten.

Wer merct Schwytz

Der herren gytz.

To the Assembly of Common Peasantry.
Full t.p., *An die Versammlung gemayner Pawerschafft*, 1525,
from Horst Buszello, *Der deutsche Bauernkrieg von 1525 als
politische Bewegung* (Berlin: Colloquium 1969), 152.

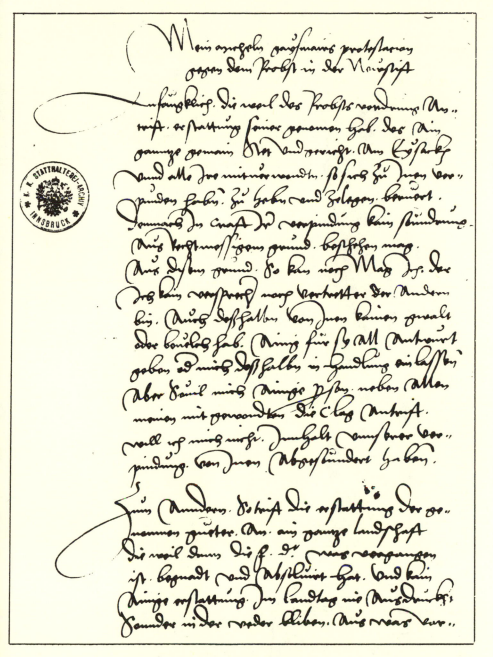

Michael Gaismair manuscript.
Protest against the provost of New Abbey, Brixen,
to Council in Innsbruck, 25 October 1525.
Made available by Walter Klaassen.

Albrecht Dürer, satirical sketch of a memorial column for the Peasants' War. A. Dürer, *Unterweysung der messung* (Nuremburg, 1525), 164. Made available by Hans-Jürgen Goertz.

Selling jewels, etc. for the Münster trek, 1534.
Lambertus Hortensius, *Het boeck … van den oproer der
weder-dooperen …*
(Enkhuizen: J. Lenaertsz Meyn 1614). Courtesy of
Mennonite Historical Library. Goshen College (IN).

Hutterite family before multi-family dwelling.
Full t.p., Christoph Erhard, *Gründliche kurtz verfaste*
Historia von Münsterischen Widertauffern …
(Munich: A. Berg 1589). Courtesy of Mennonite Historical
Library. Goshen College (IN).

Hutterite dovecote in Jesuit polemics.
Full t.p., Christoph Andrea Fischer,
54 erhebliche Vrsachen warumb die Widertauffer ...
(Ingolstadt: A. Angermeyer 1607). Courtesy of Mennonite
Historical Library. Goshen College (IN).

TOMAS MVNCER PREDIGER ZV ALSTET IN DVRINGEN.

Thomas Müntzer portrait.
Christoph van Sichem, *Historische beschrijvinge ende
affbeeldinge der vornemste hooft ketteren*
(Amsterdam: C.v. Sichem 1608). Courtesy of Mennonite
Historical Library. Goshen College (IN).

BALTHASAR HVBMOR DOCTOR VON FRIDBERG.

Balthasar Hubmaier portrait.
Christoph van Sichem, *Historische beschrijvinge ende
affbeeldinge der vornemste hooft ketteren*
(Amsterdam: C.v. Sichem 1608). Courtesy of Mennonite
Historical Library. Goshen College (IN).

JOANNES HVT — IN MERHERN.

Hans Hut portrait.
Christoph van Sichem, *Historische beschrijvinge ende
affbeeldinge der vornemste hooft ketteren*
(Amsterdam: C.v. Sichem 1608). Courtesy of Mennonite
Historical Library. Goshen College (IN).

Bernd Knipperdollinck portrait
from Die Wiedertäufer in Münster. Stadtmuseum Münster.
Katalog der Eröffnungsaustellung, 1 October 1982–
27 February 1983
(Münster: Aschendorff 1983), Kat.-Nr. 122.

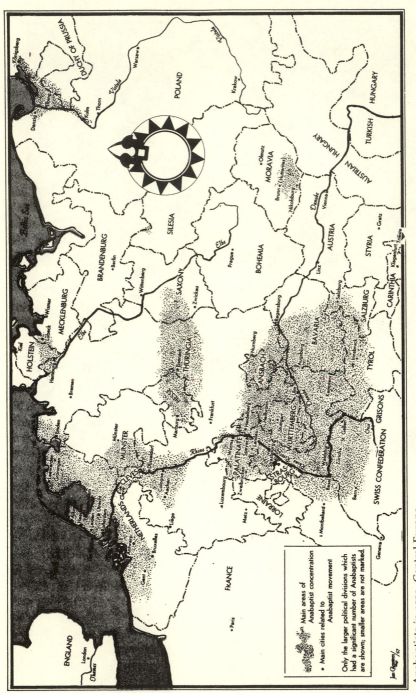

Anabaptists in 1550. Central Europe.
Map by Jan Gleysteen reprinted by permission of Herald Press, Scottdale, PA 15683. From *An Introduction to Mennonite History* by C.J. Dyck. All rights reserved.

The German Peasants' War and Anabaptist Community of Goods

Introduction

The connection between the German Peasants' War of 1525 and Anabaptism, which also began in 1525, is controversial. As recently as 1972 Claus-Peter Clasen in *Anabaptism, A Social History*, a vastly important monument of current Anabaptist research, concluded that there was no significant relationship between the Peasants' War and Anabaptism.[1] The present work undertakes to establish that Anabaptist community of goods, as it was understood and practised in Switzerland, south and central Germany and Austria, territories which experienced the Peasants' War, and Moravia, which received Anabaptist refugees from those lands, owes a crucial, if indirect, debt to the Peasants' War.

After the suppression of the commoners' resistance of 1525 and 1526, only the Anabaptists of the southern Germanic territories continued the defeated rebels' effort to carry out the concrete social commands of the divine law of the Bible. In fact, Anabaptist community of goods represented a pronounced radicalization of the Christian social objectives of the commoners of 1525. In north Germany, which had not experienced the Peasants' War, Anabaptist community of goods was experimented with in Münster during the years 1534–35. However, in Anabaptist Münster the continuing prominence of the governing estate worked against the biblical egalitarianism of community of goods as practised in the south, where the self-assertion of subjects against their masters continued from the Peasants' War into Anabaptism. The élitist distortion of Anabaptist community of goods in Münster indirectly confirms the importance of the egalitarian traditions of the Peasants' War for Anabaptist community of goods as it developed in the south.

In presenting the case for a significant connection between Anabaptism and the Peasants' War, this study does not attempt to identify the two movements with each other. Only a small minority of the participants in the Peasants' War became Anabaptists (and many early Anabaptists did not participate in the Peasants' War). Most of the rebellious commoners were adherents of the Reformation, but the theological differences over the Lord's Supper and baptism which defined the later confessional distinctions between the Lutheran, Reformed and Anabaptist positions were only beginning to take shape in 1524; and most of the commoners who resisted priests and rulers in 1525 were unaware of them. Early Anabaptism was a fringe phenomenon in a few regions of the Peasants' War. Still, as chapter 3 will suggest, the Peasants' War was a formative experience for many, if not most, of the major leaders of the original, non-Melchiorite Anabaptism of the south. Although Anabaptism is not important for understanding the Peasants' War, the Peasants' War is very important for understanding Anabaptism.

The changes in Peasants' War research since 1972 are even more important for this interpretation of the connection between the Peasants' War and Anabaptist community of goods than is new research on Anabaptism. Historians of Anabaptism, it is true, have searched out the cases of Anabaptists and future Anabaptists who participated in the Peasants' War. They have provided the data that is summarized, reviewed and assessed in chapter 3. Yet, if Günther Franz still dominated Peasants' War studies as he did in the early 1970s, the connection between the Peasants' War and Anabaptism would seem a lot more tenuous than it now does.

For Franz, the Peasants' War was primarily a political phenomenon, the culmination of a series of *Bundschuh* conspiracies.[2] Well before the Reformation the *Bundschuh* (an organization named for the peasant laced boot) had introduced the revolutionary slogan of "divine law" to replace the traditional, conservative peasant appeal to the "old law," the established custom of a political territory. Without denying either the role of the Reformation or the participation of townsmen in the Peasants' War, Franz minimized these facets of the event. They are, however, fundamental motifs in the interpretation of Peter Blickle, the most prominent historian in the explosion of new Peasants' War studies that began with the 1975 anniversary.[3]

Claus-Peter Clasen's social history of Anabaptism, for its part, adhered to the hypothesis of earlier interpreters such as Paul Peachey, according to which the original vital Anabaptism of the 1520s was a phenomenon of the towns, only driven by subsequent persecution into the countryside.[4] Drawing primarily on court records, Clasen presented statistical evidence that in the late 1520s, when the number of Anabaptists was greatest, roughly two-thirds of the verifiable Anabaptists of known residence lived in cities and towns. From 1530 onward the balance of Anabaptist population gradually tipped towards villages and farms; but this was the result of the decimation of the town movement through persecution rather than of an absolute numerical increase of rural Anabaptists.[5]

Franz's Peasants' War participants were primarily rural and militant and their objectives were social, economic and political, in other words, secular. Clasen's Anabaptists were primarily urban and nonresistant and their goals were the exclusively religious ones of withdrawn sectarians. Obviously there was no possible point of contact between such disparate movements. The actual specific cases of persons involved both in the Peasants' War and Anabaptism were necessarily random and qualitatively and quantitatively insignificant.

The new Peasants' War historiography of the 1970s and 1980s has reinterpreted the Peasants' War in ways that make it seem much more important for the Reformation and Anabaptism. To anticipate points made in chapter 1, the historiography of the last two decades sees the Peasants' War as a conflict extending beyond the social limits of the peasantry, or even of villagers, to include miners and townsmen. Peter Blickle presents it as a movement of all commoners outside the officeholding estates. Even if we accept Tom Scott's criticism of Blickle – that essential barriers of socio-economic interest kept most burghers of the larger cities and towns, commercial/industrial centres and middling-craft communities apart from the rebels of 1525[6] – the Peasants' War did bring small-town burghers together with miners, village craftsmen and peasants. What occurred in 1525 was no mere peasants' war. The Habsburgs in their previous struggles against the Swiss had used "peasant" as a disparaging epithet for their opponents, well knowing that the social reality was much more complex. If we rearrange Clasen's statistics, grouping the small-town burghers with the rural residents as was the case in the Peasants' War, 60 per cent of the Anabaptists of the 1520s came from social strata implicated in the Peasants' War. Since the persecution of the Anabaptists which produced Clasen's sources was more thorough and efficient in the larger urban centres, certainly a good deal less than 40 per cent of the early Anabaptists lived in communities that stood apart from the Peasants' War.

Among other recent interpreters of the Peasants' War, Henry J. Cohn, Justus Maurer and Franziska Conrad have emphatically seconded the older East German Marxist assertion that there is a fundamental connection between the Peasants' War and the Reformation.[7] They, however, have declined to adopt the East German thesis which holds that the Peasants' War and the Reformation add up to an "Early Bourgeois Revolution in Germany," the forerunner of all modern revolutions. The current recognition of the link between the Reformation and the Peasants' War was facilitated by the discarding of an exclusively theological perspective in Reformation studies. Thomas Brady writes hopefully of the "rehistoricizing of the Reformation."[8] If Luther's theology (considered by most Protestant theologians to be the best Reformation theology) is no longer to be the litmus test of whether someone or something belongs to the Reformation, the way is clear for recognizing that the Peasants' War was the expression of the Reformation in the countryside. As Heiko Oberman put it, the movement of 1525 must be accepted as "basically a religious movement," just like the currents originating in Wittenberg or Geneva.[9]

Oberman, too, stressed that the inner conflict between militance and non-resistance, documented for Anabaptists in my *Anabaptists and the Sword*, had its prehistory among the resisting commoners of 1525.[10] The new Peasants' War historiography stresses elements of legal resistance, carnival mockery and strike among the rebels of 1525. This non-military resistance predominated up to the beginning of April. The rebels' violence was more often against things than persons; the dismantling of a castle could be decorous and orderly, the "sacking" of a monastery could stay within the framework of celebratory rowdiness. The bloody war that began in April 1525 came not from the commoners but from the mercenary armies of the princes. The rulers restored order by violence directed against subjects who had broken the barriers of traditional deference. When historians depict the Peasants' War in such a light, then its connections with the Anabaptists no longer seem strained. The princely officials regarded the Anabaptists of the 1520s as a continuance of the commoners' resistance of 1525. Certainly the nonconformist religiosity of the Anabaptists continued to deny deference to the rich, the rulers and the professionally learned.

The Peasants' War is such a multifaceted, rich historical phenomenon that it cannot be caught in any scholar's formula. Undoubtedly, interpretation of it will continue to be elaborated and revised for a long time; in this respect, at least, it is like the French Revolution. This book's contributions to Peasants' War studies are meant to assess the Peasants' War insofar as it casts a new light on Anabaptist community of goods. The Peasants' War is presented in chapter 1 through the prism of a critical essay on Peasants' War studies in the

1970s and 1980s. Chapter 3 summarizes the growing evidence that the same persons were participants in the Peasants' War and Anabaptists. Not only have the Peasants' War scholars cited in chapter 1 reinterpreted the Peasants' War with the result that it *could* have been very important for Anabaptism, the Anabaptist scholars cited in chapter 3 have delivered empirical proofs that there *were* personal links between Anabaptism and the Peasants' War.

Chapter 2 discusses the major programs of the Peasants' War, analyzing what divine law meant to the rebels of 1525 and 1526. Starting with the fact that lay pamphleteers of the early 1520s required "works of holy mercy" from their evangelical readers, this chapter examines the social Gospel of the Reformation in the period immediately before, during and immediately after the Peasants' War. There is no absolute distinction between Reformation pamphlet literature and Peasants' War programs; to attempt to separate the two categories sharply distorts both the Reformation and the Peasants' War. It is proposed in this chapter that influential pro-Reformation pamphlets helped to define commoners' notions about divine law, and that it was also a Reformation pamphlet that used a communist utopia to crystallize the general bitterness about the way the ruling classes suppressed the commons in the Peasants' War. From 1524 to 1527 a process of radicalization occurred in statements about the social implications and applications of the rediscovery of the Word of God. At first tithes and zins contracts (rents based on the use of money or property) were criticized in a way that would continue among Swiss Anabaptists. Then, with such classical "moderate" statements as the Twelve Articles, divine law came to mean an application of Genesis 1:28–29 to uphold the extensive traditional common property rights of the rural village. After the military suppression of the commoners' resistance had begun, divine law was invoked on behalf of the equality of Christians; for the first time it was interpreted as a rejection of the traditional hierarchy of estates. The next step beyond the rejection of political and social privilege – the rejection of personal property, of "mine and thine" – was taken in early 1527 in the pamphlet *Von der neuen Wandlung eines christlichen Lebens* ("On the New Transformation of a Christian Life"). It is the argument of this book that Anabaptist community of goods was the logical continuation of the social Gospel of the Reformation described in chapter 2, a very radical, albeit non-violent, expression of the commoners' Reformation during and after the suppression of the Peasants' War. Chronologically it was practised in Switzerland before it was called for in the pamphlet literature. In many cases it was the personal contribution of Anabaptist leaders who experienced the early Reformation through the Peasants' War, who were bitterly disillusioned by the way the Peasants' War ended, and who would not resign themselves to becoming hewers of wood and carriers of water under a magisterial Reformation.

While Part I of this study approaches the Peasants' War from various perspectives, all of which inform the interpretation of Anabaptist community of goods, Part II presents a new interpretation of Anabaptist community of goods itself. Valuable studies of the economics of Anabaptism and of Anabaptist community of goods have already been published by Peter J. Klassen and Hans-Dieter Plümper.[11] A subsequent work such as the present one has the obligation to bring something new to the discussion.

Basically, previous studies have assumed that community of goods was "adopted by only a small minority of the Anabaptist movement"[12] and that the typical expression of Anabaptist economics outside of Moravia and Münster was a system of Christian mutual aid that was compatible with private property. These assumptions were the result of the way the various terms were defined.

Menno Simons regarded the community of goods described in Acts 2, 4 and 5 as an exceptional practice of the early church of Jerusalem that had no normative significance for later Christians. The Mennonites of the North Sea and Baltic lands, like the Anabaptists of Switzerland and the Palatinate from 1540 onward, wanted nothing to do with community of goods. For the Mennonites, community of goods carried the odour of Münster; and for the Swiss-south German Anabaptists, community of goods was associated with the Hutterites, who aggressively proselytized their membership.

Naturally, if Anabaptist community of goods is to be defined as some composite photograph produced by blurring together the economic practices of the Moravian Anabaptists and the Münsterites, it was a minority phenomenon. Even in this case, however, it would not be the experience of a "small minority." Historians of Swiss-south German Anabaptism have failed to realize to what extent, after the brutal persecutions of 1528 and 1529, Anabaptism was wiped out in these territories and the focus of Anabaptist history transferred to Moravia, on the one hand, and to Westphalia and the Netherlands, on the other.

The idea that the Hutterites had some sort of patent on Anabaptist community of goods, and that Anabaptists living in a *Bruderhof* (a community of large multi-family households) practised community of goods while Anabaptists who lived in a smaller single-family household did not, runs against what the early Anabaptists actually meant when they spoke and wrote of community of goods. When the early Anabaptists (or Thomas Müntzer) referred to community of goods, they were citing Acts 2 to the effect that the first Christians in Jerusalem "had all things in common" and that "they sold their possessions and goods and distributed them to all, as any had need."[13] In their eyes, it was probably more sensible to interpret the New Testament account in Acts 2, 4 and 5 as describing a process of sharing among single-family households than as something like the common life in a Hutterite *Bruderhof*. For the purposes of this book, I have defined Anabaptist community of goods the same way the early Anabaptists themselves did, namely, as the attempt to put Acts 2 and 4 into practice.

It is argued here that community of goods was at first an endeavour common to all Anabaptist groups. Later, from the 1540s onward, the Swiss Brethren, the Marpeck brotherhood and the Mennonites chose to abandon the objective of realizing Acts 2 and 4, in the course of their self-definition *vis-a-vis* Münsterites and Hutterites. At that time and among those groups, which are outside the limits of this study, it seems proper to think in terms of a transition from Anabaptist community of goods to an economics of mutual aid. The practice of mutual aid within the Anabaptist-Mennonite tradition, and of sharing with needy outsiders, have lived on through the centuries, right up to the ministrations of Mennonites and Brethren to devastated Europe in the wake of the Second World War.[14]

The present study, then, defines community of goods as a general attempt to follow Acts 2 and 4, rather than modelling it upon the specific practices of the Hutterites. In addition, adapting Peter Blickle's stress on the "common man" as the agent of the Peasants' War, it views Anabaptist community of goods as an expression of the economic and religious ethos not of some particular class or estate but of sixteenth-century commoners generally.

Anabaptist community of goods was as much the doctrine of the peasant as the craftsman. If we are to delimit the social inspiration of Anabaptist community of goods further, it would parallel the way Tom Scott describes the social reach of the Peasants' War in his debate with Peter Blickle. The rural and semi-rural groups that supported the uprising of 1525, and not the large or middling towns that stood neutral or opposed, provided the social inspiration for Anabaptist community of goods. Generally, it was not the achievement of the wealthy who successfully manipulated the sixteenth-century market, the rulers who governed the various sorts of polities, the professionally learned who presided over the old and new established churches and their affiliated universities, or those burghers whose town mentality set them apart from rural people. These were the groups of the privileged from whom Michael Gaismair distanced himself in the Tyrolean *Landesordnung* of 1526, one of the Peasants' War programs we shall analyze in chapter 2. Obviously, to define Anabaptist community of goods as the thought and work of commoners, of "ordinary people," opens this interpretation to the accusation of "romantic populism." But, in fact, like the Peasants' War of 1525, Anabaptist community of goods was the work of people who were outside the several élites of their day.

To view Anabaptist community of goods as an expression of the hopes and ideals of rural and semi-rural commoners distinguishes the present interpretation from some of the better recent studies of Anabaptist social and economic belief and practice. Hans-Dieter Plümper and Michael Mullett tend to see Anabaptist community of goods as the expression of an "artisan mentality," the protectionist outlook of small craftsmen.[15] There is much to be said for their argument. The leaders of the Anabaptist groups were primarily craftsmen, who always outnumbered Anabaptist leaders originating from the intellectual professions or the peasantry. An important factor in the background to the Anabaptists' coming to power in Münster was the rivalry of the craft guilds, combined in the United Guild, with the council. The most prominent leaders of Anabaptist Münster were craftsmen. From Jakob Hutter, the hat maker, onward to the Thirty Years' War, all but one of the Hutterite presiding elders were craftsmen. To paraphrase Trotsky, it is accurate to speak of "the leading role of the artisanry" in Anabaptism.

But the artisan leaders of Anabaptism simply articulated the economic and religious ideals of pre-capitalist, pre-industrial rural and semi-rural commoners generally. If we miss that point we are in danger of taking too urban, too "progressive" a view of Anabaptist community of goods and of incorporating it into an extended historicist cliché about the rise of the middle class. Otto Brunner stresses that until the eighteenth century economic thinking concerned itself with the management of the autonomous household rather than with the impersonal laws of the market.[16] The Hutterites conceived of themselves in the sixteenth century as a great extended household, an industrious beehive, to use one of their favourite images. Plümper commented, "The Hutterites have remained loyal into the modern period to the medieval ideal of 'Nahrung,' provision of the necessities of life without striving for luxury."[17] Although the reality of twentieth-century Hutterite life is interlocked with modern economics from agro-business to the stock market, pre-industrial ideals are very strong among them. The ideal of "Nahrung" reappears in the book Paul S. Gross wrote about Hutterites for outsiders. "We are an economic entity," Gross says, "although without any competitive interests beyond providing food and clothing and shelter for ourselves."[18]

The economies of the other, non-Hutterite Anabaptist groups who sought to implement Acts 2 and 4 were centred in single-family households, both among the Swiss and south German Anabaptists and in the polygamous households of Anabaptist Münster. The plan of chapters 4, 5 and 7 is to demonstrate how the Hutterites, as the most prominent and successful Moravian Anabaptist group, eventually absorbed, combined and developed further the community of goods of the Swiss Anabaptists and that of the Anabaptist successors of Thomas Müntzer. Each of the Anabaptist groups described in these three chapters had the Peasants' War in its background.

The Swiss Anabaptists are discussed in chapter 4. They emerged in the midst of the Peasants' War, and they took Christian community of goods to be an expression of divine law. They interpreted Acts 2 and 4 as a law that mandated sharing with the needy and that forbade human exploitation. They saw the church, the body of Christ, as a congregation of commoners who worked with their hands, in which no rulers or rentiers with their special privileges disturbed the unity of the brotherhood.

The south and central German Anabaptists, discussed in chapter 5, had somewhat different antecedents and a different expression of community of goods. Most of their leaders had been involved in the Peasants' War before they were Anabaptists, and they were direct or indirect heirs of the radical anti-materialistic piety of Thomas Müntzer. In Müntzer's eyes, the materialistic élite of his day, the "Big Jacks," made a good spiritual life impossible for commoners because they deprived them of a decent "Nahrung" and thus made subsistence economics an obsession for them. In this way he justified his participation in the Peasants' War. His Anabaptist successors, some of them figures such as Hans Hut and Melchior Rinck who had experienced the battle of Frankenhausen with Müntzer, continued his mystical search for *Gelassenheit*, a "letting go" which enabled them to break free from creaturely attachments.

Chapter 7 treats the Anabaptist refugee community in Moravia, which was eventually dominated by the Hutterite version of community. Anabaptists from all parts of Switzerland, south and central Germany and Austria found a precarious safety in Moravia. The Tyrol, which had experienced an especially fierce version of the

Peasants' War, provided the most influential leaders of Moravian Anabaptist community of goods. Jakob Hutter had been the dominant Anabaptist figure in the south Tyrol before coming to Moravia. The Hutterite genius was their ability to fuse the various earlier expressions of Anabaptist community of goods into a new synthesis. Hutterite community of goods was the divine law in the Swiss manner, but it was animated by the anti-materialist piety of south German *Gelassenheit*. Above all, it made creative use of the dire poverty of Anabaptist refugees in order to transcend the social and economic limitations of the single-family household and to achieve remarkable economic productivity. It is argued here that the Hutterites attained the social goal of Michael Gaismair's Tyrolean peasants, a self-contained, relatively egalitarian society of commoners. This victory of the commons was a conditional one, however, because it did not include political independence. Unable to protect themselves and schooled to leave such matters to God and the Moravian aristocracy, the Hutterites were largely destroyed at the beginning of the Thirty Years' War.

Chapter 6 is in a sense a foreign body in a work aiming to articulate the linkages between the Peasants' War and Anabaptist community of goods, because it treats a case of Anabaptist community of goods which had hardly any connection at all with the Peasants' War. The discussion of Anabaptist Münster and its "war communism" aims to show, however, what a different character Anabaptist community of goods could assume when its social and historical antecedents were radically different from the Peasants' War context of Anabaptist community of goods in Switzerland, south Germany and Moravia. Chapter 6 is a case study of Anabaptist community of goods without the tie to the Peasants' War.

The Anabaptists came to power in Münster in precisely the sort of community that Tom Scott argues persuasively would never have joined the Peasants' War. For reasons connected with the peculiar history and politics of Münster, once the Reformation had generated a large Anabaptist congregation within the walls, a powerful group of local notables decided that it was better to side with the Anabaptists than expel them. So the Anabaptists took power in Münster with a large debt to an urban social élite. In the first months under the prophet Jan Matthijs, as long as the apocalyptic fever focused on Easter 1534 lasted, the early Anabaptist demand for community of goods overrode all else. Later, however, the Münster notables had to be catered to as a condition of the city's continued effective resistance to the army besieging it. The royal court of King Jan of Leyden made a mockery of the egalitarian pretensions of community of goods. Ultimately, community of goods became, on the one hand, a series of practical measures to meet the needs of a city under siege and, on the other, a shabby façade which imperfectly disguised the persistence of gross privilege. Chapter 6 is intended to illustrate how differently Anabaptist community of goods could turn out when there was no tie to the Peasants' War (and instead a significant involvement by a social élite).

Many readers will no doubt be interested in the question of whether or not religious community of goods offers a practical alternative to the dilemmas of modernity. Claus-Peter Clasen, for instance, made it a part of his results to expose the "impracticality" of sixteenth-century Anabaptist social objectives.[19] This study is aimed at illuminating the past, however imperfectly, rather than at prescribing for the present. Undoubtedly, good history, like all forms of good literature, provides food for reflection on the present situation and therefore affects the choices people make about what they should do now. Yet it is doubtful whether historians (or novelists) have any wisdom that gives them a head start on other people. As current literary criticism insists, the text speaks for itself; it is a story which readers can reflect upon further, without an authoritative author's voice to cramp their imaginations.

That said, this interpretation of sixteenth-century Anabaptist community of goods does not intend to reduce the meaning of its topic in the manner of historians who have adopted some variety of historicism. (At the World Congress of Historians in Stuttgart in 1985 a Soviet historian criticized Max Weber for "taking the historicism out of history." What appeared from that Soviet perspective as a damaging objection can seem from another point of view to be a high compliment.) My study does not assume one inexorable historical process leading to the contemporary economic and social order. The Anabaptist ideal of community of goods was neither "progressive" nor "reactionary." It cut through the distinctions between a declining "feudal" socioeconomic order and a rising "capitalist" order, as they are now proposed by Marxist and other historians committed to conceptions of lock-step development into modernity. Here again, the viewpoint of current Peasants' War studies is helpful. Recent historians of the Peasants' War have reacted against traditional views that called rebel objectives "utopian" or impractical, either because they were "ahead of their time" (the Marxist view) or because they were the bizarre projections of distorted idealism (the conservative view). Communal autonomy for the villagers and integration of the villagers and unprivileged towns-people among the politically enfranchised estates of the several ter-ritories were by no means chimerical expectations in the framework of sixteenth-century society and politics. The creation of new Swiss-type confederacies of peasants and townsmen on the borders of Switzerland had been going on for more than a hundred years; there was no inherent reason why it had to stop at the beginning of the sixteenth century, why the Peasants' War could not continue this process.[20] By the same token, there was nothing either backward-looking, forward-looking or unrealistic about Hutterite communi-tarianism and its pragmatic acceptance of limitations which one scholar labels as "Christianity in one country."[21] The Anabaptist ideal of Christian community of goods was informed by the fun-damental hostility of lay supporters of the Reformation towards the luxury and avarice of the clergy. It pronounced judgment on the similar vices of both aristocrats and merchants, without an inkling that twentieth-century democrats and socialists would see the aris-tocrats as "reactionary" defenders of declining feudalism and the merchants as "progressive" forebears of rising capitalism.

Linkage of the Peasants' War with Anabaptist community of goods may seem to some to relegate the religio-theological motives for communitarianism to a secondary, or even marginal, place. This is a misapprehension that must be corrected.

Hans-Jürgen Goertz has shown in his recent general study of the Reformation, *Pfaffenhass und gross Geschrei* ("The Hate of Priests and Much Ado"), how broadly the social theme of anti-clericalism was spread among the various expressions of the Reformation and in what varied guises it could manifest itself. The strength of his inter-pretation is precisely, however, that it is not a reductionist one that makes the Reformation "only" a matter of anti-clericalism. It encom-passes everything that traditional theological scholarship has in-cluded within the Reformation, and at the same time it establishes connections with such phenomena as the Peasants' War and the Knights' Revolt, which earlier were not properly integrated into Reformation history.[22] No categories of an interpreter's mind can do full justice to a broad field of study – or at least this is the lesson that the post-positivist philosophy of science seems to have taught those of us in other disciplines. But if a broad framework of inter-pretation is always to be decried as "reductionist," the result is to assign muddle a positive value, as though it were the distinguishing characteristic of dispassionate, nonideological scholarship.

Theology will always hold a place of significance in Reformation studies. Increasingly this is an insight shared by all Reformation historians, Marxist and non-Marxist alike. As Thomas Brady expressed it, not to have a "firm grasp" of theology is to lack understanding of "the culture and self-consciousness" of the Reformation era.[23] No historians abreast of contemporary trends in historical study would willfully cut themselves off from the language of their epoch. To go further perhaps than Thomas Brady, the champion of the "rehistoricizing" of the Reformation, would go in his concessions to theology, it is possible here to concur with Bernd Moeller that – whatever the one-sidedness of the Reformation studies that dominated the period between the 1920s and the 1960s – we are in their debt for the way they deepened our knowledge of the theology of the Reformers and improved our methodological access to it.[24] But it is unacceptable to assert that a study of the full history of the Reformation, specifically including its social dynamics, somehow marginalizes its theological, or even its religious, substance. This insistence on "pure religious causation" always comes down to a form of idealism. Religious ideas (often formal theological concepts) are taken to be "causes" operating in abstraction from the social or material factors which account for their transmission or reception. There is no fundamental division among secular historians, church historians and theologians on this point. The younger generation of church historians, too, has rejected the notion of separating ideas from social forces and seeing "purely religious causes" as purely ideal causes. In current theological language this is the error of "gnosticism," which separates spirit from body, and it is not only bad secular history but poor church history and poor theology.

The present study deals both with thought and practice, and if anything the balance comes down more heavily on the side of thought. But the effort is made always to situate products of consciousness on a verifiable material horizon. Without a material context there is too little to check and anchor the interpretation of ideas, except for the limits of an author's ingenuity. Non-Marxist Western historians, unlike their Soviet-bloc counterparts, who in the years between 1945 and 1989 were usually materialists in principle, have seldom been idealists in principle. In theory, they have upheld plurality of causation – specifically, "interaction" between ideas and the material structures of human experience. In practice, however, particularly during the Cold War, their approach failed to hold the balance against a *de facto* idealism. Recently, Franziska Conrad, a young scholar introducing her first book, devoted some reflective pages to an appropriate methodology for a topic very much like the present one. Starting with the assumption of an "interaction between objective reality, intellectual processes and action," she aimed to avoid two opposing pitfalls – "on the one hand, a 'sociologism' which fails to do justice to the spiritual and religious components of the Reformation era; on the other, a 'romantic idealism' which assumes from the beginning the hegemony of religion in history."[25] The present study shares her assumptions and seeks to avoid the same pitfalls.

My perspective is neo-liberal. While my earlier work focused on the pluriform character of sixteenth-century Anabaptist experience, this one, without losing sight of the distinct religious culture of the several Anabaptist groups, concentrates on the unity of background among the Swiss-south German Anabaptists and on their common commitment to putting Acts 2 and 4 into practice.

PART ONE

The Peasants' War: Three Essays

CHAPTER ONE

The Peasants' War
Seen through the Prism of
Current Historiography

The uprising of 1525, conventionally named the "German Peasants' War," was a phenomenon whose tangled root system was political, economic, social and religious. It is so difficult to interpret because, to use Freudian language, it was "overdetermined" – it had entirely too many plausible causes, each of them necessary to the shape it took, but none of them quite sufficient to explain it. For the foreseeable future it will be impossible to do more than suggest a "provisional assessment" of the Peasants' War, following the example of Peter Blickle, now the outstanding scholar in the field. Blickle's own "provisional assessment" has provoked extensive scholarly discussion, as did the earlier East German theses "Thesen zur frühbürgerlichen Revolution" – they presented 34 theses on the subject in 1960 about an "early bourgeois revolution in Germany." The arguments of the historians, especially those of the last two decades, will provide the subtext of this chapter, so that the reader can learn about the Peasants' War through the historiographical debate and at the same time gain a critical estimate of that debate itself.

One thing that can be said is that the uprising of 1525 was an event of great importance in German social history. Friedrich Engels called it "the grandest revolutionary effort of the German people."[1] Max Steinmetz, ranking historian of the German Democratic Republic, called it "the most significant revolutionary mass movement of the German people until the November Revolution of 1918."[2] For those who suspect the authenticity of the German revolutionary tradition in the twentieth century, Steinmetz's qualification is no improvement. Engels had it right, in that what occurred in the first half of 1525, according to traditional estimates involving 300,000 persons at its high point and costing 100,000 lives,[3] was the greatest upheaval of subjects against their masters ever in German history (at least prior to the events of 1989, which we lack the historical perspective to assess). Whether it is appropriate to follow Engels and make it the first modern revolution, anticipating Puritan England, Jacobin France, Bolshevik Russia and Maoist China, is another matter entirely.

We are probably stuck with the label "German Peasants' War" for the movement of 1525, although most persons who now write on the topic do not like it at all. The chief ground for its wide acceptance is the lingering authority of Günther Franz, whose book *Der Deutsche Bauernkrieg* ("The German Peasants' War") defined and dominated the field for about forty years after its appearance in 1933. As will be explained in this chapter, the movement of 1525 was no *mere* "peasant" phenomenon, nor was it concerned with a national "Germany," nor was it intended as an act of "war" by the people who began it. These social, political, geographic and military contexts mislead us. Blickle argues that "it is high time to bid farewell to the Peasants' War, or at least to use that word with such discretion that it helps rather than hinders our understanding of the phenomenon of 1525." He proposes that we substitute the "Revolution of 1525,"[4] as Thomas Brady has done already in his writings. It is troubling, however, to call what happened in 1525 a revolution, when it seems so much more akin to England and Wat Tyler in 1381 (an event nobody wants to call a revolution) than to France and Robespierre in 1794. Blickle, of course, defines carefully what he means when he calls the Peasants' War a revolution – that it was a rational, ethical movement for human self-realization.

The approach here will be to avoid extensive discussion of terminology. Given the many different preconceptions that underlie terms such as "revolution," "capitalism," "feudalism" and so on, such discussions tend to be inconclusive. Possibly "Revolution of 1525" *is* better than "German Peasants' War," but it isn't very good; and therefore this chapter and the subsequent ones will use the older, traditional label, striving for the "discretion" that Blickle rightly demands. "Peasants' War" and "Anabaptists" were value-laden expressions in their own day but have now become neutral tags for historians, who can use them with the same ironic detachment as when they write of a "Renaissance" or an "Enlightenment."

First, the "Peasants' War" must be located in time and place.[5] The Peasants' War was primarily a phenomenon of about twenty-four weeks from late January to mid-July 1525, even though it was anticipated by a preliminary rising in the Black Forest, extending through most of the summer and fall of 1524, and had a militant aftermath that stretched into 1526 in the Tyrol and the archdiocese of Salzburg. About one-third of the twenty-four week period, the phase until the last days of March, was mainly non-violent, essentially an armed mass movement of protest aimed at binding negotiations and/or legal redress. Blickle has pointed to the half-political status of the rural "armies" (*Haufen*), which were at the same time assemblies expressing the collective will of a region (*Landschaften*): "autonomous village and urban communes [were] now bound together in 'armies,' which became political rather than chiefly military bodies."[6] They articulated grievances against landlords and rulers, withdrew obedience, refused services and sought arbitration. This period of "phoney war" was more a general strike than a war, although it did sometimes involve the dismantling of fortresses as well as the frequent sacking of monasteries. The villagers did not "take arms," since it was their tradition to be armed for local defence. The groups assembled rather to parley than to fight[7]; and the label "war" is only appropriate for the period beginning with the battle of Leipheim on 4 April, when the princes undertook to disperse or destroy the peasant "armies," often overturning previously negotiated agreements which had settled rural grievances.[8] Typical of this concern with the redress of grievances was the earliest peasant band, thirty-five hundred persons led by the ex-mercenary Hans Müller, which moved through the Black Forest in October 1524: "When they came somewhere they would have their grievances read out, do no harm to anyone but pay for what they ate and drank, and call upon all peasants to back them up in getting justice [*ina zu Recht helfen*]."[9]

The rural resistance assumed a major scale when it spread from the Upper Rhine area to neighbouring Upper Swabia, with the assembly of the tenants of the abbey of Kempten in late January 1525. In the first week in February one of the biggest Upper Swabian peasant assemblages began at Baltringen. During pre-Lenten carnival time (a period when subjects had a traditional licence to mock their betters) groups of armed peasants moved from village to village gathering support in a snowball fashion. When asked what they were doing, they answered that they were exchanging Lenten cakes.[10] By the end of February the Baltringen "army" consisted of thirty thousand persons. The atmosphere of carnival, with much wine consumption, lent a mixture of rural tradition and revolutionary euphoria to the occasion. These vignettes are far removed from the stereotype of murdering and pillaging peasant bands left to us by Luther.

By its high point in May the Peasants' War affected, besides the Upper Rhine and Upper Swabia where it began, Alsace, Württemberg, Franconia, Thuringia and the Tyrol, together with the neighbouring archbishopric of Salzburg. Where the movement spread and where it did not occur are equally significant. It did not touch the north of the Holy Roman Empire of the German nation, the ramshackle political confederation into which the German lands were gathered in the sixteenth century. The geographically limited and late rising in Prussian Samland in September 1525 should not distract us from the specifically south German character of the Peasants' War. However, the Peasants' War had a more basic relation to the structure of the empire than at first appears. Thomas Brady has recently pointed out that the centre of gravity in the empire – the location of all imperial diets, most imperial cities and imperial governing institutions – was in the south, in the area south of the Main River.[11] The northern princes and electors had already well-developed territorial states which put them at a certain remove from the life of the empire. The movement of 1525 crossed the line of the Main into Thuringia and Saxony, but it was essentially a south German phenomenon. The only part of south Germany it did not sweep over was Bavaria, a major territorial principality like those in the north. The main instrument of the eventual suppression of the Peasants' War was the Swabian League of princes, nobles and cities, which, with the Habsburgs, traditionally policed south Germany.

One of the barriers to a convincing theory of economic or social causation of the Peasants' War is the diversity of conditions in the regions where it occurred. For instance, the importance of serfdom and overpopulation has been stressed by historians such as Peter Blickle and David Sabean, whose researches have focused on Upper Swabia, where the movement appeared to "take off" and expand from a merely regional to an imperial concern. The trouble is that serfdom played no role in the uprising in the Tyrol or Thuringia, and that Alsace was apparently not overpopulated.[12] An Upper Swabian "ideal type" offers a seductive coherence in interpreting the Peasants' War. It might be said to offer a non-Marxist counter-model of a "moderate" Peasants' War, against the East German Marxist radical model fashioned on the events in Thuringia, where the uprising began late, in mid April, after patterns of mutual violence between rulers and subjects were already established. However, the recent work of Blickle and Tom Scott on the Upper Rhine region cautions us against pushing this original hearth of the Peasants' War too much to the periphery of a general interpretation.[13] Obviously, a satisfactory approach to the events of early 1525 must sort out differences among the regions affected without following Günther Franz in dissolving the movement into a series of more or less disconnected local episodes. No doubt, in one sense the empirical plurality of what happened in 1525 is inescapable. But historians cannot remain satisfied with mere empiricism. Their function is to unify and interpret, insofar as they can do so and still stay faithful to their source materials.

Given the regional differences of the Peasants' War, general interpretations were doomed to fly off into abstraction. Insofar as he had any common denominator for his Peasants' War, Günther Franz focused upon the peasant appeal to divine law as a standard for arbitration of grievances. The church historian Justus Maurer held that the Reformation was "not only in many respects the cause but in large part the content of the Peasants' War." Heiko Oberman declared that its character as a religious movement may be questioned no more than "in the case of the movements originating in Wittenberg, Geneva and Trent."[14] We will return in due course to these very influential interpretive motifs. Tom Scott, who has written a regional study of the antecedents and course of Peasants' War in the Freiburg area, as well as a number of distinguished review essays on current Peasants' War scholarship, has devoted himself particularly to the critique of Peter Blickle's attempts at a synthesis. He has underscored the continuing importance of Franz's divine law and the growing acceptance of the tie between Reformation and Peasants' War as underlying adhesives for Blickle's apparently multicausal "Revolution of 1525."[15] Scott's view of Blickle's interpretive keys to the Peasants' War has been dour. Scott is, however, an interested party. He has his own motif to give shape to the Peasants' War – early capitalism, a factor that created antagonisms between town and countryside.

Scott infers from the undoubted fact, and apparent paradox, that this "peasants' war" took place in the most urbanized areas of Germany (and was confined to them), that "the revolt was above all a response to fundamental changes in the structure of the German economy which were most acutely felt in the areas of greatest economic activity, specialization of production, technical progress and market integration."[16] At least since the researches of J.U. Nef in the 1940s, the big technical breakthroughs around 1450 in the silver and copper mines of central Europe, often financed by share capital, have been well known.[17] Likewise in the mid-fifteenth century, the organization of the new printing businesses would seem to foreshadow the capitalist distinction between owner-bosses and wage workers. Broadly in this same period merchant capital evaded the rigid control of guilds of townsmen over textile production by organizing and financing textile manufacture by rural cottagers. The first two developments began in central Europe and the third touched it. Marxist historians were the first to interpret the data of economic history as confirming that the transition from the feudal economy to an early capitalist economy occurred in the age of the Renaissance. Marx and Engels, after all, shared with other classically educated western Europeans of the nineteenth century the idea that modern times began with the Renaissance. Engels called the Renaissance "the greatest progressive transformation that mankind had up to then experienced."[18] In the period 1521–1523 the imperial diets were preoccupied not with the Reformation but with the "monopoly question," the privileges and price-fixing of great merchant firms such as those of Augsburg, an issue that was, of course, connected with the exploitation of the mines.[19] Whether this is a sign that hidden market forces were shaping the consciousnesses of the unprivileged commons who joined the armies and assemblies of the Peasants' War, remains open. It is difficult to specify the connections between these instances of economic vitality in early sixteenth-century Germany and the outbreak of either the Reformation or the Peasants' War.

Scott's objection to attempting, in the manner of Franz, Oberman or Blickle, to see the Peasants' War as the outworking of some political or religious ideals is that such an explanation is "ideological."[20] "It really is rather far-fetched to argue that burghers and peasants fought side-by-side in 1525 in the name of a *libertas christiana* based upon their shared commitment to the idea of the Christian community."[21] His goal is to take a structural, economic approach to 1525, as indicated by his recent book on the relations between Freiburg and its Breisgau hinterland in the late middle ages and the sixteenth century. Certainly he gives impressive evidence of the economic factors which predetermined that guildsmen and council in Freiburg would make common cause against the Peasants' War once it occurred. No doubt many craft towns such as Freiburg were alienated from their rural hinterlands by economic rivalries. This may be a partial explanation for the ultimate collapse of the uprising, but what needs to be accounted for is not so much the Peasants' War's failure as the event itself. As the economic history of the regions that experienced the Peasants' War takes on firmer contours, undoubtedly our interpretations of 1525 will be enriched. In the meantime, the invoking of early modern capitalism as an explanation for the Peasants' War can be at best a research frontier and at worst a species of mystification. At least it is not self-evident that political and religious explanations of 1525 should be set aside while we wait for someone to articulate the economic structures behind the Peasants' War.

That said, it is clear that the resisters of 1525 had fiscal and economic grievances against their landlords and rulers. There is a controversy going back to the sixteenth century about whether these peasant grievances accurately reflected their real situation. Were the peasants prosperous or poor? In its twentieth-century form the same issue has reappeared in the disagreement between Marxist and non-Marxist writers as to whether the south German peasants of 1525 were an oppressed or a "rising" class.

Since the Second World War a new quantitative approach to economic history has indicated broad cycles in the economic life of medieval and early-modern Europe. The early sixteenth century is now regarded as a time of rising prosperity and population after the demographic and economic disasters of the fourteenth century, which had terminated the expansion of wealth and population of the High Middle Ages.[22] But a generalization of this sort is not very helpful in determining the prosperity of particular regions and classes or estates.

Marxist and non-Marxist writers are guided, typically, by different sociologies of revolution – the Marxists inspired more by nineteenth-century revolutionary rhetoric, according to which revolutions are by and for the oppressed; the non-Marxists influenced by early twentieth-century theories of the power of élite minorities, which hold that only "rising" classes seize power, something the genuinely oppressed are simply incapable of doing.[23]

John Stalnaker has pointed out in a provocative essay that the purest case of "feudal oppression" of German peasants was to be found in the lands east of the Elbe, which were almost untouched by the events of 1525. He describes Swabia and Franconia, the heartland of the uprising, as experiencing totally opposite conditions from the German northeast:

Like the French Revolution more than two centuries later, the insurrection in Swabia and Franconia involved the collision of 'two rising classes'; ambitious lords and prosperous, assertive peasants. Furthermore, it was a collision sharpened and to an as yet unknown degree shaped by the disturbing influence of the numerous and dissatisfied rural poor. The substantial peasants had secured an enviable position in the villages and vis-à-vis their landlords during the agrarian depression of the fourteenth and fifteenth centuries. Now reaping the fruits of that strategic position with the agricultural prosperity of the later fifteenth and early sixteenth centuries, they were threatened from two quarters: from above by the intrusion of landlords and princes, from below by the growing mass of landless or nearly landless rural poor clamouring for a share of the agricultural prosperity. The essential elements which the social scientists have taught us to expect in an insurrection are here: confidence, hope, 'rising expectations,' confronted by formidable threats to those expectations.[24]

This is a model of interpretation that is explicitly influenced by the non-Marxist sociology of revolution. The substantial peasants of Germany in 1525 were projected into a position structurally similar to that of the French bourgeoisie in 1789. Blickle refers to it as "a general framework that has not been documented": "Stalnaker's hypothesis regarding the clash of two groups competing for the market will not be acceptable until it can be proved that the upswing in agriculture after 1450 took place – and it has not been proved."[25] Blickle seems to have the better empirical case in arguing on the basis of his own studies of Upper Swabia that rural oppression was real enough, not just a mirage produced by the peasantry's rising expectations: "Despite all the statistical difficulties one can probably say this much without completely distorting the situation: gradually, through the fifteenth century, the peasant's position worsened, and this process accelerated in the decades before 1525 because usage rights were restricted, services were increased, and tax burdens fell with full effect on peasant enterprises."[26]

Blickle argues that a "second serfdom" was in the process of being introduced in southwest Germany, less onerous, but not different in kind from that east of the Elbe.[27] Both reversed a tendency towards personal freedom of the more prosperous medieval centuries, and both involved an amalgamation of the rights of landlordship and legal jurisdiction. Blickle shows that 90 per cent of the peasant grievance-lists from Upper Swabia attacked serfdom; and that serfdom was the strongest grievance from the area where the Twelve Articles of Memmingen, the most famous manifesto of the Peasants' War, emerged.[28] Serfdom was stressed by Blickle far more than by previous interpreters of the Peasants' War, who tended to regard it as a peripheral issue. It poses problems for various reasons. Blickle's findings show that in the southwest, unlike the northeast, the function of serfdom was primarily political. On this point Scott's studies of the Breisgau strongly confirm Blickle's research on Upper Swabia.[29] That is, landlords enserfed formerly free peasants in order to consolidate their political power over blocs of territory. There was need and opportunity for this kind of political consolidation only in some of the areas later touched by the Peasants' War. As mentioned previously, serfdom was not among peasant grievances in Thuringia and the Tyrol. Moreover, the "second serfdom" of south Germany was most onerous in the middle of the fifteenth century and was mitigated in the period afterward, thus for the better part of a century before 1525.[30] Undoubtedly, part of Blickle's increasing interest in the connection between the Reformation and the Peasants' War stems from the inadequacy of other ways of accounting for what happened in 1525.

Another aspect of the Stalnaker thesis that attributed the uprising of 1525 to "prosperous, assertive peasants" was the implication that this group was caught in the middle between their landlords and a "growing mass of landless or nearly landless rural poor." No one who studies rural history in this period is about to deny that there was marked social and economic stratification among the villagers. Specifically, David Sabean argues from his study of Upper Swabian population and landholding in the years preceding 1525 that this stratification, worsening with population increase, was the indirect cause of the Peasants' War. He claims that the objective of the movement was to protect the traditional authority of the village commune, through which a landholding peasant élite dominated all aspects of village life, against the encroachments of officials determined to make the rulers' power a reality at the grass-roots level.[31]

In Sabean's analysis, population increase was ultimately responsible for the breakdown of social peace in Upper Swabia. Lacking demographic data for the region he studied, he worked with the assumption that data from the Swiss territories south of Lake Constance were more or less valid for the Upper Swabian territory to its north. Chronicles and other non-quantitative sources tend to confirm that Upper Swabia was at this time experiencing population pressure.[32] In this situation, rather than dividing farms into smaller and smaller acreages, lords and tenant farmers usually kept the farms unified, most often by the practice of *ultimogeniture*, by which the last son inherited the lease on the family farm as a sort of payment for taking care of his parents in their old age. The result was a striking disparity of means between the landholding peasants and brothers and cousins who had to make their living either as landless farm labourers or cottagers, who possessed only a dwelling and a small adjoining plot.[33] The rural poor, either as mercenary soldiers or simple clients of the lord, could become instruments of the aristocracy against the landholding peasants and their village communes. The rulers and their officials, Sabean argued further, were a constant threat to the prevailing system of running the village by and for the peasant landholders. For instance, they could expand their clientage by parcelling out common fields and meadows into small plots for cottagers. These tensions between the peasant élite and the rural poor could very well have prompted the general stress on village autonomy in peasant demands. They might even explain why mercenaries recruited from the rural poor were willing, after well-documented initial hesitations,[34] to slaughter their peasant brothers in the last stage of the Peasants' War.

There are many things wrong with the Sabean thesis when it is applied to the events of 1525. Above all, it is an ingenious chain of hypotheses almost entirely without empirical substantiation. The subjects of the cloister of Ochsenhausen in Upper Swabia did shape a series of articles of grievance in 1525 that reflected the interests of day-labourers and opposed those of landholding peasants, but this single case is the only one that we know about.[35] In general, despite the undoubted stratification, there was no class struggle in the villages in 1525 – instead, there was class solidarity between peasants and craftsmen, rich and poor. Tom Scott remarks that we know of few complaints about lords cutting up the commons into plots for cottagers, but many against their infringing on the commons for their own direct profit. He goes further to suggest that the lords did not frequently cut up the commons to house poor cottagers, because the cottagers were not necessarily the rural poor: "many rural artisans were master craftsmen producing independently for the market, [persons] who could amass considerable wealth, especially if they became middlemen as well." Scott's detailed study of the relations between Freiburg and the Breisgau shows the villages sapping Freiburg's earlier economic advantages throughout the fifteenth century as they developed their own craft industry and their own markets.[36] In this part of the German southwest, population increase was a sign not of misery but of relative prosperity. Finally the very notion of high rural population as an indicator of poverty and misery may be questioned. A genuinely miserable and exploited rural population tends not to reproduce itself, as some studies of medieval Italian peasantry indicate.[37] The high rate of natural increase in Upper Swabia is perhaps an indication that here, as in the nearby Breisgau, there was a measure of opportunity in the crafts for the additional sons who could not become tenants of the indivisible family holdings.

The balance of evidence from the various regions suggests that the rural population had real social and economic grievances about serfdom, rights to hunting, fishing, timber and the commons, and the burden of payments and services owed to both rulers and landlords. Nevertheless, it is true enough that persons genuinely oppressed could not have produced the early manifestations of the Peasants' War – legal actions, negotiations and measured appeals for redress of grievances that marked the conflict's first eight weeks. The resisting commoners had traditional political outlets. The socio-economic explanations of 1525 seem, almost involuntarily, to twist off in a political direction, perhaps an indication that they run against the grain of the events.

Key factors in the villagers' resistance in 1525 were certainly the traditional outlets for political expression they already possessed in south Germany. The most important of these was undoubtedly the village commune. Scott notes that "the overriding importance of the self-governing and self-aware peasant community (*Gemeinde*) as the nucleus and carrier of rebellion throughout western Europe has become a commonplace amongst historians."[38] Among the historians of the Peasants' War of 1525, this consensus embraces Günther Franz, Peter Blickle and David Sabean, despite their other extensive differences. The village communes were very powerful and relatively self-reliant in south Germany in the fourteenth and fifteenth centuries, partly because confused, overlapping and competing jurisdictions among the lords created a vacuum that the villagers had to fill. Blickle's study of late-medieval peasant revolts shows that the areas of strong communes were the lands that experienced uprisings: the alpine lands generally, Alsace, southwest Germany and Franconia. Conversely, in Bavaria, which was largely spared the uprising of 1525 as well as late-medieval revolts, the communes were especially weak.[39] The communes originally supervised cultivation and pasturage, controlled commons and forests, regulated the markets and exercised lesser judicial powers.[40] To one degree or another in the generation before the Peasants' War, this communal autonomy was being eroded as village officials came to regard themselves as servants of the lords set over the villagers rather than as representatives of the localities. Structurally, the Franz-Blickle-Sabean thesis about village communes is very similar to the Moeller thesis about the communes in the imperial cities. Just as for Moeller the Reformation temporarily rejuvenated a declining urban communalism, for them the Peasants' War was a thwarted attempt to revive rural communalism.[41]

Some of the Twelve Articles, such as Article 1, calling for village appointment and dismissal of pastors, Article 2, demanding village control and allocation of tithes, Article 4, which involved village control of water ways, Article 5, which called for village control of forests, and Article 10, on common meadows and fields, were aimed at strengthening the village commune.[42] Certainly, these grievances were directed against the lords, either landlords or princes, who often enough made the village pastor into an arm of their authority like the official, made the tithes into their property, and used water ways, forests, meadows and fields for their profit. Clearly, too, if the Twelve Articles had been put into practice, the result would have been to strengthen the authority of the "natural leaders" of the village, the landholding peasantry, against cottagers and landless labourers. Hence the issue raised by Sabean of whether, behind the resistance to the lords explicit in the peasants' demands, there was an implicit program of class struggle in the villages.

The empirical findings of Peasants' War research indicate that in the south German villages of 1525 communal solidarity prevailed and that there was little or no class struggle. As Thomas Brady remarked about the contemporary situation in the south German cities, an effective ideology could become so ingrained that the commons became its primary defenders.[43] Tom Scott, too, despite his polemic against merely ideological interpretations of the Peasants' War, recognizes the power of ideology in the village of 1525 and in earlier peasant risings: "antagonism towards ruler or landlord seems almost always to have overridden (however temporarily) tensions within the peasant community... Only when economic moderni-zation and social mobility had fully impinged upon the peasantry (in many cases not until the late nineteenth century) did village solidarity finally disintegrate. This may be true, but it ignores the degree of social control which village elders exercised (often quite ruthlessly) over women and youths, immigrants and landless."[44]

The political dimensions of the Peasants' War extended beyond local government, and its social dimensions stretched far beyond the peasantry. Unlike earlier peasant uprisings which mobilized the populations of particular rural lordships, the Black Forest band of Hans Müller and the Baltringen band, both very prominent in the beginnings of the 1524–25 uprising, paid no attention to feudal bor-ders but assembled the subjects of a geographical region. In the Upper Rhine, Upper Swabia, Franconia, Alsace and Thuringia, the bands adopted the medieval practice of a common oath that created a sworn association or confederation.[45]

The Swiss Confederation (*Eidgenossenschaft*) is the outstanding me-dieval example of rural subjects forming such a sworn association. It had previously inspired similar confederations on its frontiers, some of which succumbed once more to feudal lordship, while oth-ers were eventually consolidated with Switzerland.[46] It was politi-cally obvious to regard what was occurring in early 1525 as an attempt to set up "new Switzerlands," certainly in the Black Forest and Upper Swabia and perhaps as far away as Franconia. The manuscript variations of the "League Ordinance" that circulated in the Upper Rhine territories came particularly close to the Swiss model in declaring a perpetual confederation of towns, villages and rural areas ("stetten, flecken vnnd landtschaften").[47]

The theme of imitating the Swiss model – or inviting Swiss expansion – was very strong among the anti-feudal resistance movements in the Reich in 1525. There were more than superficial parallels between the upheaval of 1525 and the Habsburgs' disastrous anti-Swiss war of 1499, in both of which Habsburg propaganda stigmatized the enemy as "peasants," although they stemmed from various estates and classes. Maximilian I, the grandfather of Charles V and Archduke Ferdinand, had declared in 1499 that the Swiss were "crude, wicked, contemptible peasants, who have no virtue, no noble lineage and no moderation."[48] There had long been a proverb hinting at Swiss expansion into Swabia: "when a cow stands on the bridge at Ulm and moos, she'll be heard in the middle of Switzerland." In 1525 the most articulate political pamphlet on the rebel side, *An die versamlung gemayner Pawerschafft* ("To the Assembly of Common Peasantry"), repeated the saying, but with the cow moved north from Ulm to the top of the mythical Schwanberg in Franconia. On its title page stood the provocative jingle: "What makes Switzerland grow? The greed of our lords!"[49]

Yet, in regions where the territorial principality was already well established – temporal states such as Württemberg, Baden and Tyrol and ecclesiastical states such as Salzburg, Würzburg and Bamberg – the Swiss model disappeared. Here the communes and the commons hoped to graft their aspirations for power onto already existing territorial diets and governing councils. The representative assemblies had arisen in the process of "territorialization" as forums for negotiations between the dual powers in each emerging principality: the princes and the politically potent estates. This dualism of prince and estates served the interests of clerics and aristocrats, usually worked to the disadvantage of territorial towns, and generally excluded peasants. But it was not invariably the case that this dual government excluded the rural commoners. In northern Europe, peasants sat in all the Scandinavian national diets. In areas touched by the 1525 upheaval – the Tyrol, the archbishopric of Salzburg and parts of Baden are most prominent – the peasantry had won a place in the territorial diets before 1525, sometimes by armed struggle.[50]

The political programs of the rebels of 1525 aimed to win commoners, peasants and unprivileged townsmen, sometimes miners, a strong place in the diets and governing councils of the territories

– wherever the political territory was sufficiently developed that its institutions could be used effectively for redress of grievances. Often these territorial programs conceded a continuing constitutional role for the aristocracy. The one group that was not to be granted a place in the post-1525 political order was the clergy.[51]

Whether they appealed to Swiss-type confederacies or hoped to divert the dualistic institutions of territorial principalities to their purposes, the political goals of the rebels of 1525 were regional. They had no aspirations, practicable or impracticable, for German national unification. The notion that the peasants had a national program was a misunderstanding of nineteenth-century historians, of the most various political shadings, obsessed by the German national question. It was continued by Günther Franz and Max Steinmetz into the mid-twentieth century, but effectively demolished by the researches of Horst Buszello.[52] When we recognize the regional focus of rebel politics in 1525, it is clear that there was nothing "utopian" about it. This politics was based on widespread, if declining, communal institutions, which sought to extend commoners' power as had been done successfully in the past – either in the Swiss manner or within the dualistic system of prince and estates. The rebels' political agenda was not national and "ahead of its time." It was communal and regional, and whatever illusions it cherished were not those of the future or the past, but the ones current in its own day. Moreover, the southwest German peasantry were by no means completely excluded from the prevailing political order on the eve of the Peasants' War. They had some rights, and they wanted many more. Perhaps the contradiction between significant, though waning, political rights and economic oppression was what distinguished the German southwest from the northeast.

The political objectives of the movement of 1525 lend the primary substance to Blickle's presentation of it as a revolution of the commons, the amalgam of unprivileged estates.[53] According to this view, a movement that began with distinguishably peasant economic grievances articulated itself further by political programs on behalf of all commoners. Except for the absence of national consciousness, we would seem to have a sixteenth-century German precursor of the Third Estate's demand for political representation in 1789 in France. To those interpreters who see what occurred as "the Revolution of 1525," it was no more a "peasants' war" than was Maximilian's campaign against the "Cow-Swiss" in 1499.[54]

They are right. The Peasants' War united all villagers, whether they were peasants or craftsmen,[55] and its leaders were not usually peasants – among them were mercenaries, aristocrats, craftsmen, clergy and government officials.[56] But the fundamental issue is not the social composition of the leadership, nor what estates stood to benefit from the political programs of 1525, but to what extent the towns joined the rural districts in the anti-feudal resistance of 1525.

Here the result is ambiguous. Some imperial cities, particularly in Franconia, succumbed to pressure from their commons and made more or less reluctant alliances with the rebels at the high point of the movement in the spring of 1525.[57] More frequently, the imperial cities offered to mediate; the city councils lost their traditional influence in the Swabian League because of their lukewarm attitude to the military suppression of the commons. The league, for its part, was metamorphized from an alliance between the Habsburgs and the city oligarchs to preserve their mutual interests against the princes into an alliance between the Habsburgs and the princes against the subversion and heresy of the commons.[58] The notion that the "common man in town and country" was in rebellion and needed to be suppressed was that of the Swabian League itself during the crisis.

According to Blickle's very influential interpretation, in the affected regions the rebellion flowed over most "territorial towns" (towns subject to princely authority), and townsmen and miners as well as villagers (not all villagers were "peasants" in an economic sense) made up the rank and file of the rebel armies. Even the term "common man" needs to be widened, since women participated, more frequently in the plundering of cloisters and the intimidation of priests and nuns, but occasionally in military actions, as in the defence of Gmund or the association of Margarete Rennerin with the campaigns of her village neighbour, Jäcklein Rohrbach.[59]

In regions such as the Tyrol, Württemberg and Saxony, where territorialization had progressed, most towns demonstrably made common cause with the rebellion. There was also cooperation between miners and the rebel bands in Saxony, the Tyrol and Salzburg. Still, as Tom Scott insists, the townsmen and miners did not give the same whole-hearted support to the uprising as did the villagers.

Scott argues that Blickle's categories were overly political and constitutional when he came to analyze townsmen's response to the movement of 1525. Regarding the towns, it is important to make socio-economic distinctions among commerical/industrial centres, middling-craft communities and peasant-burgher towns. Commercial/industrial centres, of which Nuremberg and Augsburg were the most prominent, had interests antithetical to those of the rebels of 1525. Peasant-burgher towns, in which the occupations and quality of life were rural, as they were in suburbs outside town walls, had common interests with the villagers. But the large number of territorial towns that were middling-craft communities, such as Freiburg in the Breisgau of which Scott made a detailed study, had anti-rural economic interests. They were run by guilds that found themselves in economic strife with village artisans, who were forever breaking down their monopolies and subverting their privileges.[60]

As a research hypothesis about weaknesses in the rebel front in 1525, Scott's approach has a lot to recommend it. The armies of the Peasants' War, in fact, failed to make effective alliances with the big and middling towns, although they were able to attract recruits from agricultural guilds in those places, for example, the gardeners of Strasbourg or the vine-growers of Freiburg. Moreover, Scott seems correct when he claims – contrary to Blickle – that a town's economic function was more important than its constitutional status in determining whether it could be won to the rebellion. But Scott is less convincing when he insists that, wherever townsmen and villagers were allied in 1525, we must apply "a coherent typology of alliances," distinguishing between true "communities of interest" and "communities of action" that "were often little more than coalitions of convenience, characterized by a pragmatic (or cynical) recognition of mutual advantage."[61] Scott's criterion for a "community of interest" seems to be economic, while political and religious solidarity are dismissed as "ideological" and ineffectual. It is not surprising that, under the microscope of local political and social history, Blickle's "revolution of the common man" appears as a diversity of social and regional groups pragmatically jockeying for position. What is surprising is Scott's implied suggestion that a movement of the dimension of the Peasants' War could be invested with some sort of purer solidarity. Since the victory of the princes in 1525, most learned post-mortems have been inclined to attribute the failure of the commons to some fatal internal flaw rather than to the strength of their adversaries. Perhaps the intractable conflicts of interest between town and country were such a flaw, but they had been overcome in the earlier expansion of the Swiss Confederation, where the established order lacked the political and geographical advantages it enjoyed in the German empire in 1525.

The most universal factor in the Peasants' War of 1525, which distinguished it from the long succession of localized risings before and after it, was its connection with the Reformation. Only the one-sidedly theological and Luther-centered outlook on the German Reformation of a previous generation of scholars has obscured what would otherwise have been obvious.

Luther quite sincerely regarded the commoners' upheaval of 1525 as a carnal perversion of "his" Gospel. What seems bizarre is that Luther's honestly expressed subjective attitude has weighed more heavily in interpreting the Peasants' War, and the Knights' Revolt of 1523, than the self-understanding of the participants. In both cases, the Peasants' War and the Knights' Revolt, the protagonists thought of the enterprise as their contribution to the Reformation. To deny the connection would be very similar to holding that the creation of the French National Assembly in June 1789 and the wave of peasant attacks on manor houses that same summer were separate historical movements. No doubt, the French peasantry did not have exactly the same objectives as the lawyers of Versailles, just as the Reformation of the theologians was different from the Reformation of the peasants. But we must not exaggerate that difference. Luther was exceptional among more or less independent Reformers in denying that the Gospel could become a model for life in the civil world. Other Reformers who did not make such a rigorous distinction between the Gospel and the law, such as Ulrich Zwingli, Martin Bucer and Thomas Müntzer, shared the peasants' assumption that divine law was relevant to life in civil society.[62]

Erasmus of Rotterdam regarded the cause of the peasant movement as monastic exploitation: "Although it seems terrible that the peasants destroyed certain monasteries, the wickedness of the latter provoked them to it, since they could not be controlled by law." Certainly, the Peasants' War in the Alsatian lands adjoining Erasmus's vantage-point in Basel was a "Klosterkrieg," a series of attacks on monasteries.[63] There is a good deal to be said for the recent interpretation of Henry J. Cohn, that economic anti-clericalism was the most important element behind the movement of 1525. The revolt tended to focus in regions where a large proportion of the landlords were clerics, not only Upper Swabia, which Cohn studied most closely, but Württemberg, Franconia, Alsace and Salzburg: "Economic anti-clericalism – antagonism to the economic privileges by means of which the clergy had become a separate order within German society – in my view largely explains why Germany had a major Peasants' War at this time, and why ideas derived from the Reformers had an especial appeal for the rebels."[64]

Anti-clericalism was a traditional factor in peasant upheavals. The majority of peasant revolts in Germany from the mid-fifteenth century to the Reformation had been against clerical landlords. The slogan of the *Bundschuh* in the bishopric of Speyer in 1502 was: "We are struck down with a plague of priests."[65] The Reformation, however, presented an unusually broad and significant setting for the playing out of the traditional peasant social resentment against the clergy.

The tithe focused economic, political and religious discontent on a single issue. The year before the Twelve Articles appeared Otto Brunfels, one of the Strasbourg preachers, anticipated the tithe article by publishing a pamphlet, *Von dem Pfaffen Zehenden* ("On Ecclesiastical Tithes"), to be discussed in the next chapter.[66] To destroy the medieval ecclesiastical tithe in the way Brunfels proposed would have greatly enhanced the political autonomy of the village, given substantial economic relief to its inhabitants and, by undercutting the old hierarchy, opened the way to a religious reformation in accordance with the Gospel and at local initiative. The refusal to pay tithes was widespread in 1523 and 1524. Sometimes, as in the Zurich area, it was associated in a comprehensive program of radical reformation with the replacement of infant baptism by adult baptism; but elsewhere, as in Alsace or in the Memmingen or Nuremberg regions, this connection did not exist. Zwingli and Christoph Schappeler of Memmingen both declared that the tithe was not grounded upon divine law, and that therefore the church had no right to extort it by threat of excommunication. More radical adherents of the Reformation reasoned that, since the tithe was not based on divine law, there was no obligation to pay it.[67] Because tithe revenues were often as large as traditional ground rents, the issue was not a merely theoretical or ecclesiastical one. It pitted peasant tithe-payers against tithe-collectors from monasteries and cathedral chapters, not accidentally the most hated clerical institutions. (Of course, tithes had sometimes been purchased by laymen; but in Upper Swabia, for instance, two-thirds of them remained clerical revenues.)[68]

The evidence Cohn assembled from Upper Swabia sheds light on Erasmus's conception of the Peasants' War as in the first instance a war against the monasteries, parallel to the Knights' Revolt, which was a war upon the ecclesiastical principalities. Upper Swabia was an area of exceptionally large-scale clerical lordship. A sample area in the region between Ulm and Augsburg shows that 45 per cent of the peasants had clerical landlords and 37 per cent aristocratic ones, with the rest holding their land from townsmen or urban institutions. Moreover, in Upper Swabia the revolt began with subjects of the abbot of Kempten, then spread to subjects of the bishop of Augsburg, to other monastic lands and then to the lordships of noblemen.[69] Local resistance movements had occurred previously, against the abbot of Kempten in 1491 and against the abbot of Och-

senhausen in 1502. The monasteries of Upper Swabia were not ordinary landlords; to an extent that set them apart from lay lords,
they squeezed the peasants financially, expropriated them for debt,
attacked their heritable tenure, and reduced them into serfdom. The
monasteries that had undergone reformation in the mid-fifteenth
century, with whatever spiritual benefits to their members, were
simply more zealous and efficient in the arts of financial management.[70]

Günther Franz's traditional interpretation of the Peasants' War
explained its generality by the appearance of the appeal to divine
law among the rebels. Whereas earlier local peasant uprisings had
appealed to the old law, the traditions of their lordship, the rebels
of 1525 set up the standard of divine law, which enabled the movement to jump across territorial boundaries. Although Franz suggested that the Reformation made an appeal to divine law more
topical, he believed that he could identify the same motif in pre-
Reformation *Bundschuh* conspiracies. His approach was to minimize
the connection between the Reformation and the Peasants' War.
Subsequent historians have criticized the artificiality of Franz's distinction between programs appealing to the old law and the divine
law, arguing that in many specific cases it is quite arbitrary to declare
that a particular program does one or the other.[71] Peter Blickle has
indeed used the appeal to divine law as an important part of his
interpretation, but has connected it with the biblicism of the Reformation much more decisively than Franz.

For Blickle, the peasants' appeal to divine law, which was dra-
matically illustrated by the Twelve Articles' principle, that the Bible
would decide whether any current grievance was valid or any new
grievance justified, was the legitimizing principle of the Revolution
of 1525. As long as all grievances had to be grounded on the old
law, or established custom, the peasants could hope for a restoration
of earlier rights perhaps, but not for a far-reaching improvement of
their status. Furthermore, the appeal to the old law normally
weighted a one-sided burden of proof against the peasants. The
divine law was a new, more promising standard to apply to the
adjudication of grievances. This was especially the case since
princely jurists had for some time been applying a law of their own
to new political and social situations to which they felt established
custom did not apply. This was, of course, Roman law, "common
imperial and ecclesiastical law," by means of which a flexible ra-
tionality could be applied to new conditions – on the prince's behalf.
Blickle remarked that the divine law of the Bible was an equally

flexible standard of justice with which the commoner could counter the Roman law of the princes.[72]

Also worth observing is the coincidence of the demand for adjudication by divine law with the emergence of assemblages of peasants from more than one territory. The first call for divine law arose in the Black Forest in early December 1524 when the mercenary, Hans Müller von Bulgenbach, started to assemble peasant followers across territorial borders.[73] As long as the peasants of a single lordship were in direct negotiation with their ruler, the established custom of the territory was an applicable standard. But in the Black Forest, Upper Swabia, Franconia, Alsace and Thuringia, where great peasant bands collected the subjects of many small lordships, a less traditional standard was needed.[74]

So there were pragmatic reasons for invoking the divine law. Nevertheless, its appeal did have something to do with the Gospel of the Reformation. An echo of the sixteenth-century Catholic accusation that the Reformation caused the Peasants' War appears in Paul Herzog's local history of the Schaffhausen peasant uprising of 1524–25.[75] Herzog, like Blickle more recently,[76] identifies the exchanges between Zurich and the rebellious peasants of the Klettgau in October 1524 as the earliest cross-over point between the Reformation's conceptions of divine justice and those of the peasant movement.

In October 1524 Zurich, which had guaranteed the lordship of the ruler of the Klettgau in return for military recruiting privileges among his subjects, received appeals from both ruler and subjects when the uprising in the neighbouring Black Forest threatened to engulf the Klettgau. Zurich told the subjects to maintain their natural obedience to their ruler, and at the same time suggested that they open themselves to the Gospel as proclaimed in Zurich's Zwinglian Reformation. The Klettgauers that same month both accepted the Gospel as proclaimed in Zurich, swearing an oath to God and the saints (!) to uphold it, and declined to provide further services or payments to their lord until he could present them with legal justification of the same.[77] By the year's end they were protesting in the name of God's law against "new, unjust impositions and burdens" – a classic instance of how blurred Franz's categories of old law and divine law could become in actual practice. In March the Klettgauers specified the Old and New Testaments as their standard in all negotiations with their lord: "Because there is no true judge in heaven or on earth other than the Word of God, and our whole cause, action, life and being rest on the Word of God and not on us inconstant, ambitious human beings."[78] When by summer and fall 1525 the peasant resistance in the Klettgau was obviously doomed to suppression by the superior force of the Habsburgs and the Swabian League, the Klettgauers protested that the most important, unnegotiable issue was their newly purified allegiance to the Word of God, and that the most offensive demand in the articles of capitulation presented them was that they should return to "the old Christian order." Zurich stood aside when the Klettgau's version of the Zurich Reformation was suppressed militarily in November 1525.[79]

Paul Herzog concluded from the events in the Klettgau that a general Peasants' War would have been "unthinkable" but for the subversive ideas of the Swiss Reformation, which were in this way injected into southwest Germany.[80] Blickle's point was a more limited one – namely that the close association of the Reformation and peasant programs was widespread. He was challenging the argument that the appeal to divine law was just some rhetoric accompanying the Twelve Articles – at the most a peculiarity of the Upper Swabian Peasants' War, mindlessly repeated due to the widespread reprinting of the Twelve Articles.[81] The traditional German Lutheran point of view presented the earlier Upper Rhine movement as Catholic, citing just such oaths to "God and the saints" as we encountered in the Klettgau situation.[82] Obviously, by late 1525 the Klettgauers had learned to speak the language of the Reformation much more competently.

In general, the movement of 1525 used the language of the Reformation. One of the versions of the Upper Swabian League Ordinance adapted by rebels on the Upper Rhine pledged itself to the preaching of "the Word of God, without any human additions."[83] This was the language of the Reformation, or at least of the transition to the Reformation, in the Swiss and south German towns.[84] The well-known prologue to the Twelve Articles claimed that "the basis of all the articles of the peasants" was "to hear the Gospel and to live accordingly."[85] These ideas were to have a very real, paralytic, effect. One reason why the Baltringers, who were most directly associated with the Twelve Articles, were easily defeated and disbanded in mid April was, no doubt, the pacific notion of their mission, to which their leaders clung, under the guidance of Reformation preachers, until the very last weeks. They claimed that they aimed to create no disturbances; they had decided "to act only in accord with the text and substance of the Word of God, as elucidated and expounded by learned, Christian men."[86] The theological mediators to whom the peasants appealed likewise demonstrated their identification with the Reformation. They were Martin Luther, Ulrich Zwingli, Philip Melanchthon, Andreas

Osiander, Conrad Billican, Matthew Zell and Jakob Strauss.[87] No Catholic arbitrators were proposed; the obvious radical names, Carlstadt and Müntzer, were missing, although Strauss was certainly a maverick figure. On the whole, the universal authority of 1525 was the Word of God as interpreted by the major Reformers. The symbols of authority had changed; earlier peasant uprisings had often appealed to the pope and emperor jointly as the distant universal heads of Christendom. Some peasant banners continued to carry the traditional emblems of earlier revolts, the Virgin and St. John, but more often, besides the *Bundschuh* itself, the symbols of the Reformation replaced them. Now peasant banners contained the figure of Christ, the only mediator, or the letters V.D.M.I.E. (*Verbum Dei Manet/Maneat In Eternum*: "The Word of God Remains in Eternity" or "May the Word of God Remain in Eternity").[88]

The idea that the language the rebels spoke and wrote can be distinguished from their "real motives" or their "real interests" has had a steady appeal to some interpreters on both the idealist and the materialist sides. Tom Scott, one of Blickle's most effective critics, puts the case moderately for a sort of "false consciousness" among the rebels. On the basis of his research of the Breisgau situation he says that he would not deny "the incontrovertible evidence for the spread of reforming doctrines throughout the Upper Rhine," but he wonders "whether the peasants' understanding of these doctrines may not have been as much instrumental – serving the subjective aims of communal defence – as idealistic – committed to objective truths valid for all Christians everywhere." Franziska Conrad, a student of Blickle who made a careful investigation of the Alsatian lands just across the Rhine from the Breisgau, obviously working from somewhat different premises and asking a different question from Scott's, concluded that the peasants' appeal to the Reformation was entirely sincere, and that "the Peasants' War is accordingly the consequence of the new faith among the rural population, who saw in the realization of the Word of God the way to the salvation of their souls and to the honour of God."[89] The linguists who have invaded the historical discipline would deny that historical actors can escape the self-referential framework of the language they use, while sociologists of knowledge would contend that all understanding is instrumental. Once we give the rebels the benefit of the doubt about "subjectively" meaning what they said when they appealed to the Reformation, can we deny Conrad's conclusion?

The fall from the heights of biblical exultation came quickly and brutally. April 1525 marked the high-water mark of the peasant-resistance movement and the beginning of its inexorable military suppression.[90] By the end of the month there was little further basis for peaceful idealism about a new social order based on the Gospel. By late April Franconia, Alsace, Württemberg and Thuringia had joined the Upper Rhine and Upper Swabian heartlands of the rebellion, often republishing the Twelve Articles. But in the same month the Swabian League, with Habsburg support, began its carefully prepared military campaign in Upper Swabia itself. Now in place of the occasional peasant siege of a threatening castle came the operations of an army of well-seasoned *Landsknechte* (German mercenary infantry) under Seneschal Georg of Waldburg, one of Upper Swabia's most propertied noblemen. In the new warlike atmosphere the peasants gradually abandoned their illusions of a negotiated, legal settlement. They undertook the extensive demolition of castles and monasteries which has given them the largely undeserved reputation for destructive violence. As already noted, the dismantling of these potentially hostile strongholds could be a very orderly process, as accounts from Franconia inform us.[91] The peasants undertook ambitious but ineffectual siege operations against major fortresses like that belonging to the bishop of Würzburg or against the Habsburg stronghold of Radolfzell on Lake Constance. Even in this period the commoners' military actions were hesitant and defensive. With the normal double-standard of aristocratic-dominated public opinion, much was made of the "massacre of Weinsberg," an isolated instance of rebel ruthlessness in which noble prisoners were killed after a military action on 17 April. It was considered only fitting that the peasant commander responsible should have been slowly roasted to death when he was captured a month later. Seneschal Georg's army was successful in April, after small-scale fighting, in accomplishing the negotiated disbanding of the Baltringen and Lake Constance groups. This provisional pacification of Upper Swabia freed the league's army for bloody one-sided military operations against the commoners in Württemberg and Franconia in May and June, while Philip of Hesse and Duke Antoine of Lorraine conducted similar massacres of rebels in Thuringia and Alsace in mid May. Now it was war indeed, a massive military response to a general strike that had aimed to change the economic, social and political system more or less non-violently in a legalistic manner. When on 15 July the last remnants of Upper Swabian resistance in the Allgäu fled from Seneschal Georg's triumphant returning army without daring to offer battle, the Peasants' War was over. Later rebellions in the Austrian Alps, beginning in May and June in the bishopric of Brixen in the south Tyrol and in the archbishopric of Salzburg, provided the rebels, now assisted by miners and *Landsknechte*, with their small portion of military glory. Associated with the name of Michael Gaismair, these uprisings were not suppressed until 1526.

The traditional historiography of the Peasants' War, noting the deaths of 100,000 peasants and the large fines following the movement's suppression, assumed that the peasantry of the Holy Roman Empire was finally crushed in 1525, and remained so until the nineteenth century. But on the contrary, a tabulation of research results in 1980 documents sixty-six peasant revolts, some of them quite major, in the empire and the Swiss Confederation between 1525 and 1789. The outbreaks of German popular unrest continued more or less steadily from the beginning of the fourteenth century to the beginning of the nineteenth, even though no other uprising matched that of 1525 in generality, scale and importance. It was to peasant wars what the Great Depression of the 1930s was to economic crises. [92]

It was said until recently by virtually all historians that the beneficiaries of 1525 were the German territorial princes, who consolidated their political absolutism and dominated the churches of the Reformation, which had no further appeal to the commoner. [93] At present there is a consensus, however, that absolutism was a product of the seventeenth and eighteenth centuries, not the sixteenth century. [94] In fact, many of the peasants' economic grievances of 1525 seem to have been responded to. The participation in territorial diets demanded on a great scale by the peasantry in 1525 was achieved in some places, notably in Kempten, where the Upper Swabian movement began, and a number of neighbouring territories. Moreover, in territories such as Baden, Salzburg and the Tyrol, where the diets had schooled the peasants for political resistance, the peasant representation continued after 1525. [95] The instruments of power of sixteenth-century governments were fine for military slaughters like Frankenhausen or Zabern, but there were not resources for anything like a police state. The rulers redressed peasant grievances for the same reason many of them accepted the Reformation – it was unsafe most of the time not to keep one's subjects relatively happy. The age of absolutism did not begin in 1526.

Franz Lau has argued that the older historiography was equally wrong in denying that Lutheranism continued to be a spontaneous popular movement after 1525. He cited ample evidence of the popular imposition of Lutheranism in north German cities after 1525. [96] The obvious point, however, is that popular disillusionment with the Reformation was much stronger in the regions that had direct experience of the Peasants' War than in those that viewed it from a distance. The north German and south German experiences of the Reformation were not synchronized.

Tackling another side of the question, Peter Blickle argues that the events of 1525 proved the politically and socially subversive potential of the Reformation, and that, since it was unthinkable to suppress the Reformation totally, the princes had to gain control of it:

Now the princes had to take over the Reformation. Only if they could bring it under political control could revolt be eliminated root and branch. They had to shear the Reformation of its revolutionary components, which they did by denying the communal principle as a mode of Christian life both in theory and practice... The proof of this is a glance at the history of the Anabaptists. They sought to save the remnant of the communal Reformation by withdrawing from the realm of this world, but the rulers mercilessly exterminated them.[97]

The last statements will be explored in subsequent chapters. It is an exaggeration to describe 1525 as the end of the communal Reformation, even if it did provide – for the reasons Blickle gives – one of the primary impulses for a magisterial Reformation. Among the Reformed in the imperial cities a magisterial Reformation could and did preserve elements of the communal ethos. In the original version of the Moeller thesis, which still has a lot of staying power, the Reformed churches of the Swabian and Alsatian imperial cities, to which Bucer acted as a sort of travelling bishop, continued to legitimate themselves on the basis of communal ideals until the era of the Schmalkaldic War, in which they were the big losers.[98]

So what remains to be said of the "Peasants' War"? Despite its undeniable economic and political facets, which include but are not exhausted by economic anti-clericalism and political anti-clericalism, its most important context was the Reformation. Without the powerful ideas and emotions generated by the Reformation a commoners' protest against the bulwarks of economic and political privilege such as occurred in 1525 would simply have been inconceivable. The military suppression from April onward was all too predictable. What needs explanation is the remarkably peaceful, remarkably widespread social-protest movement of the commoners in January, February and March 1525. No economic, no political factor was general to it in the way the Reformation was. The "Peasants' War" was the form of the Reformation in the south German villages. It was just as much an expression of the Reformation, even though it was short-lived, as the movements stemming from Wittenberg or Geneva. The advocates of a capitalist root cause of the Peasants' War (a mystery of the early-modern market, only waiting to be decoded) view an explanation of it that leans on the Reformation as an appeal to a superficial common denominator. But this "capitalism" is in the sixteenth-century context, for all its materialist (or structuralist) trappings, an ultra-idealist fiction. And *that* the Reformation, with its powerful ideas, was not.

CHAPTER TWO

The Radicalization of the Social Gospel of the Reformation, 1524–1527

The German Reformation was accompanied by a "social Gospel" well before the outbreak of the Peasants' War. It is true that Luther, at least in his 1523 tract *Von weltlicher Oberkeit* ("On Temporal Authority"), had forged a distinction between spiritual and temporal life which implied that the Word of God was not directly relevant to human society.[1] Alert followers, such as Wenzeslaus Link, pastor of Altenburg, digressed from their anti-clerical tirades to warn the followers of the Reformation not to seek a merely "fleshly freedom," as had the Jews who expected a temporal king as their Messiah.[2] However, another face of the Reformation is revealed by Paul Russell's recent analysis of lay pamphleteers lacking a Latin classical education. Such different figures as Hans Sachs, the Lutheran shoemaker from Nuremberg, Haug Marschalck, the imperial army paymaster from Augsburg, and Sebastian Lotzer, the journeyman furrier of Memmingen and the primary author of the Twelve Articles, all wrote pamphlets in 1523 and 1524 which highlighted Christ's social commandments in Matthew 25.[3] Rather than renounce "works-righteousness" for justification by faith alone, these lay advocates of the Reformation wrote that the essence of the Gospel was to replace the ceremonial holiness of the discredited papal cult with the six works of holy mercy that Christ himself had prescribed. Christians should prepare themselves for the last judgment by "providing housing for the poor, giving them food and drink, clothing the naked, caring for the sick, ministering to prisoners and burying the dead." The three self-educated laymen went different ways in the Peasants' War: Marschalck fulfilling his duty to his imperial master by joining in its suppression, Sachs lending his muse to the anti-populist rhetoric of his "Wittenberg nightingale," and Lotzer composing the Peasants' War's most influential programmatic statement. The early years of the Reformation contained many anticipations of the appeals to divine law or Christian Reformation that became the trademark of the rebel programs of 1525 and 1526.

A tract of special interest for the movement of the Reformation from educated humanist circles into the early Peasants' War and early Anabaptism was Otto Brunfels's *Von dem Pfaffen Zehenden* ("On Ecclesiastical Tithes"), published in 1524 in Strasbourg in German although first composed in Latin. Brunfels had fled a Carthusian monastery in 1521 and sought the protection of Ulrich von Hutten, who appointed him to a benefice in the gift of the Hutten family, thus involving him in the system of lay appropriation of tithes. After he had to flee the Rhineland in the course of the Knights' Revolt in 1522, he managed to secure a pastorate in Neuenburg in Breisgau. The Habsburg government intervened against this outbreak of the Reformation in its territories at the same time and for the same reasons that it acted against Balthasar Hubmaier in Waldshut. In February 1524 Brunfels fled to Strasbourg, bringing with him drafts of his tract on tithes, the most extensive one to appear in the Reformation era. He remained in Strasbourg until 1533; his departure was partly triggered by his opposition to the suppression of the Anabaptists there.[4]

The refusal to pay tithes was already widespread at the time Brunfels wrote; for instance, the future Anabaptist Wilhelm Reublin had stirred up hostility to the tithe in the rural environs of Zurich. At the beginning of his pamphlet, Brunfels mentioned the active resistance to the payment of tithes as one of the reasons he had decided to write on the subject.[5] He also stressed that he was writing only against ecclesiastical tithes, not those in the possession of the laity: "I have not denied tithes to princes, lords and nobles, since, if they perform their duties properly, they have a much better right to them than do chapters and monasteries." Futhermore, he wrote, he was not calling on just anyone to act against the tithe system but only the legitimate temporal authority.[6]

A learned treatise of 142 theses, Brunfels's pamphlet repeatedly contrasted Scripture with canon law to the detriment of the latter. To begin with, the tithe lacked any foundation in the New Testament. It was surely commanded in the Old Testament, but was no more a part of the divine law for Christians than circumcision or Old Testament dietary prohibitions.[7] Therefore, the provisions of canon law which extorted tithes on pain of excommunication and damnation were a betrayal of Christ: "Those who compel the poor to pay tithes with their godless, devilish ban, and have no better justification for this than to sing mass seven times daily, are viler betrayers of Christ than Judas, yes worse than the godless priests of Baal."[8] Brunfels's anti-clerical arsenal included references to Lorenzo Valla's literary demolition of the Donation of Constantine and to John Hus, who paid with his life for teaching "that it was against the Gospel for the clergy to have temporal goods."[9]

Besides stressing that the tithe was not a divine command in the New Testament dispensation, but an alms that should flow from voluntary Christian charity, Brunfels was much concerned to distinguish who could properly receive it and who should be denied it. Proper recipients of the tithe were temporal rulers, preachers of the Word of God, the poor and the aged.[10] "If the tithes were sufficient, it would not be a bad idea that they be used for the public welfare, and that the common man should not be further burdened with special taxes ..."[11] Brunfels made it clear that the objectionable clerical tithe-takers were not the working clergy in the parishes, but, above all, the chapters and monasteries. If the Peasants' War did indeed begin as an assault on chapters and monasteries, Otto Brunfels was one of its early cheer-leaders.

For Brunfels, the corruption of the church began when lay people donated large sums to chapters and monasteries with the good intention of helping the poor and establishing schools for the young. But these regular clerics did nothing useful; instead, by amassing benefices "they robbed the parishes, leaving them with small pittances."[12] Brunfels called upon temporal rulers to act against "these idle, rich, fat beggars, who ride on great horses, who collect tithes from all the farms, who grasp and devour the best houses, fields, grasslands and meadows, who skin and steal from the whole world."[13] Originally a collection of Latin propositions offered for reasoned debate, and ostensibly a proposal for intervention by legitimate magistrates, Brunfels's tract was nevertheless a popular manifesto of economic anti-clericalism.

In the same period, 1523 and 1524, the pastor of Eisenach, Jakob Strauss, wrote his tracts against usury. He was third, following Luther and Melanchthon, on the list of Reformers proposed by the Memmingen peasant assembly of March 1525 "for the pronouncement of divine law."[14] His ideas about usury and zins contracts not only anticipated some of the Peasants' War programs but also continued to be lively concerns among early Anabaptists, as we shall see in the case of the Strasbourg notary, Fridolin Meyger, and in the formal disputations between the Reformed pastors and the Anabaptists in the territories of Bern in the 1530s.

Like Brunfels, Strauss eschewed any appeal to violence or direct action by commoners, leaving the suppression of usury to the action of the ruling classes.[15] Given that, he left his popular readership hamstrung, because he insisted, against traditional scholastic teaching, that it was a sin to receive a usurious loan as well as to lend at interest. He declared that in usury the devil murdered the souls both of lender and of borrower.[16] Besides referring to Luke 6:34–35, the traditional text against usury, Strauss stressed the ethical argument that a loan at interest was always an unequal contact – it put the borrower at risk but not the lender, to whom it guaranteed "profit without work and worry."[17] He described the usual zins contract, in which a rich man conferred a piece of property on a poor man in return for yearly payments, and the man who worked the property could free himself from this arrangement only by paying the owner the stipulated capital value of the property. Such a contract, wrote Strauss, was but a thinly disguised instance of usury. Again it was a case of unequal risk; the property owner was assured of his rent in perpetuity unless the peasant could somehow buy the property, but the peasant was subject to all the risks of bad weather, war, illness and tax increases. A fair bargain would be one that secured "the subsistence and maintenance [*narung und undterhaltung*] of the worker" before rent could be collected. Any other contract was "usurious and tyrannical, against God and nature."[18]

Strauss applied his argument not only to the exploited condition of ordinary people but to the alleged exploitation of the rulers themselves by the great merchant companies. He had earlier been a preacher in the Tyrol. Like Friedrich Weigant and Michael Gaismair during the Peasants' War, he was very well abreast of the debates about suppressing the merchant companies, the Fuggers, Welsers, Hochstetters – an issue more prominent even than the Luther affair in the reichstags of the early 1520s.[19] Writing about Jakob Fugger, the Rich, Strauss thundered: "I know very well what I'm saying here. It is unfortunately the case that many great and mighty principalities are burdened right now to the point that, for each one penny per year that the prince receives an important arch-usurer gets ten. I don't have to name that land destroyer because he is well known to the whole world."[20] Strauss ended with the paradoxical juxtaposition of an appeal to non-violence and a prediction of revolution: "There can be no good fruit, no furthering of the Gospel, with crime or violence. There would be no improvement of the world, even if the pope, the bishops, priests, monks and nuns and their whole following were slain and wiped out ... For the words that our lord Christ spoke in Matthew 20 are now at work in many men and women: The first will be last and the last will be first."[21]

The deference to the *Obrigkeit* – the generic term for civil authority in the empire – in these early social applications of the Gospel had its limits. Even Luther had acknowledged that a subject need not follow his ruler into war when he was morally certain that the war was unjust.[22] Wenzeslaus Link did not go beyond a right of passive resistance, but he switched from Luther's emphasis on the ruler's high calling (Romans 13:1–2) to an emphasis on his duty (Romans 13:3–4), a reversal of exegesis usually associated with Thomas Müntzer.

If someone were to say, if [the *Obrigkeit*] has power over my life and goods, it can at its pleasure kill me and take my property, just as it is said that in some countries the people are so subjected that if a nobleman or a prince were to say to his subject: Go hang yourself!, he would have to do it. That would be a bestial, tyrannical system. St. Paul answers this in II Cor. 13, writing that God gave him power in order to improve, not to destroy. In the same way God gives the temporal ruler power only so far as it serves the maintenance and improvement of the public welfare and the peace of his land and subjects.[23]

Rather than being lost in some utopian dream world, the authors of the peasant programs were in general very sensitive to the topical issues of their day – the noisy campaign against the merchant companies, the widespread rejection of tithes, the questioning of the terms on which land was rented, and the hesitant expression of reservations about princely authority. Of course, all of these issues intersected with the great watchword of 1524 and 1525, the exclusive authority of the Word of God as the foundation for all human actions. Since the view that the Word had been newly rediscovered after a long eclipse was widespread in the Germanies at that time, it seemed natural to expect that this rediscovery would have some dramatic effect upon the way people lived.

The Twelve Articles and the League Ordinance, the two printed peasant manifestos that originated from the assembly of the leaders of the united Upper Swabian peasantry at Memmingen in early March 1525, are without doubt the most influential statements of the resisting commoners. It has long been recognized to what a great extent the Twelve Articles served as a model format for subsequent local statements of grievance that remained in handwritten form. Peter Blickle called them the "conceptual glue" that unified the whole

Peasants' War.[24] Recent research by Gottfried Seebass has increased our awareness of the significance of the Memmingen League Ordinance.[25] If not used as extensively as the Twelve Articles, it did serve as a model for various organizational statements of commoners in the Upper Rhine region, and the Letter of Articles, once interpreted as a separate peasant program of a very radical character, now seems to have been an appendix that accompanied the League Ordinance.

The League Ordinance and the Twelve Articles began with statements that underscored their indebtedness to the Reformation. The League Ordinance described the united commoners of Upper Swabia as a "Christian union and league" set up "for the praise and honour of the almighty, eternal God, to call upon the holy Gospel and the Word of God, and to protect justice and the divine law." It mentioned the names of fourteen doctors upon whom it relied to give substance to the principle of divine law, all of them well-known supporters of the Reformation, with Dr Martin Luther in first place.[26] Similarly, the introduction to the Twelve Articles denounced the enemies of the Reformation, who claimed that the new Gospel was a cause of rebellion and disorder. It stated that the Twelve Articles would present a Christian justification of the peasant uprising, declaring that "the basis of all the articles of the peasantry is to hear the Gospel and to live accordingly."[27] Hence the twelfth of the Twelve Articles offered to withdraw any article that was not in harmony with the Bible, and threatened to introduce new demands as the commoners' understanding of the Scriptures improved – not the least radical aspect of this supposedly moderate document.[28]

The pro-Reformation standpoint of the Twelve Articles and the League Ordinance is obvious, but a tradition of denial of the Reformation character of the Peasants' War continued to be strong at least until the 1970s.[29] As indicated, the argument was made that many apparently evangelical statements in the peasant programs were but unthinking repetition of the Twelve Articles, which had themselves been superficially legitimized by proof texts supplied by the Memmingen pastor, Christoph Schappeler. It was also contended that the Peasants' War cut across all confessional parties of the Reformation.

These arguments are incorrect. It is true that occasional references to the saints or to the saying of mass can be found in programs associated with the Peasants' War,[30] sometimes even in these cases inconsistently connected with expressions of support for the Reformation. Nevertheless, the overwhelming majority of the programs, coming from all regions affected by the uprising, use the language of the Reformation. Besides the programs produced by the urban uprisings of Mühlhausen, Frankfort and Erfurt,[31] and the well-known case of Michael Gaismair's *Landesordnung* for the Tyrol,[32] this generalization applies to the Franconian programs, which expressed the "Protestant" character of the commoners' movement in terms still more unmistakable than the Upper Swabian statements. The Tauber Valley program of April 1525 began by declaring that "this common assembly will raise up the holy Word of God, the evangelical teaching, which henceforth will be preached purely and clearly without adulteration by human teaching or additions; and what the holy Gospel raises up shall be raised up, and what it casts down shall be cast down and remain so."[33]

The very term "Reformation" was often used in the programs or in participants' statements to describe the object of the movement. The Tauber Valley program stipulated that "neither zins, tithes, nor taxes of any sort may be paid to any lord, until the learned men have set up a Reformation from the holy, divine, true Scriptures, stipulating how far one is obligated to temporal and spiritual rulers."[34] Heinrich Pfeiffer, interrogated after his capture in May 1525 about the objective he and Müntzer had sought, replied that after all *Obrigkeit* had been destroyed they "wanted to make a Christian Reformation."[35] The Reformation called for by Friedrich Weigant in that same month in Heilbronn responded to the events of the day but at the same time continued the older theoretical format of a project of *Reichsreform*.[36] Thus, the declaration of a "Reformation" combined and confused elements that later centuries would distinguish as religious reformation, social reform and political revolution.[37] The peasant programs reflected the power of the Reformation in their territories and among their following, and at the same time served as a vehicle for the spread of the Reformation into deeper strata of the commons.

The content of the divine law writ into the slogans of the uprising was in part to be left to the determination of the Reformation theologians, but a good deal of it was spelled out in the Twelve Articles and similar documents. Müntzer's disputable statement in his interrogation that "omnia sunt communia" (everything is in common) was almost the sole reference to Acts 2 and 4 in the whole literature of the commoners' uprising. Otto Brunfels, demanding in his tract on the tithe that secular governments restore the clergy to apostolic poverty, skirted over Acts 2 and 4 as a passing phase in the history of the early church and explicitly rejected any literal community of goods.[38] On matters of property the main concern of the Twelve Articles was to advance a religiously grounded rejection of property in people (Article 3), as well as an affirmation of the traditional common property of villagers (Articles 4, 5, 10). Besides that, the arguments of Reformation pamphleteers such as Brunfels and Strauss were adapted for the criticism of tithes and rents (Articles 2, 8). Other articles, such as 6, 7 and 9, involved a much less specific appeal to divine law as a decent, flexible and reasonable protection against the growing demands for labour services, taxes or court costs by landlords and territorial rulers. Here the old law and the customs of older generations could often be appealed to as a standard of how the commons hoped the Reformers would pronounce divine justice.[39]

The attack on serfdom in Article 3, with its appeal to Christ's redemption as a foundation for human freedom, was a radical departure from the learned tradition of Scriptural exegesis, which observed that slavery was taken for granted in the New Testament and therefore continued to defend it until the time of the anti-slavery movement in the eighteenth century. "It has been custom hitherto that we have been regarded as belonging to people [*das man uns für ir aigen leüt gehalten haben*], which is distressful, seeing that Christ redeemed and ransomed us with the shedding of his precious blood – there are no exceptions, from shepherds to persons of the highest rank. Therefore it is mandated in the Bible that we are free and want to be free."[40] Peter Blickle has shown that in local lists of grievances the demand to abolish serfdom was the one with most widespread support throughout Upper Swabia.[41] Perhaps for this reason its ringing appeal to the atonement stands out in the Twelve Articles. Interestingly the Treaty of Ortenau, on 25 May 1525, the result of negotiation between the peasant assemblies of Baden, on the one side, and the Margrave of Baden and the councilmen of Strasbourg on the other, chose to evade the issue of whether or not serfdom was in violation of divine law. Instead it abolished the most offensive practical consequence of serfdom, the restriction upon freedom to marry, and eased regulations regarding the movement of serfs.[42]

To judge from the way it was taken up in other regions, the demand for common use of game, fish, woods, waters and meadows, scattered over three separate articles, was the most prominent grievance of the Twelve Articles. It was based on a widely shared perception that the villagers were subject to worsening economic exploitation by lords and princes; their crops were destroyed by protected game and their water ways, forests and meadows were forcibly expropriated. The divine law seemed to bear with particular force on those encroachments by the Big Jacks against the traditions of the village. Genesis 1:28–29 was cited three times in the Twelve

Articles, for instance: "When the Lord God created people he gave them power over all animals, over the birds in the air and over the fish in the water."[43] The peasants viewed these lower creatures as their common property unless the lord could show that he or his ancestors had acquired them by purchase.

In *To the Assembly of Common Peasantry*, a pro-peasant pamphlet published in Nuremberg in early May 1525, the issue of whether or not the aristocracy could properly claim to own wild animals occupied a central place and was used to illustrate the usurping nature of the rulers, which in turn justified military resistance.[44] The subject of serfdom received only passing mention. There is good reason to think that this pamphlet was of Franconian origin,[45] hence the primary application of Scripture to game rather than to serfdom, which was rare in Franconia. When the rebels in Bamberg were temporarily in control in May, they dictated an agreement that gave them the right to hunt wild birds and animals.[46] Typically, the Ortenau Treaty resulted in a more complex settlement, in which the villages were able to reclaim such fish-ponds and common pastures as they could show to have been extorted from them. The commoners could gather firewood and building wood from the forests, within reason and consistent with the conservation of the forests. Hunting rights, too, were divided, with the peasants receiving an absolute right to protect their crops and domestic animals, but with the choicer game, such as deer, ducks and pheasants, reserved for the aristocracy.[47] The Ortenau settlement of quarrels between villages and lords over forests, waters and commons granted substantial redress of the economic grievances which made the Twelve Articles so relevant to the daily life of the commoners. Still, it must have had a flat taste in the mouths of leaders who wanted "to make a Christian Reformation." In the case of Müntzer, compromises such as the one at Ortenau (he did not live to comment on the Ortenau Treaty itself) probably informed his final disparaging appraisal of the rebellious commoners, that "everyone sought his own profit rather than the justification of Christendom."[48]

In other respects, too, the Twelve Articles pressed for considerable economic improvements for commoners in areas that the Reformation had highlighted, yet within the existing hierarchy of estates. Except for the demand for total abolition of the small tithe on animals and animal products, the second article was fully anticipated in Brunfels's pamphlet. It restricted payment of ecclesiastical tithes to support of a pastor and the village poor, and it recognized the need for the communities to buy back tithes purchased by laymen.[49] Article 8 recommended, in a watered down version of Jakob Strauss's argument, that a tenant burdened with an impossible rent should have it mitigated, "so that the peasant does not have to work for nothing, for every worker is worthy of his wage (Matthew 10)."[50] The Ortenau Treaty agreed with the Twelve Articles on this point and went further, allowing a tenant simply to withdraw from a disadvantageous zins contract by giving the owner three-months notice that he was leaving the property.[51] The Erfurt program of May 1525 was a rare instance in which one of Strauss's ideas – that anyone who had made interest payments sufficient to equal the original capital sum was to be deemed free of all obligation – was taken up. Martin Luther denounced the Erfurt program in general and this provision in particular.[52]

The Ortenau Treaty stands out for its willingness to deal with the commoners' assemblies in the terms that they originally proposed, recognizing that "the assemblies came together without angry or wicked intention, and in no way in opposition to their rulers" and accepting the Twelve Articles as a basis for "amicable negotiation [gütliche underhandlung]."[53] Obviously, among rulers this was a minority response to the relatively peaceful gatherings of February and March. The combination of duplicity, brutality and self-righteousness on the side of their betters naturally led to social and political radicalization among the commons. It was in this historical situation that the traditional hierarchical society was challenged and a much more radical social Gospel emerged than had been visible in the pamphlets of the early 1520s, the Twelve Articles, the Memmingen League Ordinance and the Ortenau Treaty.

One sign of the transition to radicalism can be observed in the numerous articles in the rebel programs devoted to castles and monasteries, the "Schlösserartikel." In early March 1525, in the Memmingen League Ordinance, the concern had been primarily about the military threat posed to the peasant assemblies by castles, although monasteries were mentioned as an afterthought. The nobles who held castles were requested not to equip them with provisions and guns in preparation for siege, nor to occupy them with persons who had not joined the League.[54] The object of the League was at the time limited to taking defensive precautions against surprise actions from the military estate of the sort that later occurred.

A more radical attitude was evident when the Black Forest peasants sent the Letter of Articles to the town of Villingen on 8 May, probably together with their own amended manuscript version of the League Ordinance. The Letter of Articles called for a boycott, – a total breaking off of economic and personal intercourse with the possessors of castles, monasteries and chapters, given that they were the source of "treason, compulsion and destruction" directed against the common people. However, to maintain the possibility of a non-violent settlement of the boycott, nobles, monks and priests were offered the chance to abandon the strongholds, taking with them their movable property, and to join the commoners' "Christian Union." A certain political and social levelling of the privileged estates was implied in the demand that they live in "ordinary houses," but the non-violent resistance of a boycott was preferred to military action.[55] At this stage the commons of 1525 pioneered tactics of non-military resistance borrowed from the medieval ecclesiastical ban and foreshadowing the practices of the nineteenth-century Irish Land League or Gandhi in twentieth-century India.

Adolf Laube and Hans Werner Seiffert regard the Letter of Articles as "the most revolutionary document of this period of the Peasants' War"[56] – an assessment that reveals the continuing influence of M.M. Smirin, who believed that a program with an economic component was necessarily more radical because it approximated later Marxist views of the historical process.[57] In fact, however, this argument is at best misleading. The Letter of Articles (which will be discussed more extensively in chapter 3 in light of its probable Anabaptist authorship) did not go as far toward either military action or levelling of the hierarchy of estates as did the more or less contemporary Tauber Valley program. That program assumed a state of war. It called for the demolition or torching of military strongholds and confiscation of their weaponry, although movable personal property could still be kept by nobles willing to join the commoners' union. Directly connected with this was a demand for the end of privileged estates: "Henceforth all spiritual and secular, noble and common persons shall observe common burgher and peasant law, and not raise themselves above any other common person."[58] When we consider the related statement in Michael Gaismair's Tyrolean *Landesordnung* of early 1526, it is clear how an originally defensive concern about castles evolved into the vision of a realm of commoners stripped of all privileged estates, even that of town burgher: "All city walls, as well as all fortresses in the land are to be broken down, so that there be no more cities but only villages, in order that there be no distinctions among men, and that no one consider himself more important or better than anyone else, for from this may flow dissension, arrogance and rebellion in the whole land. There is to be absolute equality in the land."[59]

Hanging over the social Gospel of the commoners of 1526 and 1527 was a tone absent from the more limited visions of 1524 and early 1525. It was the radical stridency produced first by the unequal war forced upon them and then by the bitterness of defeat. In Michael Gaismair's *Landesordnung* and the subversive pamphlet *On the New Transformation of a Christian Life* we are not far either from Thomas Müntzer's invocation of Acts 2 or from Swiss Anabaptists who would not compromise the unity of the body of Christ and their equality as members by permitting rulers or rentiers to associate with them.

In the very days of the slaughter at Frankenhausen in May 1525 *To the Assembly of Common Peasantry* was printed in Nuremberg and began to be distributed to travelling book dealers before being confiscated by the city government.[60] It gave an unequivocal endorsement of military action against rulers who had not been true to the moral purpose for which God established them, called on the rebels to remain constant in their cause, and promised that God would help them just as he had helped Swiss common folk against their proud aristocratic oppressors:

And so often as the Swiss fought for themselves, for their land, their wives, their children, and had to defend themselves in the face of arrogant power, they usually won the victory and achieved great honour. All that without doubt occurred through the will and power of God, how else could the Swiss Confederation have grown up from three simple peasants? And it still increases daily without abating, so that the insolent arbitrary power and all *Obrigkeit* will have no rest until perhaps the prophecy and old proverb will be fulfilled – that a cow shall stand on the Schwanberg in the land of Franconia and look and bellow, so that it can be heard in the middle of Switzerland. Truly the saying does seem to be true. In this way the proverb may well be fulfilled: for what makes Switzerland grow? The greed of our lords![61]

During the first three months of 1526 a bitter Michael Gaismair, temporarily driven out of his homeland by the Habsburg government's successful tactic of sowing division in the burgher- and peasant-resistance movement, penned his sketch of an egalitarian, liberated Tyrol. At the time he had sought safety in neighbouring Graubünden,[62] whose confederation had been defended within living memory by the greater Swiss Confederation in a brutal war, in which Maximilian, the Habsburg emperor, suffered a humiliating defeat in his attack on the "cow Swiss," the "peasants." Gaismair's Tyrolean *Landesordnung* would, if it had been put into practice, have "increased Switzerland" just as surely as the defence of Graubünden in the Swabian War of 1499.[63] It set out the model of a land of "masterless men" governing themselves, inspired both by the practical example of the Swiss and the divine law of the Reformation.

Gaismair's constitution would have destroyed the hierarchical order of estates in a way that went far beyond social conditions in the real Swiss Confederation of his day. He portrayed a "wholly Christian order" in which "all special privileges will be abolished since they are contrary to the Word of God and pervert justice."[64] This applied in the first place to the privileges of the old church. Religious images were to be destroyed; the chalices and the other precious objects of the churches were to be confiscated by the government and melted down into coins; the mass was to be forbidden; books of scholastic theology and canon law were to be burned. Nevertheless, this was not intended, like similar measures in later revolutions, as dechristianization – the Word of God was to be preached everywhere and the Scriptures made the sole basis of instruction in the land's one university.[65] The privileges of nobles, townsmen and merchants were also to disappear. Like preaching, government and exchange would continue, but as functions performed by ordinary, unprivileged people in the service of the community and subject to a common law. Gaismair foresaw the public expropriation of the silver, copper and salt mines and hoped that their income could support the government of the Tyrol. His statement echoed the general complaints of the time against the great merchant companies (the Fuggers, Hochstetters, Baumgartners and Pimels were mentioned by name), who were denounced as usurious monopolists, exploitative employers and warmongers.[66]

The monasteries would be transformed into hospitals, homes for the aged and orphanages. Gaismair proclaimed an ambitious project for the reclamation of swamp and moorland for agricultural uses, a concentration of craft manufacture under governmental supervision at Trent, and a standardization of weights and measures. Tithes, as in the Twelve Articles, were to provide support for the pastor and parish poor relief. At the head of this polity in Brixen, the Tyrol would be governed by regents elected from all areas of the land and from the mines; they would be advised by three councillors learned in the Scripture and chosen from the university. There were no illusions about immediate peace – a liberated, economically self-sufficient Tyrol would need money for continuing war, and expropriation of emigré nobles was assumed, as was the need for a substantial war treasure, presumably to hire mercenaries as they were needed.[67]

However idealized the Tyrolean state projected in Michael Gaismair's *Landesordnung*, it was intended to be a real, functioning state,

like neighbouring Graubünden and Switzerland, only informed by
the newly discovered Reformation Gospel, and therefore better. Its
principle was the abolition of all *freyhaitten* (special privileges), not
the abolition of individual property.[68]

The step of identifying the abolition of the special privileges of
the estates with the abolition of private property came as a sort of
postscript to the Peasants' War. *On the New Transformation of a Christian Life*[69] was brought to press in Leipzig in late 1526 or early 1527,
after the last peasant armies had disbanded. Its publisher (possibly
its author) was Hans Hergot, who had been Thomas Müntzer's
printer in Nuremberg. He was apprehended, tried and executed in
May 1527 by Duke Georg of Saxony's government.[70]

The *New Transformation* looked back on the Peasants' War as history, reminding the nobility and princes of how frightened they were
in the ten weeks at the height of the rebellion.[71] It called Luther to
account for his bloodthirsty encouragement of the princes: "This
shout has been heard enough: 'Slay and strangle whoever has
hands ...' God says: 'Be merciful, as my Father is merciful to you.'
If that is the mercy of the scribes, I will let the peasants have it, I
can do without it. But, if God is merciful to the scribes in that way,
none of them will enter his kingdom."[72] The accusation that the
scribes would like to forbid the Holy Spirit to speak – "Do you think
that the Holy Spirit will remain forever mute and let himself be
buried as though he no longer has the right to speak?"[73] – shows
how close the author of the *New Transformation* stood to Thomas
Müntzer. Like Müntzer, he warned his readers that it was high time
to take refuge with God, who would now remove the tares from
the wheat.[74]

What the Holy Spirit was expected to do specifically was to usher
in the new age (the "new transformation"), which was to succeed
the age of the Father in the Old Testament and the age of the Son
in the New Testament.[75] The tract ended with a parable of three
tables: "There were three tables in the world, the first overflowing
with too much on it. The second was moderately filled with a modest
sufficiency [*bequeme notturfft*]. The third had very little [*gantz
notturfftig*]. Then the people from the abundant table came and
wanted to take the bread from the needy table. From this there arose
a fight and God will upset both the abundant table and the needy
table, and he will establish the middle table."[76] This, too, was
Thomas Müntzer's hoped-for solution for the materialist obsessions
both of those who were too rich and those who were too poor.

The proof text for the age of the Spirit came not from Acts 2 and
4 but from John 10 (especially 10:16): "There will be one shepherd

and one sheepfold." The one elected shepherd of the 144,000 lands of the world, one third of them Latin, one third Greek and one third Hebrew, would mint coins with the inscription *Eyn hirt und eynerley schaffstal* to signify that he had replaced the two shepherds, the emperor and the pope.[77]

When it moved from its grandiose projection of a federated world to the sphere of its basic unit, the *fluer*, the rural field, the *New Transformation* had striking similarities to Gaismair's projected government for the Tyrol and even more startling anticipations of Jakob Hutter's "New Tyrol" in Moravia. The effect of the new era would be "that no man will remain in his present estate, for all will enter one order."[78] This was not only to mean the abolition of the distinction between noble and commoner but also of that between townsman and peasant, as in Gaismair's Tyrol. The new order would be "Protestant," with four of the current seven sacraments reduced to the status of "good works."[79] As in Gaismair's *Landesordnung* there was to be generous provision for the aged and the sick. It was to be a self-sufficient world with food and clothing produced in each agricultural village, which also supervised the common use of woods, water and meadows.[80] More realistically than in Gaismair's Tyrol, the craftsmen were not to be removed from the village to some manufacturing center: "They will have craftsmen such as tailors, shoemakers, weavers of wool and flax, smiths, millers and bakers and whatever will be required in each *fluer*."[81]

But the mark of the new order was that no one would say any longer, "That is mine."[82] "Everything will be in common, so that they will eat from one pot, drink from one keg and be obedient to one man, in so far as the honour of God and the public welfare require it. They will call him a 'parish provider' [*gotshaus ernerer*]. And the people will all work in common, everyone doing what he does best and what he can, and everything will be in common use, so that no one will live better than the other."[83] The parish providers would get together two or three times yearly to organize the collection of the surplus from particularly productive villages into storehouses, for use either in their own land or in other lands.[84]

The *gotshaus ernerer* of the *New Transformation* anticipates the *Diener der Notdurft* who emerged in 1528 among the Anabaptists in Moravia. Likewise, the education of children starting at three or four years of age foreshadows Hutterite practice.[85] Even more important was the stipulation that people would live together in a large assemblage like Carthusian monks.[86] Undoubtedly the main reason the later Anabaptist colonies in Moravia broke away from the traditional pattern of living in single-family houses was the need to shelter large numbers of uprooted refugees. Nevertheless, the utopian tradition growing out of the Peasants' War, which foresaw a new age in which married people would live together in large communities like monks, cannot be entirely disregarded as a possible inspiration for the patterns of living established soon afterwards by Anabaptists in Moravia. For, as the next chapter will show, a striking number of Anabaptists and future Anabaptists, particularly their leaders, did participate in the Peasants' War.

The result of this study of the social Gospel of the commoners, as it flowed into and out of the Peasants' War, cautions against any simple identification of it with Anabaptist community of goods, or against any attempt to efface the distinction between the Peasants' War and Anabaptism. The Peasants' War was a vast movement that, however often or vehemently Luther said otherwise, brought the Reformation to the countryside. Its first peaceful and moderate notions of divine law, as expressed in the Twelve Articles and the Memmingen League Ordinance, aimed only at a religiously justified extension of the political, social and economic rights of the commoners. When the lords bit the extended hand of the commoners, a process of radicalization set in that broke through the traditional deference of subjects and the hierarchical order of the estates, all the more so since the Swiss experience seemed to demonstrate that masterless men could govern themselves. But it was only coincident with the final defeat of the commoners that an unreconciled minority trusted to God to break down the hierarchy of estates entirely, and the order of property together with it. In the historical circumstances of 1526 and afterwards they had to abandon military self-defence; but their conception of the social meaning of the law of God was not moderated by military defeat; instead it underwent a further stage of radicalization.

CHAPTER THREE

Anabaptists and Future Anabaptists in the Peasants' War

In his classic social history of Anabaptism,[1] Claus-Peter Clasen counts only 32 to 37 peasant rebels[2] among the 3,617 Anabaptists he has identified in the years from 1525 to 1529,[3] about one in a hundred. There are some odd omissions: Balthasar Hubmaier, who as pastor of Waldshut enthusiastically endorsed the town's alliance with the rebels, is not one of Clasen's thirty-seven. Subsequent scholarship has turned up some new names. But no large number of known Anabaptists can be identified by name as participants in the 1525 upheaval. Nevertheless, most scholars currently active in Anabaptist studies think that there is a significant connection between Anabaptism and the Peasants' War. John Oyer, Walter Klaassen, Gottfried Seebass, Arnold Snyder, Hans-Jürgen Goertz, Martin Haas, Werner Packull and I have affirmed this position in our publications.[4] It is time to assess how much – or how little – we have proved or plausibly suggested.

Like other radical adherents of the Reformation, the persons who broke with Zwingli and the Zurich magistrates over whether infants or adults should be baptized anticipated some of the socio-economic demands of the peasant resisters. Three of the radicals who challenged Zwingli – Conrad Grebel, Simon Stumpf and Wilhelm Reublin – were also prominent in the campaign against tithes. Stumpf opposed the payment of tithes to his monastic collator, the abbot of Wettingen, as early as 1522, the year of the first open manifestations of the Zurich Reformation. He told his parishioners in the village of Höngg that the monks who collected their tithes were "worthless" persons who had "stolen their sustenance for long enough."[5] In June 1523 Reublin, with explicit support from Grebel, led six villages in the vicinity of Zurich in refusing tithes to the Grossmünster Chapter, which was the major institutional pillar of the Zurich church. The villagers' petition to the Zurich council said that they were "now informed and instructed by the holy Gospel that the tithe was nothing else but an alms, yet it is common knowledge that some of the canons misuse it for useless and frivolous purposes."[6] At the height of the tithe controversy the council investigated the character of Reublin's preaching to his congregation in Witikon and neighbouring villages, and discovered that he had, like Thomas Müntzer and the peasants, extended an attack on the clergy into a denunciation of the lay rulers who protected them. From the theme of the masturbating nun, who would better be decently married, he went on to the "murdering, heretical and thieving priest" and the "stinking patricians and bailiffs," feared so long as they held office: "You pious peasant, you should know how good you are – but then it would not be good for him to find out."[7]

In responding to the tithe controversy of 1523 Zwingli acknowledged that the tithe could not be justified on the basis of "divine law" or "divine justice," but upheld it on the basis of a lesser "human justice" appropriate to sinful human beings.[8] This began the estrangement between him and Conrad Grebel, who condemned the council for its "tyrannical and Turk-like" behaviour in maintaining the collection of tithes.[9] At stake behind the quarrel over the tithe was whether the Reformed church in the rural Zurich territories was to be centrally controlled by the council or transformed into a series of independent congregations locally directed by village communes. The obvious link between the radicals' agenda of reconstituting the church through local direct action and the desire of the 1525 rebels to free local communities from the heavy hand of territorial authority explains how the proto-Anabaptists anticipated articles 1 and 2 of the Twelve Articles.

The most important surviving programmatic statement of these early Zurich radicals was a letter they wrote to Thomas Müntzer in September 1524, a few months before he became a leader in the Peasants' War. They agreed with him on what they regarded as essential to the Reformation, although distancing themselves from his militance, much as Carlstadt did.[10] The letter, apparently composed by Grebel, makes it clear that they opposed the regular system of ecclesiastical benefices as a usurious burden on the poor. They told Müntzer: "If your benefices, like ours, are based on zins contracts and tithes, both of them pure usury, and the whole congregation doesn't support you, please get loose from your benefices. You know very well how a pastor should be nurtured."[11]

The letter addressed to Müntzer at Allstedt, seems never to have reached him. At the time he was taking a journey to Switzerland and southwest Germany that would put him in the Klettgau, the region whose early version of the Peasants' War was so prominently influenced by Reformation ideas from Zurich. The days in late January 1525 when the Zurich radicals defied Zwingli and the council by starting the baptism of adult believers were the same ones during which the Peasants' War was beginning in earnest in the Upper Rhine and Upper Swabian regions. In the Upper Rhine area and south of Lake Constance, spreading Anabaptism and the spreading Peasants' War indisputably intermingled, particularly in border areas between the Swiss Confederation and the empire – Waldshut, the Schaffhausen territories and the lands of the abbey of St Gallen.[12]

Wilhelm Reublin and Johannes Brötli, priest of Zollikon, a village prominent in the 1523 tithe-resistance and the earliest Anabaptist centre in 1525, were two of the first individuals to forge links between a Reformation involving believers' baptism and the peasants' campaign of disobedience against the lords. Both Reublin and Brötli were exiled from Zurich territories because of their agitation for the baptism of adult believers. A debate on baptism before the Zurich council on 17 January 1525 occasioned their exile, and they were probably participants in the first adult baptisms on 21 January.[13] They immediately moved into the rebellious Klettgau, at just the time that Thomas Müntzer's eight-week stay there would have been concluding. The village of Hallau, where they settled, was the scene of recent Swiss territorial expansion, having been conquered from the bishop of Constance by Schaffhausen in 1521. In 1525 it was the hearth of massive political, social and economic discontent. Hallau took the lead in convening the rural subjects of Schaffhausen, probably in February, to present their grievances against serfdom, tithes and compulsory labour services.[14]

Brötli and Reublin usurped the place of the pastor of Hallau, Hans Ziegler, an unpopular man involved in quarrels with his parishioners.[15] While Brötli settled in the inn at Hallau and began to preach, Reublin moved about the region, baptizing burghers of two strategic towns, Schaffhausen and Waldshut.[16] Both Sebastian Hofmeister, pastor of Schaffhausen, and Balthasar Hubmaier, pastor of Waldshut, were sympathetic to an Anabaptist reformation of their towns. Waldshut had been cooperating with peasant rebels since the summer of 1524, and in Schaffhausen the plebeian vinegrowers' and fishermen's guilds pressured the council to implement a radical reformation and economic concessions based on "divine justice."[17] "Virtually the whole population" of Hallau underwent adult baptism.[18] At Easter, Hubmaier and sixty Waldshuters accepted baptism from Reublin, after which Hubmaier baptized most of the town's mature population.[19] As long as the peasants' movement controlled its rural hinterland, the Schaffhausen council temporized with Hofmeister and the vinegrowers and was unable to exercise its authority in Hallau. But by the late summer of 1525 the war was definitely going against the peasants. In a pre-emptive action against the vinegrowers' guild on 9 August, the Schaffhausen council smashed the commoners' opposition, exiled Hofmeister and launched a patrician Catholic reaction which lasted until 1529, when reformation on the Zurich model was instituted in Schaffhausen.[20] The newly assertive council sent an armed party to Hallau to bring Brötli and Reublin "imprisoned, living or dead, into our hands." As the complaint against Hallau later said, the villagers "kept the priests away from our men with violence and weapons."[21] Hallau submitted to Schaffhausen only after the suppression of the Klettgau peasants in November and the Austrian occupation of Waldshut in December. At that time Brötli and Reublin fled Hallau, just as Hubmaier fled Waldshut. Reublin, Brötli and Hubmaier all eventually found their way to Moravia. All three appear in Hutterite writings, Brötli and Hubmaier as Anabaptist martyrs, Reublin in a less favourable light, as we shall see in Chapter 7.[22]

Anabaptist Waldshut sent a contingent to join the Lake Constance peasant army in the siege of Radolfzell, which lasted until the Austrians lifted it on 1 July 1525. Anabaptist Waldshut also gave armed assistance to Anabaptist Hallau in one of its quarrels with its overlords in Schaffhausen.[23] Of these hundreds of militant Anabaptists, only one name appears in Clasen's list of Anabaptists who participated in the Peasants' War – Hans Rüeger, executed in Schaffhausen in 1527.[24] He is included within the framework of Clasen's study because he appears in court records.[25] Obviously, calling the Hallauers individually to account for their religious intercourse with Brötli and Reublin was beyond the resources of the Schaffhausen government. It was enough that the village submitted and paid its fine. Rüeger's execution was justified by his unrepentant Anabaptism and an equally unrepentant partisanship for Cläwi Hainemann, the guild master of the Schaffhausen vinegrowers, who had been in exile since August 1525. As it turns out, Rüeger was a very important member of the Hallau community, and his life is well documented years before his final trial and execution. In December 1525 he was one of the twenty representatives of Hallau who submitted to Schaffhausen and accepted its terms.[26] In May he was one of the three congregational plenipotentiaries who negotiated the dismissal of Hallau's former pastor, clearing the way for Brötli and Reublin.[27] Still earlier, in September 1518 he is listed in papal nuncio Antonio Pucci's record of papal pensioners in the Schaffhausen area, receiving fifteen florins in payment for recruiting Hallauers to join the Swiss soldiers who fought papal battles in Italy.[28] The profile that emerges is of a man of influence in the political and religious life of his village, a "leading layman" who endorsed the connection of the Peasants' War with Brötli's and Reublin's Anabaptism. He had great hopes for the peasants' rebellion – a destruction of the Schaffhausen patriciate, an end of tithes and zins contracts, and a new era when "all things would be common, with everyone sharing with everyone else in a friendly and loving way." He had even bought a house that he could not afford, since "when the Gospel won the day he would not have to pay for the house any longer." Whether this last statement correctly represents Rüeger, who was certainly not a naive man, or was an attempt by his captors to discredit his motives, must remain undecided.

Brötli and Reublin were not the only Anabaptist preachers in this area who availed themselves of the protection of rebellious peasantry. The same was true of Hans Krüsi, a former schoolmaster, who was chosen as pastor by Tablat, a centre of rebellion against the authority of the abbot of St Gallen. Krüsi assured his followers that, according to "God's living Word," they did not have to pay tithes, and he baptized so many that he could not remember them all. Less fortunate than Brötli and Reublin, Krüsi was arrested at night and hurried off to Luzern for execution, after peasants had threatened the fortress in the abbey's territory where he was at first imprisoned.[29]

But by far the most prominent Anabaptist leader who was associated with the Peasants' War while he was an Anabaptist (instead of joining the Anabaptists after the end of the Peasants' War) was Balthasar Hubmaier of Waldshut. A rich source of information about Hubmaier's Waldshut career is Johannes Faber's *Ursach warumb der Widertauffer Patron unnd erster Anfenger Doctor Balthasar Huebmayer zu Wien auff den zehenten Martij Anno 1528 verbrennet sey* ("Cause why Dr Balthasar Hubmaier, the Patron and Founder of the Anabaptists, was Burned at Vienna on 10 March 1528").[30] I have elsewhere examined the credibility of Faber's *Cause* against the background of our present knowledge of the Peasants' War and concluded that its specific claims about Hubmaier's role in the rebellion are not to be dismissed out of hand, although it may not be possible to prove or disprove them conclusively.[31] Faber wrote for the learned community to justify the execution of one of its prominent members, much as others would later feel called upon to discuss the execution of Michael Servetus, *pro* and *contra*. His main point, which does seem extravagant, is that Hubmaier "takes second place only to Luther in being responsible for the sad slaughter of a hundred thousand peasants and the making of many hundred thousand widows and orphans."[32] Since Faber was vicar general for the bishop of Constance and later became bishop of Vienna, his affiliations were Habsburg and papalist, and these loyalties coloured his notions of the Peasants' War. However, he did visit Waldshut in December 1525, immediately after Hubmaier fled before the Austrian troops, and his investigations there formed the basis of his specific allegations.[33]

Recent church historians have found themselves in the awkward position of accepting Faber's account of Hubmaier's actions during the Peasants' War in Waldshut but at the same time denying his circumstantial connection of Hubmaier with the authorship of peasant programs.[34] Waldshut was under threat of Austrian military intervention because of Hubmaier's introduction of the Reformation there. According to Faber, Hubmaier told the Waldshuters that they had the right to remove themselves from Austrian authority, encouraged fortification of the town and himself carried weapons. He also was said to have opposed tithes and zins contracts. He promoted military cooperation between Waldshut and the Klettgau peasants, and preached to the armed peasants when they were in Waldshut "that game, fish, fowls, wine, meadows, woods, etc., were free."[35] On these matters Faber's *Cause* confirms and complements our other historical sources.

Hubmaier's confession in his final trial in Vienna, produced verbatim in *Cause* and universally accepted by subsequent scholarship, contains the admission that he was somehow involved in the drafting of peasant programs: "I elaborated and interpreted the peasant articles that they brought to me from the armed assembly [alternative reading: from Upper Swabia] and led them to imagine that they could be accepted as Christian and just."[36] Thomas Müntzer made a similar admission to his interrogators after the battle of Frankenhausen. But Faber went much further than this. He wrote in *Cause* that he had discovered documentary evidence of Hubmaier's authorship, which the pastor left behind when he fled Waldshut. Faber found a manuscript booklet belonging to Hubmaier that contained eight folios written in his own hand and other pages "written by others but improved upon by him."[37] In another publication, Faber supplied additional data about this booklet, saying that it contained thirty folios,[38] from which we may infer that eight were in Hubmaier's handwriting and twenty-two edited by way of his written insertions. Faber then summarized two documents, one of them clearly the Black Forest peasants' Letter of Articles, whose full text we know from elsewhere,[39] as well as a second that we know only from the summary in *Cause*, referred to by modern scholars as the "Draft of a Constitution."[40] Farther on, Faber continued: "He produced particular peasant articles, circulated in print, which had the consequence that the peasants in Stühlingen and the Klettgau were the first to rise up against their rulers, which was the cause of the pitiable terrible rebellion and slaughter..."[41]

It is not clear whether, as in his foregoing description of the Letter of Articles and the "Draft of a Constitution," Faber was referring to documents he had read in Hubmaier's house or merely, as in many of his other statements, passing on what he had learned from Waldshuters about Hubmaier's activities. At first glance, Faber seems to be contending that Hubmaier was the author of the famous Twelve Articles, since they were usually described as the peasant articles "which circulated in print."[42] The other printed peasant articles were those of the Memmingen League Ordinance, agreed to in Memmingen on 7 March 1525, as a basis for cooperation between the Baltringen, Allgäu and Lake Constance peasant bands of Upper Swabia. Manuscript adaptations of the Memmingen League Ordinance were circulated among armed peasant assemblies on the Upper Rhine, so Hubmaier's confession that he elaborated peasant articles brought to him from the peasant armies of the Upper Rhine (or, according to another reading, from Upper Swabia) seems to fit Faber's statement, whatever its basis. Still, Faber's statement cannot be accepted as it stands. If the printed peasant articles that Hubmaier worked with were ultimately of Upper Swabian origin, they could not, certainly, have provoked the first peasant uprisings of mid 1524 in Stühlingen and the Klettgau as Faber alleged.

Before the work of Günther Franz in the 1930s, it was seriously debated whether the Twelve Articles originated with Hubmaier in Waldshut, as Faber seemed to say, or with Sebastian Lotzer in Memmingen. From Alfred Stern in 1868 to Wilhelm Mau in 1912 a tradition of scholarship took Hubmaier's authorship seriously and tried to prove it.[43] Franz, seemingly decisively, established the case for Lotzer, possibly assisted by the Memmingen pastor, Christoph Schappeler, as the author of the Twelve Articles.[44] In the 1980s the issue was reopened with the discovery by Peter Blickle and Tom Scott of manuscript versions of the League Ordinance in Basel and Karlsruhe, which, unlike the Memmingen printed ordinance, contained statements of grievance summarizing the content of the

Twelve Articles. Blickle argued that an "Upper Rhine League Ordinance," circulating in manuscript, had preceded the editorial work of March 1525 in Memmingen, which then separated the printed statement of grievance, the Twelve Articles, from the printed Memmingen League Ordinance.[45] It seemed an exciting, plausible idea; I have already endorsed it in my published writings.[46] However, it has just now been convincingly discredited by the careful research of Gottfried Seebass on the major texts of the League Ordinance.[47] It was an old assumption, never challenged, that longer manuscript drafts (all of them, as it happened, of Upper Rhenish origin) preceded the two printed editions of the Memmingen ordinance. But both internal evidence and comparison with the narrative of the commoners' resistance make it clear that the printed ordinances from Upper Swabia were adapted and enlarged in various ways by a number of regional editors in the Upper Rhine area. In some versions the enlarged Upper Rhine League Ordinance incorporated within it summaries of the Twelve Articles. If Balthasar Hubmaier had been the author of the Twelve Articles, that would by itself have established a significant connection between Anabaptism and the Peasants' War. But, after Seebass' work, such a conclusion seems more out of the question than ever.

What Faber may have meant was that Hubmaier had a hand in the peasant articles of the League Ordinance, although his elaborations of that document were apparently never printed. Hubmaier's confession seems to confirm such an explanation, even if his role in composing these peasant articles and their weight in the Peasants' War were a good deal less significant than Faber contended. One of the peculiarities of the Upper Rhenish League Ordinances in manuscript, as opposed to the Upper Swabian prints, was their goal of a perpetual confederation of towns, markets and rural territories.[48] This was, of course, organization on the Swiss pattern, and Switzerland had expanded historically by absorbing copy-cat versions of the original confederation, like the one in Graubünden. If Hubmaier contributed this touch to the League Ordinance used by the Black Forest peasantry, he was coordinating it very closely with Waldshut's foreign policy. In order better to protect its Reformation, Waldshut requested in early March 1525 to be accepted under the protection of evangelically inclined Zurich, Basel and Schaffhausen and thus to "turn Swiss."[49] In contributing articles to a regional version of the League Ordinance Hubmaier would merely have been doing something he has long been understood to be doing, defending Waldshut's Reformation with the assistance of its rural neighbours.

In regard to the Letter of Articles and the "Draft of a Constitution," there is no good reason to doubt that Faber saw what he said he saw. It has sometimes been suggested that Hubmaier was merely copying the Letter of Articles and annotating the "Draft of a Constitution."[50] But Faber's description of what Hubmaier did to the "Draft of a Constitution" was that he "improved" (*gebessert*) it.[51] Certainly, the point was that he was taking editorial responsibility for the document, not annotating it in the sense of jotting down detached observations about its contents. Concerning the Letter of Articles, *Cause* says that Hubmaier composed it, indicated that it was written in Waldshut, dated it and sent it to "Hall and other places."[52] In sum, Faber thought he had documentary evidence that Hubmaier was the author of the one peasant program and the editor of the other.

There is a surprisingly broad consensus that the "Draft of a Constitution" was the handiwork of Thomas Müntzer during his stay in the Klettgau.[53] This is not impossible but neither is the case for it a very strong one. Textual comparisons between Faber's summary of the document and Müntzer's writings are necessarily unsatisfactory. The document's topic is the political structure of a *Landschaft*, a territorial assembly of the south German sort, an institution not discussed in Müntzer's known writings. Gottfried Seebass has recently joined those who hold that Müntzer probably wrote the original version of the "Draft of a Constitution."[54] He argues persuasively that the Letter of Articles was the elaboration of one of the sections of the "Draft of a Constitution."[55] Since the Letter of Articles was used publicly by the Black Forest peasants on 8 May 1525, the reference in the "Draft of a Constitution" to the battle of Zabern, which occurred on 17 May, must accordingly have been an editorial addition by Hubmaier. This point serves to demonstrate that Hubmaier was engaged in sympathetic "editing," rather than neutral or hostile "annotating," of the "Draft of a Constitution," but it does not advance the case for Müntzer's original authorship. Still, the proponents of Müntzer's authorship can handily dismiss evidence to the contrary as the result of Faber's paraphrasing and Hubmaier's editorial work. Such arguments are impossible to disprove but neither do they have much positive substance.[56]

If Hubmaier was indeed its editor, the "Draft of a Constitution" does not provide dramatic new insight into his ideas. It received its name because it proposes a process of removing and replacing rulers. The people of each *Landschaft* were to constitute a covenant, brotherhood or union (the terms were used interchangeably) and summon their ruler to join. If he did not comply, the power of government could be taken from him and given to someone else. In choosing a new ruler, the ordinary peasantry were to nominate twelve candidates of whom one would be chosen. In this selection process, members of the aristocracy would be excluded from consideration, or at least they would be given no preference – the text is ambiguous. The new ruler, too, was removable. In case a ruler resisted deposition by his people, he was to be subjected to the general boycott of secular excommunication elaborated upon in the Letter of Articles. If necessary, the new ruler might summon his people to arms or even hire mercenaries to expel the deposed "tyrant."[57]

The idea of getting rid of a tyrannical, "childish" (as Hubmaier referred to Ferdinand of Austria) or otherwise unsuitable (*ungeschickt*) ruler turned up in various circles connected with the Reformation. The statement in the "Draft of a Constitution" that, if subjects failed to depose a bad ruler, "they are becoming accomplices in the ruler's vices,"[58] seems to be echoed in Hubmaier's 1527 statement in *Von dem Schwert* ("On the Sword"), which is also very similar to Zwingli's commentary on Article 42 of the Zurich Reformation disputation of January 1523.[59] Thomas Müntzer voiced the same view when he preached in the rebellious Klettgau and Hegau, saying "that where there were unbelieving rulers there would also be an unbelieving people, so that a proper reordering must occur there."[60] The idea behind the "Draft of a Constitution," that unbelieving rulers should be deposed or else God would punish their subjects for tolerating them, was expressed around this time by Hubmaier, Müntzer and Zwingli. It is probably wrong to think that their ideas on this subject were widely different in the beginning of 1525. Indeed, it seems entirely reasonable to assume that the edited "Draft of a Constitution" summarized in Faber's *Cause* expressed Hubmaier's viewpoint at that time, although how much he and how much others had to do with its composition remains an impenetrable mystery.

If one accepts Seebass's argument that the Letter of Articles expanded upon a theme to be found in the "Draft of a Constitution," Hubmaier becomes its likely author.[61] He edited the "Draft of a Constitution," and then wrote the Letter of Articles in his own hand. There is internal evidence that the text of the Letter of Articles used by the Black Forest peasants was a revised and abridged version of Hubmaier's original.[62] Even so, it provides an adequate basis for comparison with the writings Hubmaier published in Nikolsburg, and the majority of contemporary scholars do find significant textual similarities.[63]

The Letter of Articles (a document that apparently circulated with a version of the League Ordinance) sought to unite the rural assemblies and towns of the Black Forest in a "Christian Union" (a Swiss-type confederation) which would remove financial and other burdens that clerical and lay lords had imposed upon "the poor commoner in the towns and countryside."[64] In harmony with the practice of the peasants in the early weeks of the uprising, the Union wanted to achieve this objective "without any fighting or bloodshed."[65] Its primary device was a sort of general boycott, referred to as "the worldly ban." Holders of castles and monasteries, who had been the main cause of the peasants' misery, were to be placed under this boycott immediately, and to be released from it only if they would withdraw from these strongholds of past oppression.[66] Presumably the castles and monasteries were to be torn down. The secular and clerical lords, as well as anyone who assisted them or refused to join the Christian Union, were to be totally shunned. "Absolutely no intercourse should be maintained or carried on with those who refuse and decline to enter the brotherly Union and to promote the general Christian welfare – neither by way of eating, drinking, bathing, grinding meal, baking, tilling the soil, mowing hay."[67] When Hubmaier, in his Nikolsburg period, wrote of the ban of religious excommunication, he used strikingly similar terms: "The Christians should have no intercourse with such a person – neither in conversation, eating, drinking, grinding meal, baking or in any other way."[68]

Those scholars who regard the part of the Letter of Articles on the "worldly ban" as a natural secular application of Hubmaier's views on religious excommunication have a strong case. Although it is impossible to establish the authorship of these peasant programs in any final, conclusive way, it seems reasonable to conclude that Faber's *Cause* (unless we regard it as a tissue of lies, which no one has yet proposed) makes Hubmaier the probable author of the Letter of Articles and an important editor both of the "Draft of a Constitution" and of one of the versions of the League Ordinance circulating in the Black Forest-Upper Rhine region. All in all, Hubmaier emerges as an important regional leader of the commoners' resistance while he was an Anabaptist, even if he was much less significant than Faber claimed or historians such as Wilhelm Mau undertook to prove. The nineteenth-century myth of heroic individual leadership – whether in the case of Hubmaier or Müntzer – may be inappropriate for a mass movement such as the commoners' upheaval of 1525, but it dies hard.

In some manner connected with Waldshut's participation in the Peasants' War was the Zurich baker Heini Aberli, a long-time radical adherent of the Reformation. Aberli was among the group at the printer Froschauer's house that first broke the Zurich Lenten fast in 1522, and he was one of the cosigners of Grebel's September 1524 letter to Thomas Müntzer. In October 1524 a few hundred Reformation partisans from Zurich organized a volunteer force to assist Waldshut's resistance against the Habsburgs. Apparently a few days after the Zurich contingent reached Waldshut, its humanist secretary, Rudolf Collin, wrote to Aberli requesting his help in organizing reinforcements – "Bestir yourself, with the help and advice of good friends, to send us forty or fifty honest well-armed Christian fellows." We do not know how Aberli responded to this appeal. As one of the first Zurich Anabaptists in early 1525, he did visit Waldshut, and when Hubmaier fled to Zurich after Waldshut's resistance collapsed he took refuge with Aberli.[69]

Schleitheim, so famous in traditional Anabaptist history for its Brotherly Agreement on Seven Articles of February 1527, which John Yoder has convincingly labelled "the crystallization point of Anabaptism,"[70] was one of the rebellious Schaffhausen villages led by Hallau in 1525. In 1525 and afterward it refused to pay its tithes.[71] Reublin likely baptized there[72] and picked it for the 1527 assembly, as he was almost certainly one of the participants in that assembly. Shortly after Michael Sattler and Reublin journeyed from Schleitheim to Horb, Sattler was arrested, while Reublin escaped to become one of the major memorialists of Sattler's martyrdom.[73]

Schleitheim's geographical location within the Christian Union of Black Forest, Schaffhausen and Klettgau peasant villages, which Hubmaier, Brötli and Reublin had turned into a territorial base for Anabaptism for a few months in 1525, certainly suggests connections between the Seven Articles of the Swiss Anabaptists and the articles of the Upper Rhine League Ordinances, as well as the Letter of Articles. That commoners should assemble to draw up articles of agreement was the practice of the Peasants' War, and Article Four of the Seven Articles, the keystone article on *Absonderung*, or Separation, echoes the "worldly ban" of the Letter of Articles.[74] All of this lends support to Arnold Snyder's hypothesis that Michael Sattler's turn to the Reformation was conditioned by the Peasants' War – that he renounced his former monastic status and joined the Reformation when the Black Forest peasant army occupied St Peter's in Staufen in May 1525.[75] The recent scholarly exchange between Snyder and Heinold Fast, both of whom have shown an impressive knowledge of historical sources in trying to disentangle references to two early Swiss Anabaptists named Michael – Michael Sattler and Michael Wüst[76] – is implicitly about the plausibility of connecting Sattler's Anabaptism with the Peasants' War. I do not think that Snyder has established the likelihood that Sattler left his position as prior at St Peter's in connection with the Peasants' War, although that is one possible explanation for his adherence to the Reformation. At most, Sattler was a non-militant peasant sympathizer, but this is only a guess.

Later Anabaptists provided a more important connection between Anabaptism and the Peasants' War than the instances we have examined so far of individuals and communities who were, or might have been, involved simultaneously in Anabaptism and the Peasants' War. The Peasants' War was a much broader historical phenomenon than Anabaptism. Most of its supporters were not involved in the campaign for believers' baptism. Also, it spread faster than Anabaptism, reaching other parts of Switzerland, the Tyrol, Franconia, Hesse and Thuringia before Anabaptism. (The case of Barr in Alsace, where Anabaptism preceded the Peasants' War and helped precipitate it, is a unique exception. There a peasant joined the rebels because the local official was seeking to banish the peasant's wife, an Anabaptist.)[77] In most regions affected by the 1525 uprising, after an interval of some months or years, former peasant rebels became Anabaptists, sometimes prominent ones. This fact permits us to examine the possibility, suggested by Marxist historians and obliquely confirmed by Peter Blickle,[78] that Anabaptism was to some degree a religious after-effect of the Peasants' War.

Heini Soder, from the village of Liestal in rural Basel, is included in Clasen's listing of Anabaptists[79] but not numbered as a participant in the Peasants' War. He never joined an "army" but he played a prominent and typical role in village resistance to higher authority in May 1525.[80] The Liestalers had broken into a cloister and a wine cellar belonging to the Basel cathedral canons and helped themselves to what they found. Soder said that he had not been involved in these goings-on, but had heard his neighbours say that it was reasonable for them to break into the wine cellar, because if they had not done it other peasants would have.[81] So the carnival accompaniments of the Peasants' War were prominent in Liestal. There was also encouragement of the villagers by an earnest priest committed to the Reformation at a time when Catholicism still prevailed in Basel. Some hundreds of Liestal villagers and neighbouring peasants from other Basel territories formed a ring in the manner we read of so often in accounts of the Peasants' War. Soder was chosen as spokesman in the ring. He gave a speech that itemized local grievances against the Basel government, mostly concerning taxes and internal customs dues but also against marriage restrictions connected with servile status. Worst of all from the standpoint of the Basel council, he suggested that the villagers send a letter to the guilds in Basel proposing that guildsmen draw up a statement of their grievances against the government and make common cause with the rural subjects. Soder was reported to have said, "It is our object to present a friendly petition to our rulers. I can't say that this is not against our rulers, because whatever burdens they remit from us result in losses for them. But we do not at all want to combine against our rulers to compel them, overrun them, harm them, take what rightfully belongs to them or throw off their rule."[82] Soder was pardoned after the rural subjects of Basel reaffirmed their allegiance; he reappears in government records as an Anabaptist in 1527 and again in 1533.[83] The Liestal peasant resistance, with its atmosphere of carnival, somewhat hesitant presentation of financial grievances and assurances of non-violent intentions, was a typical episode in 1525. Peasant resisters as well as Anabaptists oscillated between non-violence and militance.

Even in the rural territories of Zurich, peasant uprising sometimes preceded Anabaptism. An uprising in the territory of Grüningen began in late April with the flight of the abbot of Rüti, an enemy of the Reformation. He took some of the monastery's valuables with him, contrary to previous promises to the Grüningers, and thus provoked a mob scene in which twelve hundred villagers spent two days consuming the food supplies and wine stores of the monasteries of Rüti and neighbouring Bubikon. Thereafter sixty representatives of Grüningen drew up a far-reaching statement of grievances, twenty-seven articles in all, which went beyond the content of the Twelve Articles to a virtual demand for local independence.[84] Two messengers represented the Grüningen assembly to the council of Zurich, the innkeeper Hans Girenbader[85] and the shoe-maker Hans Vontobel,[86] both future Anabaptists. Jörg Berger, Zurich's governor of Grüningen, accused Girenbader of leading a radical minority in the Rüti assembly which objected to the last of the twenty-seven articles, the now standard provision, borrowed from the Twelve Articles, according to which the previous articles had to be in accordance with the Word of God in order to be valid. He proposed, "We should simply stand by these demands, and not reduce any of them."[87] Charges were brought against Girenbader because, after having caused the government trouble at Rüti, he went on to become an Anabaptist.[88] Besides Girenbader and Vontobel, another leader of the Grüningen commoners, the miller Hans Maag probably joined the Anabaptists.[89]

When Girenbader set out from Rüti to Zurich he was accompanied by Uli Seiler, "the Anabaptist with one hand."[90] This was probably the "bad Uli," a particular thorn in the side of Zurich officialdom in Grüningen. He was described by the governor Berger as one of the first Anabaptists in the area; he led a prison breakout in Grüningen in February 1526 and repeatedly denounced the disputation of November 1525 with which the government had tried to silence the Grüningen Anabaptists. He went around with a gun and carried through one of the more imaginative disruptions of a sermon in the early Zurich Reformation – according to Berger, a pigeon shoot directed at the church tower, "while the priest was proclaiming God's Word ... which was a terrible shame and disgrace!".[91] Uli certainly does not fit the stylized requirements of a non-resistant Anabaptist, but in the beginning of the movement rejection of the world and its "Big Jacks" could express itself in ways more exuberant than those that became conventional later.[92]

Grebel,[93] Mantz and Blaurock all occupied themselves with recruiting Anabaptists in Grüningen in the months following the uprising. They were undoubtedly as effective as they were because of the vacuum left by six radical priests in the Grüningen territory, who at first supported peasant opposition to the collection of tithes and sometimes rejected infant baptism, only to make a rapid peace with Zwinglian theology and Zurich's territorial authority as soon as Grüningen's separatist movement collapsed. This was the situation of Hans Brennwald, pastor of Hinwil, whose pulpit was usurped by Blaurock and Grebel one Sunday in October 1525.[94] As for Grebel himself, although he *may* have inspired the decision of Jacob Gross and Ulrich Teck to contribute to Waldshut's defence only as non-combatants (for which they were exiled and their property confiscated),[95] he buzzed around scenes of peasant uprising like a bee seeking pollen. He was active not only in Grüningen and Waldshut but at Schaffhausen and St Gallen – to judge from his movements he regarded the commoners' uprisings on behalf of divine law as an ideal preparation for winning Anabaptist converts.

There were only loose connections between Anabaptism and the Peasants' War in Alsace and Swabia, two major regions where they overlapped, no doubt because so many of the Anabaptists we know about in those regions in the 1520s came from imperial cities. Of the 716 Anabaptists Clasen has enumerated for the 1520s in Swabia, 324 come from Augsburg alone; and when we add Esslingen and its territories we have accounted for 428. Aside from the 138 Strasbourg Anabaptists he has identified for the 1525–29 period, we know of only a few Alsatian Anabaptists.[96]

One of the most interesting cases of a future Anabaptist participating in the Peasants' War in this region involves Oswald Leber, later to become the evil genius who inspired the apocalyptic fantasies of Augustin Bader. A priest in Neudenau in Baden, Leber encouraged the rebellious peasants of the Odenwald by preaching from anti-clerical Reformation pamphlets but insisted that he had been ill when they marched off to Weinsberg.[97]

Another case is that of Michael Jungmann. He was arrested in 1555 in Kürnbach, one of the border territories of Württemberg. Claiming to be seventy years old at the time, he had been baptized *circa* 1530–32. One of the few later Anabaptists to consider the possibility that rulers could be Christians, like sympathetic Romans in the New Testament, he remembered the Peasants' War as something he had been forced into by, among others, the notorious Jäcklin Rohrbach, who executed noble prisoners at Weinsberg. Jungmann had taken "no pleasure" in it, it was "a cross on his heart." He had spent about fourteen weeks in Moravia as a day-labourer, probably at Auspitz, shortly before the restoration of Duke Ulrich in 1534 when Württemberg went Protestant. Jungmann said that he had disliked Moravia, but one of his interrogators remembered him praising the ideal of community of goods.[98]

A few Anabaptists from the Esslingen area are known to have participated in the Peasants' War: Hans Feigenbutz, Michel Spruer and possibly Lienhart Wenig. Wenig emigrated to Moravia in 1531[99]; Spruer appears as an Anabaptist only in 1539.[100] The one individual who may present a biographically significant connection between Anabaptism and the Peasants' War in Alsace and Swabia is Feigenbutz, who was imprisoned and fined in Esslingen for having joined the rebels, was baptized by Reublin in 1527 and became one of the deacons of Esslingen's large Anabaptist congregation. He was a second-rank Anabaptist missionary in Swabia and the Rhine valley until his recantation in 1529.[101]

Jean Rott's careful study of Boersch in Lower Alsace compared the names of sixty-four townsmen implicated in rebellious activities in 1525 and the names of twenty Anabaptists subjected to hearings over more than a decade following 1529, of whom at least thirteen would have been responsible adults in 1525. The probe revealed a more or less dry well. Two names appeared in both lists, Diebolt Esslinger and Hans Müller. Diebolt Esslinger the Anabaptist turned out to have been the son of the Diebolt Esslinger who lost his position as burgomaster through involvement in the Peasants' War; and the difficulties of sorting out the three (or four) Hans Müllers who appeared in Boersch records turned out to be insuperable.[102]

Thus, the evidence we have for Alsace[103] and Swabia shows some interesting personal histories linking Anabaptism and the Peasants' War – those of Oswald Leber, Michel Jungmann, Hans Feigenbutz and the two Diebolt Esslingers – but no significant connection between the two movements. A certain number of the Anabaptists in places such as Strasbourg and Augsburg probably were refugees from the Peasants' War; but refugees in large imperial cities attracted less attention than persons who stayed at home and embarrassed the same magistracy first as 1525 rebels and then as Anabaptists.

The south German variety of Anabaptism, actually the Anabaptism of south and central Germany and Austria, has a profile distinct from that of the Anabaptism of Swiss origin. In 1975 Klaus Deppermann, Werner Packull and I tried to express the pluriform character of Anabaptism by positing a separate origin for south German Anabaptism – when Hans Denck baptized Hans Hut in Augsburg on the Day of Pentecost, 1526.[104] Denck and Hut were certainly the most prominent figures of early south German Anabaptism, and the Augsburg baptism was a dramatic beginning of a new, distinct Anabaptist movement. Nevertheless, before his baptism Hut had received vague reports of people baptizing adult believers elsewhere[105]; and Denck may indeed have been baptized in the St Gallen region when he spent some time there in 1525.[106] What was important was more the separate character than the separate origin of south German Anabaptism. South German Anabaptism was "a completely different Anabaptism" from the one spreading from Switzerland, and a lot of the difference lay in the prominence of the legacy of Thomas Müntzer for south German Anabaptism.[107] Müntzer was dead and he never became an Anabaptist, but his most important continuing impact was among the south German Anabaptists. The contribution of Müntzer's anti-materialistic piety of *Gelassenheit* to the articulation of Anabaptist community of goods is a topic of major importance, but it belongs in a subsequent chapter. The focus here is on the tie between Müntzer's local version of the Peasants' War and the missionary impulses which began Anabaptism in his native Thuringia and in neighbouring Hesse and Franconia.

The tradition of Anabaptist non-resistance led earlier scholarship to explain away the presence of important future Anabaptist leaders at Mühlhausen and Frankenhausen. Harold Bender long ago conceded the anomaly, but gave it little significance: "We know also that some who were under the spell of Müntzer, later became Anabaptists, that, e.g., a Hans Hut, who as an itinerant book dealer participated in the distribution of Müntzer's writings (but also of the Wittenberg writings) and was in Frankenhausen with his books, later, in 1526–27, united with the Anabaptists as an apostle of the peaceful faith and accomplished much for the movement. Also a Melchior Rinck, a former Lutheran preacher, who had even taken part in the battle of Frankenhausen, played an important role as a zealous Anabaptist apostle in Middle Germany in 1527 and later."[108]

If it was not clear at the time Bender wrote in the early 1950s, it is obvious now that these two, Hans Hut and Melchior Rinck,[109] together with Hans Denck, were the major leaders of early Anabaptism in south and central Germany and Austria. Moreover, their Anabaptist careers were interlocked in 1526 and 1527, with Denck baptizing Hut and possibly Rinck as well – at any rate having great influence on him in the period at the end of 1526 and the beginning of 1527 when Rinck first emerged as an Anabaptist.[110] It seems entirely plausible that not only Hut and Rinck were linked by the experience of Müntzer's Thuringian Peasants' War, but Denck as well.[111] Denck was expelled from Nuremberg in January 1525, on the eve of the Peasants' War. Oecolampadius wrote from Basel to the Nuremberg patrician Willibald Pirckheimer in April 1525 that Denck had gone to teach in Mühlhausen, then under the leadership of Müntzer and Pfeiffer. Oecolampadius had helped Denck get his post as schoolmaster in Nuremberg in 1523, and the prevailing view is that his information makes it probable that Denck did go to Mühlhausen.[112] If so, he managed to save himself when the city was occupied after the Peasants' War on 19 May 1525. Denck would have been the schoolmaster with whom Pfeiffer said he wanted to flee to Basel after the collapse of the resistance in Mühlhausen. We know from other sources that Denck did head for Switzerland at that time. After surprisingly mild treatment in Catholic Schwyz, which exiled him for heresies for which it executed others, he appeared in September 1525 among Anabaptists in St Gallen.[113]

Hut's role in the Peasants' War was a good deal less innocent than Bender presented it. As "Hans of Bibra" he was enrolled in Müntzer's "Eternal Covenant" in Mühlhausen, thus becoming part of Müntzer's "vanguard of true believers" at the start of Mühlhausen's involvement in the Peasants' War in the spring of 1525.[114] At the hill outside Frankenhausen where the famous battle occurred, Hut heard Müntzer preach about the covenant of God; and when the latter pointed to his rainbow banner, Hut saw the confirming rainbow in the sky. When there was shooting all around him, Hut fled into the town of Frankenhausen, where he was captured by Hessian soldiers but was one of the lucky ones to be let go. On his return to his home territory in Bibra he preached in the church that the war should continue: "We subjects should slay all our rulers. This is the right moment because we have power in our hands!"[115]

We know less about Rinck's role at Frankenhausen. He owed his position as pastor at Eckardtshausen to Jakob Strauss. Strauss certainly was a Reformation radical and was regarded as a friend of the commoners because of his attacks on usury, but he avoided the stigma of rebellion by last-minute denunciations of Müntzer. Probably the decisive experience that led Rinck to the camp of the rebels was his expulsion from Hesse at the beginning of 1524. At Hersfeld in Hesse, Heinrich Fuchs had been pastor and Rinck his chaplain. They preached in what they certainly regarded as the spirit of the Reformation against "Big Jacks, monopolists and usurers," but found themselves left in the lurch by the Hessian government when their enemies worked to have them removed.[116] This must have seemed to them very similar to what had happened to Müntzer at Allstedt. Fuchs and Rinck fought at the side of Müntzer and the commoners at Frankenhausen; Fuchs was killed and Rinck survived. Eberhard von der Tann, captain of the Wartburg, the fortress in which Luther spent his exile after the Diet of Worms, and an advocate of strict punishment for Rinck's Anabaptism, claimed that Rinck was one of the rebel captains at Frankenhausen.[117]

Some other prominent Anabaptists were alumni of the Mühlhausen-Frankenhausen experience: Hans Römer, the furrier from Eisenach,[118] the schoolmaster Alexander,[119] Klaus Scharf from Mühlhausen[120] and Heinz Kraut of Esperstedt[121] were all important leaders, if not figures of the dimension of Hut, Rinck and Denck. These leaders directed their Anabaptist mission to persons who shared with them the experience of the Peasants' War.

Hans Römer's Anabaptist career forms a more militant, less influential parallel to Hans Hut's. There may have been direct connections between Hut and Römer, because Römer's plot for his band of Anabaptists to seize Erfurt on New Year's Day 1528 and to renew the Peasants' War corresponds to one variant of Hut's apocalyptic timetable.[122] A firm adherent of Thomas Müntzer, Römer escaped from Frankenhausen[123] to Franconia, where he preached continued resistance in the Bildhausen peasant army. His advice was not heeded, since the Bildhausers capitulated early in June.[124] Probably through their mutual association with the Bildhausen band Römer learned to know Andreas, a master tailor, "who started the uprising in Meiningen," and whom he baptized.[125] The shoe-maker from

Eisleben, Dionysius Mansfeld, had been at Frankenhausen and had his life spared by the nobleman who captured him. Baptized by one of Römer's lieutenants and later arrested and interrogated in December 1527, Mansfeld supplied the authorities with information about the Römer group shortly before the aborted attack on Erfurt.[126] Georg Fuchs, involved in the Peasants' War in one of the villages outside Erfurt, also received baptism from Römer.[127] Less definite evidence connects two of Römer's inner circle with the Peasants' War. The peasant Volkmar Fischer from Rohrbronn,[128] another Erfurt village, and Christoph, the shoe-maker's journeyman from Meissen or Mühlhausen,[129] both principals in the plot against Erfurt, may have been Peasants' War veterans.

Although more violent than most Peasants' War survivors who became Anabaptists,[130] the Römer group had definite connections with other Anabaptists in central Germany. Aside from an eschatology that sounds like Hut's, Römer had links with the Anabaptist congregation at Sorga, a village ministered to by Melchior Rinck and the schoolmaster Alexander, both of whom had been with him at Frankenhausen. He directed Ludwig Spon, another Anabaptist leader, to Sorga, telling him that "in a village near Hersfeld called Sorga there is a congregation that leads a good Christian life. Everyone helps everyone else with goods and food when someone is in need. Forty or fifty people get together there."[131]

The villagers from Sorga participated, probably *en bloc*, in hostilities in April 1525, during which they first forced the abbot of Hersfeld to accept the Twelve Articles and then submitted almost without resistance to the mercenaries of Philip of Hesse.[132] When the Hessian government eventually exiled the Sorga Anabaptists in the late summer of 1533, members of the congregation were interrogated, among other things about their participation in and attitudes towards the Peasants' War.[133] The twelve families of landholding tenants resident in Sorga had given refuge to at least nine other families "fugitive" from Franconia, Fulda and elsewhere. The Hessian chancellor wrote, "Whoever cannot stay anywhere else turns up here at Sorga." The fugitives were fleeing persecution for Anabaptism, to be sure, but most of them were probably on the run even earlier because of their participation in the uprising. Only one of the group questioned, Marx Baumgart, who had come to Sorga from Herda, denied involvement; nine explicitly admitted participating in the uprising of 1525, including the tailor Gilg, the most prominent among the refugees, and the four leaders of the Sorga tenants, Hans Koch, Hans Ziese, Hans Plat and Heinz Hutter. Ziese and Plat mentioned that they had been punished, apparently for a prominent role in the uprising. Several Sorga Anabaptists claimed that their pastors had blessed the Peasants' War and led them astray in 1525. But only three of the ten persons questioned were willing to admit clearly that the uprising had been ungodly. The rest chose evasive answers, of which the most provocative came from a husband and wife named Groshen: "The past rebellion was for the sake of temporal goods, therefore it was ungodly. If it had taken place for the sake of the Gospel, we wouldn't know what to say." This of course gets close to the post-mortem assessments of the Peasants' War of both Hut and Müntzer, clarified by Müntzer's reference to John 7 in his last letter to Mühlhausen – "My time is not yet come."[134]

The congregation gathered in Sorga was the most important fruit of Rinck's work from the time of his return from the Rhineland to Hesse in 1528 until his first imprisonment in April 1529. Heinrich Beulshausen argues persuasively that Rinck lived there and made it the center of his mission elsewhere in the region.[135] Rinck was followed in Sorga in 1532 or 1533 by the schoolmaster Alexander from Einbeck, who had earlier been an Anabaptist apostle in northern Thuringia and the southern Harz area.[136] Alexander was described by two of the Anabaptists who knew him as "put to flight [vorjaget] at Frankenhausen." Beulshausen says this probably means that he was a survivor of the battle,[137] which fits well with Alexander's Anabaptist contacts. Alexander had associations with Peasants' War veterans in the Mühlhausen area as well as in Sorga. Claus Scharf, "a rebel and principal figure" in the Peasants' War, received instruction in Anabaptism from Alexander and visited Sorga with him.[138] Another member of the same Mühlhausen group was Heinrich Hutter, denounced as the instigator "who provoked the rebellion of the other commoners" in 1525 in his home village of Ammern. Hutter was punished by mutilation of two fingers on his right hand but was allowed to stay in Ammern, outside Mühlhausen.[139]

Alexander was executed in 1533 after having been run to ground at Frankenhausen of all places. In the years following Alexander's death his followers experienced a schism over whether divorce from non-Anabaptist spouses was to be permitted, with two veterans of Frankenhausen, Klaus Scharf and Heinz Kraut, leading the opposing sects.[140] Kraut received additional historical notoriety by being interrogated by no less a figure than Philip Melanchthon in December 1535. He upheld the traditions of commoners' resistance by addressing his social betters, the learned theologians, with the familiar du (in the manner Germans speak to God, loved ones, children, animals and persons they wish to deflate). He cut through the formal hypocrisies of a process that he predicted (accurately) would lead to his execution. On the scaffold in Jena he repeated the old watchword of peasant resistance, "When Adam delved and Eve span, who then was the gentleman?"[141]

Following Kraut's execution, both Jakob Storger, Kraut's successor as sect-leader, and Klaus Scharf were brought to trial in Mühlhausen with some of their followers in October and November 1537. Both leaders were subsequently executed. A number of Scharf's followers said they had not received communion in the twelve years since the Peasants' War.[142] The trial brought into special relief the continuing reverence in which Storger and his followers held Thomas Müntzer. One said that Anabaptism was a continuance of the faith she had learned from the teaching of Müntzer and Pfeiffer. Another made the distinction that Müntzer's teaching was right but the Peasants' War was not.[143] Storger was apparently drenched in Müntzer's writings. He said that Luther was worse than the pope, quoting Müntzer about Luther's "beshitten mercifulness": "Müntzer was one of the prophets foretold in the Revelation of John. I also put a high value on dreams, which lead to the Gospel. Müntzer's teaching was right and I follow him as one who grasped the inner Word so well, in the sense that he wielded the outer sword with the inner Word."[144] True to Kraut's example of disdain for the world, Storger told the Mühlhausen priests that he held their disputing with him as worth no more than a louse and that he would not change his views if they talked the whole day.[145]

On their expulsion from Hesse in September 1533 the Sorga Anabaptists went to Auspitz in Moravia. Jörg Zaunring, one of the founders of the Auspitz community in 1531, had been a missionary to Sorga in 1532 and had urged such a move, even before the Hessian government required the villagers to recant or leave Hesse. In the fall of 1533 the Sorga Anabaptists arrived in Moravia in two groups: first eighteen refugee-settlers from Sorga led by the tailor Gilg, and then twenty-four Sorga tenant-residents led by Heinz Hutter. At the time, Jakob Hutter had just broken with the other Anabaptist leaders in Auspitz. The minority supporting him numbered less than four hundred; so the addition of the Sorga contingent appeared to be a signal indication of divine favour. As it happened, quarrels about dress and food between the Hessians and the Tyrolean Hutterites led to a schism in 1534, after which the Sorga group affiliated with Jakob Hutter's rivals, the Philippites. In the doctrinal quarrels accompanying this split the Hessians invoked the authority of Melchior Rinck, in their eyes a greater teacher than Jakob Hutter. The Sorga congregation was driven out of Moravia in 1535 by the same general persecution that victimized all Moravian Anabaptists. In February

1535 the Peasants' War veteran Hans Plat, who had returned to his native Sorga, was turned over to Hessian authorities by the new tenants who had been settled there to replace the expelled Anabaptists.[146] Thus we can trace in Sorga a particularly clear case of the three-stage pilgrimage from the Peasants' War through Anabaptism to the communal life in Moravia.

What happened to the congregation of Sorga repeated itself in the life of Erhard Steus, a journeyman tanner from Mühlhausen. In 1525 he had been enthusiastic about Müntzer and followed him to Frankenhausen. More than ten years later, still in Mühlhausen, he became convinced that the Anabaptists had the right way. So in late 1538 he went to Nikolsburg in Moravia and received baptism. Back in Saxony the next year, he at first stuck to his beliefs when he was arrested, saying that the twelve thousand Anabaptists in Moravia could not all be in error; but in the end he recanted.[147]

The common experience of Frankenhausen, too, supplies the link, perhaps the only one, between Anabaptism and a band of 170 murderers and arsonists in the Fulda region, referred to as "Anabaptists" in the confession of Hans Krug in 1533.[148] In this case, there was not the same overlapping of contacts with other groups that ties Römer and his followers to other central German Anabaptists. But the parallel experience a few years later of the Batenburgers in the Netherlands shows the possibility at least that disappointed apocalyptic enthusiasm can, against a background of persecution, sour into a quasi-criminal struggle for survival and vengeance. Krug said that his real leader was a peasant, Hans Schott, who lived in a small village near Frankenhausen before the Peasants' War. One of the peasant captains at Frankenhausen, Schott escaped to Franconia, like Römer, and became a captain of a peasant band there. For a while after the Peasants' War he took refuge in Bohemia, after which he returned to organize terrorist activities.[149] Krug reported that "the genuine Anabaptist cause depends on an insurrection to drive away princes and lords, like that which occurred in the Peasants' War."[150]

Aside from Hans Schott, veterans of the Peasants' War in Müntzer's immediate locality – Hans Hut, Melchior Rinck, Hans Römer, Alexander, Klaus Scharf, Heinz Kraut, Dionysius Mansfeld, Heinrich Hutter and Erhard Steus (we may probably add Hans Denck, assuming that he worked on the "home front" in Mühlhausen) – had all sorts of important roles in central German Anabaptism. Moreover, as Anabaptist missionaries they were drawn to others in the area and beyond it who, like them, survived the Peasants' War. The village of Sorga and the early Franconian missionary travels of Hans

Hut provide the clearest, but not the only, cases of Anabaptist leaders recruiting Peasants' War participants. In terms of the history of Anabaptism, the Frankenhausen-Mühlhausen alumni were a very distinguished group – not counting Denck, they included six significant leaders – and Hut, Rinck and Denck were the *most* significant leaders of south and central German-Austrian Anabaptism as a whole.

Hans Hut returned home to Bibra in Franconia immediately after Frankenhausen to call upon his neighbours to continue the Peasants' War. Likewise, after his baptism he again went home to Franconia to begin his mission to assemble the apocalyptic elect, so that they could be spared (in order to punish the wicked) when the world ended in 1528, three and one-half years after the Peasants' War. Gottfried Seebass holds that Hut first of all sought out persons who, like him, were fugitive survivors of the Peasants' War and who longed most ardently for a divine rescue from the fiasco of 1525.[151] In Haina, the village neighbouring Bibra, he found Georg Volk (sometimes referred to as Volckmer or Volkhaimer[152]), one of his most important early Anabaptist co-workers, who "bragged that he had to flee Count Wilhelm [of Henneberg's] land in the rebellion,"[153] that is, the lordship in which Hut and he lived. Volk's flight, then, was a result of the Peasants' War, not Anabaptism. When he had fled his home, Volk abandoned his wife and four children. One of the children asked their mother, "Where is our father?" She answered "He is in misfortune [*im Elent*]." The conversation continued: "When will he return?" "When the bad people perish."[154]

Seebass has argued persuasively that figures who were fugitives before the hunt for Anabaptists had begun should be assumed to be persons who feared to return to their homes because of what they had done in 1525. Most of the leaders of Hut's Franconian mission were, in fact, fugitives from their homes. In some instances we know that this was because of the Peasants' War, as in the case of the three brothers Hans, Marx and Michael Maier. They had lived in the bishopric of Bamberg at Herzogenaurach and were leaders in the destruction of court records and tax rolls and the plundering of church properties during the Peasants' War in their home area, after which they fled to Alterlangen in Hohenzollern territories, where Hut won them for the new baptism.[155] Eukarius Kellermann from Coburg, whom Packull calls "Hut's most faithful companion from Franconia,"[156] also described himself as a fugitive like Hut and Volk, who "were both fugitive since the time of the Peasants' War."[157]

Hut and his lieutenants sought out Peasants' War veterans. Besides the Maier brothers, a wagoner named Peter and a brick maker named Konz were involved in the 1525 disturbances at Herzogen-aurach and later became Anabaptists.[158] The Anabaptist Heinz Schare, a linen weaver from Burglauer, was a brother of an executed captain of the Bildhausen band.[159] Fritz Harscher from the Nuremberg village of Reutles, captain of an assembly of Nuremberg rural subjects in 1525, accompanied Volk when he came to baptize in the area.[160] At Uttenreuth, a Hohenzollern village involved in the Peasants' War, Hut and Volk baptized four persons whose names appear on lists of 1525 rebels, Hans Beck from Rosenbach and Hans Grueber from Egenhof together with Grueber's sons Heinz and Jörg.[161] Seebass says that "besides Hut himself Jörg Grueber must be numbered one of the more important missionaries of Hut's Anabaptism."[162]

Hut was also an active missionary in 1527 in Upper and Lower Austria and Salzburg, where he and his followers began to recruit for Anabaptism. He visited Austrian cities such as Melk, Steyr, Freistadt and Wels, which had been near the centres of the rather weak Austrian peasant uprising in 1525 and which had generally maintained a friendly neutrality toward the rebellion.[163] Hut, Eukarius Kellermann and other associates were also active in Salzburg,[164] where the Peasants' War had been long and fierce. There is not enough evidence to establish that Hut's mission was directed at Peasants' War survivors in these regions as it was in Franconia.

A Franconian, Georg Nespitzer from Stadtlauringen, was probably Hut's first convert in Passau on the Danube, where he was baptized in the presence of his brother-in-law Eukarius Kellermann, the husband of Nespitzer's sister. This happened "in the year after the Peasants' War," Nespitzer later confessed, and his well-documented enthusiasm for the vengeful aspects of Hut's apocalyptic teachings led Seebass to speculate about whether Nespitzer "came or fled to Passau" after the rebellion.[165]

In the Augsburg meeting of Anabaptist leaders in August 1527 (styled the "Martyr Synod" in earlier Anabaptist historiography) Nespitzer received the assignment to rebuild the dispersed Anabaptist group in the area of Staffelstein, an important focus of Hut's early Franconian mission. In 1525 the peasants of the area had participated in the rebellion with a similar uniformity as in Sorga in Hesse, plundering the chapel on the Staffelberg and the monastery at Langheim. Hut's converts from this region expressed his apocalyptic expectations in their most threatening form: a Turkish invasion would destroy the victors of the Peasants' War. While it was underway the Anabaptists, as God's particular elect, were to go into hiding; but afterwards they were to emerge to carry out God's judgment on princes, lords and the ungodly in general.[166] Nespitzer's own confession shows him drenched in the expectation of this not-quite-natural day of vengeance, to occur "three and one half years after the Rebellion."[167] In 1529 and 1530 a Franconian Anabaptist leader named Georg from Staffelstein, possessed by similar apocalyptic hopes (even though the date Hut set was past), worked successfully to win Anabaptist converts in the borderlands between Hesse and Thuringia. Beulshausen points out that there was no precedent for an Anabaptist leader unknown in his own region to establish such authority so quickly in a new territory of activity. He suggests that Georg from Staffelstein, a vineyard labourer, was none other than Georg Nespitzer, the linen weaver, who probably worked in the vineyards during his mission in Staffelstein.[168] This hypothesis has some difficulties,[169] but whether or not it is ultimately accepted, the mission of Georg from Staffelstein illustrates the way Hut's message knitted connections among Franconian, Hessian and Thuringian Anabaptists, and suggests that the content of that message was apocalyptic vengeance for the Peasants' War.

The same connections are indicated in the case of the Anabaptist Philip Tuchscherer from Windsheim, who worked with both Georg Nespitzer and Melchior Rinck. Tuchscherer originally came from Rothenburg; in his house the hapless fugitive Andreas Carlstadt hid himself, and there, too, the meetings took place which led to the uprising against the Rothenburg council.[170] Involved in these events was the tailor Hans Hartmann, who first got himself into trouble for "following Dr Carlstadt, although the council forbade it," and then was permanently banished for receiving baptism from Tuchscherer.[171] The eccentric Anabaptist Claus Fry, who later was executed for bigamy in Strasbourg, was also prominent in the Rothenburg uprising.[172] Another case of an educated figure who participated both in the Franconian Peasants' War and in Anabaptism was the former Augustinian monk, Friedrich Pretscher, executed in Würzburg in 1528.[173]

Two of the Tyrol's most famous sons were the Peasants' War leader Michael Gaismair and the Anabaptist leader Jakob Hutter. In the 1520s their activities centred in the same limited area of the south Tyrol. Hutter's home village, Moos in the Pustertal, is only a short distance from the episcopal city of Brixen, which Gaismair ruled from May through August 1525. Gaismair is important in the history of the Peasants' War not because he had a vast following, which he did not, but because of his military daring and social radicalism.[174] Several recent scholars[175] have argued that Hutter's movement should be regarded as the successor to Gaismair's, even though as in other regions only a small number of personal connections can be documented. (A point of some interest is that Michael Gaismair's nephews, Kaspar and Erhart, escaped the Habsburg government's systematic persecution of their family by joining the Anbaptists in Moravia.[176])

We find a particularly important personal connection between Gaismair and South Tyrolean Anabaptism in the case of the former cleric and Reformation sympathizer Mathias Messerschmied, jailed by the bishop of Brixen in 1524–25 and later, from 1527 to 1531, active as an Anabaptist preacher in the nearby Eisacktal. Gaismair's biographer, Jürgen Bücking, counts Mathias Messerschmied as one of the preachers who supported Gaismair and identifies him as the brother of Paul Messerschmied, one of Gaismair's close circle of original supporters.[177] In 1528 King Ferdinand wrote that his local officials reported that Peasants' War participants were now re-emerging as Anabaptists. Government correspondence of that year mentions the pursuit of four Anabaptists resident on the Ritten, an inaccessible high plateau between the Sarn and Eisack rivers. These persons, named as rebels in the Peasants' War, were Hans Portz, Ulrich Kobl, Hans Gasser and his wife, Anna. The Innsbruck government insisted upon confiscating their property, a measure which was doubly justified, it claimed, by their being not only Anabaptists but also followers of Gaismair.[178]

Mission activity from eastern Switzerland, led by no less a figure than Georg Blaurock in 1527, gave a specifically Anabaptist confessional content to a nonconformist religious movement that was already underway in the south Tyrol. Blaurock penetrated the Etsch valley as far as Bozen, close by the wild Ritten area that had provided shelter for Peasants' War veterans.[179] One of the Anabaptists first arrested at Bozen was Bartlmä Dill, a painter, whose father had been active in the uprising.[180] Erhard Urscher from nearby Sarntheim, executed as an Anabaptist in 1533, confessed that he had participated in plundering a granary during the Peasants' War.[181] In the south Tyrol, as earlier in Grüningen, Blaurock was conducting a successful mission in a region that the Peasants' War had alienated from the government and the established church.

In September 1532 excitement was aroused in Austrian government circles in Innsbruck by the statements of a prisoner under interrogation, Friedrich Brandenberger from Cologne. Apparently he had been a confidant of Michael Gaismair's during the Peasants' War in the Tyrol and Salzburg, and now, just before his arrest, he was travelling about with Jakob Hutter conducting baptisms.[182] Brandenberger mentioned Portz and Kobl and a Peter Wirt who lived on the Ritten Plateau as receiving a promise from Gaismair that they would each be paid twenty florins if they could kill or capture Christoph Herbst, the governor of Welsperg, a well-known enemy of the Anabaptists who was devoting himself to chasing Hutter. Wirt was supposed to have said, "I still have four oxen, and I'd give them all to see Gaismair march through the land once more!" Kobl, supposed to have earlier fled the Tyrol to Bern, was now said to be in contact with Gaismair in Padua.[183] It is at least interesting that one of the early testimonies of Tyrolean martyrs in the *Hutterite Chronicle* is by Barbara, the wife of Hans Portz.[184] As late as 1545 the erstwhile Tyrolean peasant leader and Gaismair partisan, Christian Lex, fled to Moravia to join his Anabaptist wife there.[185]

Wolfgang Lassmann, the most recent scholar to study the subject, suggests that the Habsburg central government was regarded by the Tyrolean countryside as a more or less foreign system, levying tribute and offering very little of value in return.[186] He illustrates the poverty of the Tyrolean rural areas with the example of Michelsburg, one of the centres of later Anabaptism, which had an average peasant indebtedness of 59 per cent. The Tyrolean church was closely connected with the government, sometimes exercising political authority directly as it did in Brixen. The failure of the Peasants' War in the Tyrol did not automatically restore the legitimacy of the Habsburg government or the Roman Church. In the Zurich highlands, particularly in the territory of Grüningen, the government had been frightened by the possibility that *Freundschaften*, clan-type associations, might frustrate its suppression of Anabaptism. In fact, in Grüningen the *Freundschaften* tended to convince their Anabaptist members to recant.[187] But just the sort of danger the Zurich government feared became a reality in the Tyrol, where subject-ruler relations were far more hostile than in Switzerland. According to Lassmann, the Anabaptists had the great advantage in the Tyrol that, because of the ferocity of Habsburg legal action against "heresy," they were the sole beneficiaries of the anti-clerical energies of the Reformation. Some of the last evangelical pastors fled the south Tyrol in 1526 with Gaismair's rebel army, leaving the field to commoners preaching a nonconformist version of the Reformation that soon adopted Anabaptist ideas. In large parts of the Tyrol the authorities were confronted with a wall of silence in their anti-Anabaptist activities. It was analogous to the protection that the sympathizers (the *credentes*) of Toulouse had once rendered the Albigensian *perfecti*. The certain execution with which the Tyrolean government threatened the rebaptized led to a pragmatic response, in which baptism and flight into exile took place more or less at the same time, if baptism was not delayed until safe arrival in Moravia.

Lassmann insists that Tyrolean Anabaptism was no mere sect that the government might have safely ignored. As the only vehicle of dissent of an angry, subjected population, it was the one genuine religion of the commoners and it threatened to become the religion of the Tyrol: "Since particularly in the south Tyrol there was virtually no radical Reformation alternative to Jakob Hutter's Anabaptism, this movement, despite its 'vulgar' character, achieved hegemony in the sphere of serious religiosity, ready for sacrifice. This effect extended into circles of the social élite, but, in contrast to the institutionalized Reformation, it generally stopped short of the politically powerful and the educated."[188] Critical scholarship in the important area of Tyrolean Anabaptism is relatively young. It will be interesting to see how others develop Lassmann's suggestions.

What, then, has current Anabaptist scholarship established (or plausibly suggested) about the relation between Anabaptism and the Peasants' War? First, Anabaptism is not a way to account for the Peasants' War. As scholars have tirelessly pointed out, many – indeed most – of the Reformation spokesmen who supported the Peasants' War did not become Anabaptists.[189] With the important exception of the Tyrol, Anabaptism never achieved the dimensions required for it to possess comparable social energies to those of the defeated commoners' rebellion. Thus, Marxist scholarship in the tradition of Gerhard Zschäbitz, which gives it the leadership of the last stage of the "Early Bourgeois Revolution in Germany," exaggerates Anabaptism's social and political importance.[190] Moreover, the Peasants' War had the greatest effect on Anabaptism in the regions where it came earlier rather than simultaneously with Anabaptism.

That said, it is hard to understand Clasen's evasion of the natural connection between the Peasants' War and the insurrectionary, vengeful elements of two of his six major groups of Anabaptists, the followers of Hans Hut (at least at the beginning of his mission) and the Thuringian Anabaptists.[191] One might expect a historical theologian or an intellectual historian, but not a social historian, to believe that the plans of Hans Römer and of Hut resulted simply from bizarre speculations about the apocalypse. The more we know about how widespread apocalyptic projections were in the Reformation era, even among social conservatives, the more cautious we become about their value in explaining seditious actions. Römer was quite explicit about revenging Thomas Müntzer, whom he called his "father," and renewing the Peasants' War.[192] For Hans Hut, the apocalyptic tribulation of God's people began with the Peasants' War. A significant sign of the moderation of Hut's movement was the decision of his follower, Leonhard Schiemer, to calculate the "judgment on the house of God" and the three and a half years to the parousia from the first persecutions of Anabaptists in Switzerland rather than from the Peasants' War.[193] When we are dealing with the Römer group and the early followers of Hut during his mission in Franconia, a good research hypothesis would be that most of them were Peasants' War veterans and all of them were Peasants' War sympathizers. How else is one to account for their actions and beliefs? To argue that this was a bitter reaction to persecution of Anabaptism does not do, because often the vengeful ideas preceded rather than followed the persecution. It seems a reasonable assumption that people do not join a religion of vengeance simply because of its intrinsic appeal; the vengeance yearned for by early Anabaptists in Thuringia and Franconia was vengeance for the Peasants' War.

Clasen concedes that "we may be certain that there were more than 37 Anabaptists who had been involved in the uprising."[194] His tabulation and correlation of vast amounts of significant data should rightly put his scholarly peers in awe, but this ought not to close our eyes to the spurious clarity and certainty of statistical arguments. For instance, in arriving at his census of 4,356 Anabaptists in the years from 1525 through 1529, Clasen counts the 360 persons in Waldshut baptized by Reublin and Hubmaier.[195] Yet, though Waldshut was involved in the Peasants' War, none of them, not Hubmaier or anyone else among the Waldshuters, appears in Clasen's enumeration of Anabaptists involved in the Peasants' War.

Studying Clasen's and other later scholars' work on Anabaptists in the Peasants' War, and using somewhat different ideas about the meaning of the Peasants' War, I have arrived at a list of sixty-six names of certain or probable participants (counting only Hubmaier for Waldshut). This list appears in Appendix A.

In fact, Clasen's book names only thirty-five Anabaptists who participated or might have participated in the uprising of 1525. Four of Clasen's possible participants have been eliminated, in three cases because I found the evidence unconvincing,[196] and in one because I could not check it.[197] Subsequent scholarship, then, has approximately doubled the number of Anabaptists known by Clasen to have participated in the Peasants' War,[198] suggesting at least a bit of the fluidity that hides behind the apparent certainty of numbers. Only five of my "certain or probable partipants" are "probables," statistically not very important, but important given who they were: Heini Aberli, Hans Denck, the schoolmaster Alexander from Einbeck, Eukarius Kellermann and the less important Hans Maag from

Grüningen. Four fall into the category of "spiritual leaders" of the Peasants' War, by which I mean not persons, like Grebel, who made converts in its aftermath but those who gave apparently non-military support to the commoners' rebellion,[199] although they are not known to have looted monasteries and led armies (like Müntzer, not an Anabaptist) or to have spoken in favour of military measures (like Hubmaier). Wilhelm Reublin, Johannes Brötli and Hans Krüsi availed themselves of the military protection of the armed commoners while they propagated Anabaptism, even if they did not personally "take the sword" (a matter about which we are uninformed). Hans Denck (probably) was schoolmaster of Mühlhausen while that imperial city was allied with the rebellion.

Of the sixty-six names I have listed, sixteen appear in Clasen's list of Anabaptist leaders. Five others – Gilg, leader of the refugee element in the Sorga congregation in 1533, Hans Feigenbutz from Esslingen, Augustin Bader's lieutenant Oswald Leber, Hans Hut's co-worker Jörg Grueber and the terrorist leader Hans Schott – have some claim to be regarded as Anabaptist leaders. Of the sixty-six persons, ten could be considered Peasants' War leaders, four of whom were also Anabaptist leaders (Rinck, Hubmaier, Schott and Girenbader) while the other six were not. Hence, twenty-seven of the sixty-six names are of persons of special distinction, either in Anabaptism, the Peasants' War or both. Two of every five participants we know by name were especially important persons, which implies that rank-and-file participants tend not to appear in our sources, unless we have a congregation investigated as in Sorga, and even there only prominent Anabaptists were questioned. Clasen counted 269 Anabaptist leaders in the 1525–29 period, 13 of whom appear on my list of Peasants' War participants – not a large percentage but a much larger proportion than that of all known Anabaptist Peasants' War participants among all known Anabaptists in the same period. When we start naming the most important leaders, the point becomes more obvious. Hans Denck, Hans Hut, Balthasar Hubmaier, Melchior Rinck, Wilhelm Reublin, Johannes Brötli, Hans Krüsi, Hans Römer, Alexander from Einbeck, Heinz Kraut, Klaus Scharf, Georg Volk, Eukarius Kellermann, Marx Maier and Oswald Leber were probably or certainly involved in the Peasants' War, all but four of them certainly. This does not count possible participants such as Georg Nespitzer, Michael Sattler and Römer's chief lieutenants. Clearly, we are looking at the tip of an iceberg, unless we are to conclude that the rank and file of early Anabaptists were peaceful persons with an aversion to the rebellion of 1525 who inexplicably became involved in a movement frequently led by Peasants' War veterans. Perhaps it is time to shift the burden of proof and to ask ourselves how many Anabaptist leaders can be proven with certainty *not* to have been involved in the Peasants' War. Arnold Snyder has created a stir by asking what Michael Sattler was doing in May 1525. What was Jakob Hutter doing in 1525? When did he stop carrying a gun under his arm?[200] Grebel, Mantz and Blaurock were definitely not themselves Peasants' War participants, but they evidently developed a mission strategy calculated to appeal to Peasants' War participants in Grüningen, northeastern Switzerland and the Tyrol. Pilgram Marpeck, attending Rattenberg council meetings and lending money to King Ferdinand, would certainly have been an enemy of the commoners' resistance.[201] Clasen mentions a similar instance, in which Konrad Sachs helped shape the Stuttgart council's anti-rebel position in 1525 and was by 1530 at the head of the Anabaptist circle in Stuttgart.[202] But there are not many future Anabaptist leaders whose movements and opinions are well enough documented to show that in 1525 they were on the side of the princes, like Luther, or at least neutral.

The Peasants' War, then, was significantly connected with the beginnings of Anabaptism. In the Waldshut-Schaffhausen-St Gallen area, particularly in the rural villages, it caused a temporary breakdown of magisterial authority for most of 1525, thereby enabling Swiss Anabaptism to spread behind its smoke-screen. Much more important, in eastern Hesse, Thuringia and Franconia, veterans of the Peasants' War provided the major leadership and probably most of the rank and file of the early Anabaptist movement. Thus was created "a completely different Anabaptism" from the Swiss one, imbued with memories of Frankenhausen and Thomas Müntzer. Perhaps most important of all, but still an hypothesis awaiting documentation, the Tyrolean Peasants' War may have alienated the mass of the population so completely from the Habsburg government and the Roman Church that it shaped the indispensable preconditions for the creation of Jakob Hutter's "New Tyrol" in Moravia.

PART TWO

Anabaptist Community of Goods

The Swiss Brethren and Acts 4: A Rule of Sharing and a Rule against Exploitation

The first Anabaptists in the Reformation era initiated believers' baptism in Zurich in January 1525 in an effort to create immediately a complete, uncompromising and uncompromised reformed Church.[1] Persecuted and scattered, rent within and without, they crystallized their sectarian distinctives in the Seven Articles of Schleitheim in February 1527.[2] From the beginning in Zollikon and St Gallen they referred to themselves as "brothers in Christ."[3] Later, from some time in the 1540s, they were called the "Swiss Brethren," the name being coined by two other Anabaptist groups that wanted to maintain an identity distinct from them – the Hutterites and the Marpeck brotherhood.[4] The term "Swiss Brethren" was not primarily a geographical designation; it referred to all Anabaptists who were direct successors of Conrad Grebel, who initiated believer's baptism, and Michael Sattler, who authored the Schleitheim articles. Anabaptists in Swabia and Alsace, and even in Moravia, as well as Swiss Anabaptists were called Swiss Brethren. Marpeck brothers resided in Switzerland for a time and Hutterite missionaries came there trying to convince Swiss Brethren and others to follow them back to Moravia.

After the baptisms of 1525 in Zurich, the first important stronghold of Anabaptism was the village of Zollikon on Lake Zurich, one of the peasant communities that had refused to pay its tithes in 1523. According to *Sabbata*, the chronicle of Johannes Kessler of St Gallen: "Now because most of Zollikon was rebaptized and held that they were the true Christian church, they also undertook, like the early Christians, to practice community of temporal goods (as can be read in the Acts of the Apostles), broke the locks off their doors, chests, and cellars, and ate food and drink in good fellowship without discrimination. But as in the time of the apostles, it did not last long."[5]

Certainly the early Swiss Anabaptists were repeatedly accused of practising community of goods. Some of this was only the malicious gossip to which all Reformation radicals were subjected, as in the comment of Cochlaeus in a letter to Erasmus: "They make everything common, wives, virgins, temporal goods."[6] Zwingli insisted repeatedly that community of goods was part of the program of his Anabaptist opponents.[7]

In 1527 the governments of Zurich, Bern and St Gallen made this accusation part of a formal indictment in their mandate against the Anabaptists: "They hold and say that no Christian, if he really wants to be a Christian, may either give or receive interest or income on a sum of capital; that furthermore all temporal goods are free and common and everyone can have full property rights to them. For we are reliably informed that they repeatedly declared such things in the beginning of their arbitrarily created brotherhood and in this way moved the poor simple-minded souls to adhere to them."[8]

Because of the later Mennonites' association of an acceptance of private property with Christian mutual aid, and their justified suspicion of descriptions of early Swiss Anabaptism in hostile, Swiss Reformed sources, these accounts of an early Swiss Brethren commitment to community of goods have been treated skeptically by Mennonite and free church historians.[9] To them, community of goods is simply a Hutterite peculiarity in the Anabaptist spectrum – and community of goods can only mean what the Hutterites made it mean.

In fact, there is good evidence of a major preoccupation with Acts 2 and 4 at the very beginning of the Swiss Anabaptist movement, as might be expected of a religious group entangled with the contemporary peasant resistance to the established social order. An early Anabaptist congregational ordinance, probably dating from 1527, is now preserved in Bern archives. Written in the same hand as the earliest version of the Schleitheim Articles, it considered a common fund and alms to the poor as the proper expression of community of property: "Of all the brothers and sisters of this congregation none shall have anything of his own, but rather, as the Christians in the time of the apostles held all in common, and especially stored up a common fund, from which aid can be given to the poor, according as each will have need, and as in the apostles' time permit no brother to be in need."[10] The practices of the early church as depicted in Acts could not be a matter of indifference to a group so dedicated to the radical, literal restoration of the true church as were the first Swiss Anabaptists.

The contention of Kessler and the Swiss governments that there was a particular preoccupation with community of goods at the beginning of Swiss Anabaptism is confirmed by the experience of one of the Zollikon Anabaptists, Heini Frei. Frei complained that in the first Anabaptist meetings he was almost persuaded to sell his land and support himself solely from his trade, weaving: "It was their opinion that everything should be pooled together as common property, and whatever someone lacked or needed he should take from the common store ... and they also would gladly have brought in and attracted rich people and great families."[11] Felix Mantz had a similar concern to implement community of goods in early 1525. In a letter in his defence written to the Zurich council less than a month after the first adult baptisms, he stated that, immediately after he baptized people, he "taught them further about love and unity and community of all things, as in Acts 2."[12] Two years later, near the time of Mantz's execution, Mantz and Blaurock in parallel statements rejected the accusation that they taught community of goods. Mantz explained that "whoever is a good Christian should share with his neighbour when he is in need."[13]

A deadly semantic game was in progress here. At the time of writing his *Apologeticus Archeteles* ("Defence called Archeteles") in 1522, Zwingli, like his humanist brothers, recognized community of goods as a Christian ideal. Now it had become part of a capital indictment he was launching at Mantz. In 1522 he wrote that among true Christians "no one calls any possession his own; all things are held in common."[14] In a tract on the preaching office in June 1525, he said that "the greater part of devout, quiet Christians will find no pleasure in the Anabaptist cause because they see at once that the Anabaptists are aiming at community of goods and the abolition of government."[15] At the same time that the princes' armies were busily slaughtering commoners in Alsace, Swabia, Franconia and Thuringia, Zwingli was at last gaining full security for himself and his type of Reformation in the internal politics of Zurich.[16] The result was the acceleration of conservative changes in his outlook already in evidence for some years.

Because of Zwingli's partisanship, the question of how to use his statements about the early Anabaptists has always been a problem for historians.[17] He is a rich but not entirely reliable source. Certainly when he is using the polemical rhetoric of the prosecuting attorney, as in the statement above combining community of goods and abolition of government, we are dealing with an opinion, partly political and social, partly theological, not a matter of fact. But what should we do with Zwingli's account of the procession of Zollikoners in June 1525, who, filled with apocalyptic excitement, cried "Woe! Woe! Woe to Zurich!"? From the writings of Fritz Blanke onward, this event has become part of the narrative for historians sympathetic to the Swiss Brethren.[18] No one, to the best of my knowledge, has remarked upon the part of Zwingli's description in which he goes on to say that these same Zollikoners "boasted that already they hold all things in common," uttering vague threats against people who resisted community of goods.[19] But if the "Woe-criers" are to be accepted as historical fact, why not the early community of goods, especially since we have independent corroboration of the latter?

The weight of evidence from early Swiss Anabaptist leaders elsewhere than in Zurich indicates that community of goods and suspicion of private property were indeed part of their program. Hans Krüsi, the third Swiss Anabaptist martyr, chosen in 1525 to preach his version of the commoners' Reformation by the rebellious villagers in the territories of the abbot of St Gallen, said in his final confession before he was burned at Luzern that "all things should be held in common, in the love of God and in faith."[20] Johannes Brötli, who was a missionary for the communitarian Anabaptists in Moravia at the time of his execution in 1530 by the Waldburg family of Peasants' War notoriety,[21] was a co-signer of Grebel's letter to Müntzer, former pastor in Zollikon and a likely participant in the first believers' baptisms in January 1525.[22] Writing in February 1525 from Hallau, where he was soon to become the minister chosen and protected by a village active in peasant rebellion, he warned the Anabaptists in Zollikon that their attachment to temporal goods made it difficult for them to stay loyal to the true baptism. "But oh, oh woe to temporal goods! They hinder you! Christ said it in the holy Gospel."[23] The allusion would have been to Matthew 19:21–24, with its story of the rich young man whom Christ told to sell his possessions and give to the poor.

There was no thought among the Swiss Anabaptists of going beyond the single-family household as the focus of living and of the economics of production and consumption.[24] Community of goods meant what was described in Acts 2 and 4 – and in the early Swiss congregational order associated with the Schleitheim Articles – the creation of a common fund intended to avert poverty in any of the family households. To judge from the Heini Frei case, the belief of the Zollikon Anabaptists was that persons with capital of some sort should, as in Acts 4, put it at the disposal of the congregation. The egalitarian principle here was that of a congregation without either poor people or idle *rentiers*, with all members supporting themselves by work. At this early stage in the Swiss Anabaptist movement we probably have the expression of an ideal for life among reformed Christians, an interpretation of the meaning of the Reformation, rather than an order for the life of a gathered, separated minority. However, 1525 ended with widespread persecution of commoners, Anabaptists among them, who had made the mistake of believing too literally in the ideals of the early Reformation.

Martin Haas has described the convoluted process in which Swiss Anabaptism ceased to be a mass movement and inexorably took the path towards separatism.[25] At first the issue of the tithe and the zins contract, for instance, was conceived in terms of whether, in a reformed Christian world, Christians should or should not pay and profit from tithes and zins contracts. This did not, usually, imply violence against owners of tithes and beneficiaries of zins contracts, but it did involve the innocent expectation of a biblical reorganization of property relations as part of the Reformation. Then the cruel realization dawned that there would be no reformed Christian order, that persecution would continue until the end of the world and that true Christians were necessarily a scattered flock not at home on this earth – an insight that had something to do with the simultaneous slaughter of the peasants and persecution of religious dissenters (particularly when they were commoners – exceptions were made for a nobleman such as Caspar von Schwenckfeld; and many of the humanely learned thought that an exception should have been made for Michael Servetus). At that point, without any particular change in economic and social ideals, it became necessary for the Swiss Anabaptists to clarify that, for them, community of goods did not mean seizing the property of the rich, and that Christians must pay what they owed under such wicked arrangements as tithes and zins contracts, even though, as real Christians, they would never turn them to their own profit. This later position was not exactly more conservative than that of early 1525 and the preceding years; it is more precise to label it a disillusioned radicalism, no longer innocently hopeful about a general commoners' Reformation.

In this context Conrad Grebel responded more with a clarification than a denial to Zwingli's accusation that he had taught community of goods among Christians: "I do not admit that I ever taught that one should have to give his property to anybody for nothing."[26] Looking back on his interrogations and forced recantation in Zurich from the safe vantage of Nikolsburg at the end of 1526, Balthasar Hubmaier wrote a tract replying to Zwingli's various accusations. Here he took a position substantially the same as the one that appears in Zwingli's earlier writings: "On community of goods I have always and ever said that each person should take care for the other, so that the hungry are fed, the thirsty given drink, the naked clothed. For we are not the masters of our goods but rather the stewards and administrators. Certainly there is none of us who says that we should seize what belongs to someone else and make it common. Rather, when someone asks for your coat you should also give him your cloak."[27]

The Swiss Anabaptist rejection of usury and zins contracts, mentioned in the 1527 mandate, continued into the 1530s. It left its mark in the formal disputations in Bernese territories between Swiss Brethren and representatives of the official Reformed church.

There were definite differences between the two sides in the debates. Despite their already well-established separatism, the Swiss Brethren thought that usury was a proper issue for Christians to discuss, but the Reformed pastors were much less certain. It was surely necessary to discuss the topic because the Anabaptists had taken a position on it; but Christ's kingdom was not of this world – he had avoided judging the two brothers' dispute about an inheritance (a favourite Swiss Brethren proof text in a different connection) and, basically, Christ "never involved himself with temporal things or undertook to change them."[28] The Christian approach to economic matters should be to apply the principle of love, taking account of human sinfulness.

The Swiss Brethren at Zofingen in 1532 and Hans Meyer from Aarau in 1531 at Bern were much more definite in their views about what they regarded as "usury." Hans Meyer, referred to as "Pfistermeyer," made the longer, more interesting argument. His statements are important particularly since he was baptized in Zollikon in August 1525 and thus is close to the early Swiss Anabaptist position on property, denounced in the 1527 mandate. In one important, but predictable, respect he differed from the position described in the mandate. "I have never taught anything other than that everyone should pay what he owes"; and it certainly did not damage a Christian's soul to pay interest on borrowed capital: "A person should pay interest, but not receive it."[29] This was in harmony with the postion of Georg Blaurock – that Anabaptists did not receive income from zins contracts or tithes, because they were evil, but, as Christians who did not resist evil, they paid them[30] – and this was the more or less standard opinion among Anabaptists in Bern and Aargau.[31]

Meyer stressed the command of Christ in Luke 6 to lend without hoping for return. The pastors replied that that was a fine expression of love from the lender; but, they asked, did not the borrower have a similar obligation of love that could be met by paying the lender a moderate yield on his invested capital? Meyer saw the borrower's obligation of love in a different light. He said repeatedly that the borrower had a Christian obligation not to borrow unless he was in need – so the whole issue of the profit that he could make with borrowed money did not arise; in effect, it was unchristian to borrow money with a view to making a profit. Taking interest from money was wrong, because money was unproductive. Indeed, should the lender himself later come into distress, the borrower had a duty of love to lend to him, not just as much as he once borrowed, but to the full extent of his property.[32]

Fundamentally, for Meyer, Christians always had a duty to help when they could: "A Christian does not borrow unless he is in need. Anyone who borrows without present need does wrong, since Christ forbade us to take care for the morrow. And thus, if someone who lends is not in need, he, too, should not receive interest from the person he helped, since he was able to do it, for we are only stewards of the property that God has given us."[33]

What seems to a twentieth-century reader to be mere ignorance of economics had a stronger rationale in the sixteenth century. "Nahrung," the ideal of modest sufficiency, was the object in fact of the greater part of the economic activity of peasants and craftsmen, and their activity was outside or only loosely connected with the market and its laws. The market had been present, of course, in the ancient world and through much of the middle ages, but only with the eighteenth century did it begin to dominate the economic lives of most Europeans.[34] For people living and working in a primarily subsistence economy, the principle of not borrowing without immediate need, and of not lowering oneself to take advantage of one's needy neighbour if you had more than "enough" for the time being, seemed to be fundamental Christian ethics. Since the Bible repeatedly denounced usury, as Meyer reminded the preachers, their evasive position was not easy for him to understand.[35]

The Reformed pastors replied with what John Yoder has unkindly labeled as "a casuistry of compromise," and what Walther Köhler has referred to more sympathetically as an attempt to reconcile the imperatives of Christianity and culture.[36] To begin with, the term "usury" in the Old Testament, they said, drawing upon their knowledge of Hebrew, referred merely to exacting *excessive* interest on loans; usury occurred only in cases of "skinning and scraping [*schinden, schaben* – the same language used by Müntzer and in rebel documents of 1525] and grievously exploiting." The ecumenical

Council of Basel had permitted returns of 5 per cent (they had it wrong – it was the Council of Constance), not exactly as a godly measure, but to avoid the greater evil of 8 per cent or 9 per cent zins contracts. Then, in a discussion that applies exactly the same reasoning used in Zwingli's *Von göttlicher und menschlicher Gerechtigkeit* ("On Divine and Human Justice"), they explained that the Bible's injunction to "lend, hoping for nothing again" (Luke 6:35) should be taken in the same sense as Jesus's "Be perfect, as your heavenly Father is perfect" – a goal never to be lost sight of, but never literally attainable in this sinful world. To elaborate, they gave an interpretation of the various levels of ethical demands in the Old Testament's approach to poverty. The highest command, in Deuteronomy 15:7, was to let there be no poor among the people of Israel. But since God knew that this would not be obeyed, he set a lower standard, a command to lend to the poor and needy. Because God knew that even the lesser command would not be perfectly obeyed, he further commanded mercy and kindness for those poor people who found themselves in such dire straits that they had to sell themselves into slavery. If even the least demanding of God's laws was ignored, human laws must intervene to put a limit to wickedness. But people who do not reach the level of God's highest laws will nevertheless be saved, if they recognize their miserable condition, cry out to God and console themselves with the merits of Christ.[37] At the end of this lengthy exposition, Meyer replied with one sentence: "With this speech of yours, you've opened the door for the avaricious and the usurers to become still wickeder and continue with their avarice and usury."[38]

Meyer, as was more or less required, recanted, saying that though he could not grasp the preachers' stretching love as far as they did on the matter of loans of money, he would pray for God to give him the grace of a wider understanding.[39] The next year the Anabaptists of Zofingen prepared a specific answer on the topic of the obligations of love that a borrower owed to his creditor. "He should not be stubborn, should repay the money he borrowed as quickly as possible and recognize the goodness and love that has been compassionately extended to him. That a loan should, beyond that, yield advantage and profit – for that we would like to hear reasons."[40] The burden of the new magisterial Reformation weighed on the Reformed pastors. "Usury" was still a bad word, and "Nahrung" was their economic ideal, too; but they had religious obligations to people who lent and borrowed as a matter of business. The sectarians, they thought, should realize that Christ stayed clear of making pronouncements about property. They felt obliged to interpret

Christ's law of love so that the specific act of love required from borrowers to their creditors was the payment of a moderate rate of return.

The arguments of Meyer and the Zofingen Anabaptists centred on the taking of interest for loans of money. But this was not the only kind of zins contract; in another kind, property, such as a field or vineyard, could be lent against a specified annual return, which would be guaranteed by a piece of the borrower's property as a surety. Meyer did not object to this type of contract, but another Anabaptist, the Strasbourg notary Fridolin Meyger, did.

Meyger provides a case in point of a peaceful Anabaptist broadly associated with the Swiss tradition who had quite a radical social conscience. Arrested in 1528 together with such Anabaptist notables as Pilgram Marpeck, Wilhelm Reublin and Jakob Kautz, Meyger wrote to Martin Bucer a summary of his views on land leases and zins contracts, which he denounced as usury. All his life, he recounted, he had been zealous about morality and religion, first as a papalist and then as a follower of the new Gospel, after Erasmus and Luther exposed abuses in the Roman Church. Yet he found himself disturbed and troubled when the Reformers began to split into separate factions and denounce each other in books. "Then these brothers who are called Anabaptists, sent by God (I cannot call it anything else) and without my own doing, led me to a middle way between the papacy and Lutheranism, removed me from all schism and directed me to a good, upright, Christian life."[41]

What most disturbed Meyger about the transactions he notarized was their role in allowing the idle *rentier* class to abuse the working poor. Meyger complained that zins contracts were really usurious, because the lender shared none of the borrower's risk. For instance, if the peasant put up his house as a surety and it burned down, or offered one of his fields to guarantee the loan and the course of the Rhine changed and washed it away, the lender had an absolute right to expropriate some equivalent property of the victim of such an "act of God": "So it is seen to that the usurer is certain of his return, even if God died or the sky fell! No matter what happens to the poor working drudge!" This usury, moreover, was the foundation of the idleness of the aristocracy, repeatedly forbidden by God. "Isn't idleness a wicked thing?" Under the circumstances, wrote Meyger, "I was not at all sorry about the Peasants' War when it first broke out and had a promising appearance." He had thought that God might through a miracle erase the common people's debts, something he thought was done every seven years in Old Testament Israel. After seeing the Peasants' War turn destructive and come to a bad end, Meyger concluded that God would indeed right social and economic wrongs, "but not before his Great Day, I fear."[42]

Meyger was a typical Anabaptist, to judge from the Anabaptist leaders he associated with in Strasbourg and from his gratitude to them for showing him the way to a good, moral life. Although a city person with an urban occupation, he identified with the wrongs of the peasantry. Indeed, he approved of the original, non-violent aims of the commoners' uprising, although he apparently turned against the peasant bands because of the indiscriminate pillaging and mass slaughter with which their movement ended. Meyger is an example of a non-violent early Anabaptist who was not so separated from the world as to be resigned or oblivious to usury, tithes and the exploitation of the common people on the land. He voiced the rejection of the idle rich which we have previously seen implied in Swiss Anabaptist attempts to restore the church of Acts 4.

Earlier, in 1526, another Strasbourg Anabaptist, Jörg Tucher, had summed up what community of goods meant among the Swiss Brethren: "that things should be common, and that we all sustain ourselves by our work. And if someone is needy, that we should share with the needy person out of the common treasure."[43] Until the clash with the Hutterites, this sort of Christian mutual aid was not seen by the Swiss Brethren as a less demanding alternative to the community of goods described in Acts 4 but as its proper, biblical expression. It is probably not too much of an inferential leap to conclude that the Swiss Brethren would have regarded a *rentier* among their number as just as much of a disturbance of the unity and equality of the body of Christ as the Schleitheim Articles declared a ruler would be. In both instances it was a moot point, because rulers and *rentiers* were not rushing to join the persecuted brotherhood. Still, at least one early Swiss Anabaptist connects the cases of rulers and *rentiers*. Heinrich Seiler from Aarau said in 1529, "No Christian can be a ruler, because rulers collect tithes and get income from zins contracts, and people who do that cannot enter the kingdom of God."[44]

The relaxing of the ideal of community of goods is evident early, however, in Bern, the eventual centre of Swiss Anabaptism. Hans Hausmann, an emissary from the Basel congregation commissioned to baptize in Bern, offered serious qualification to the principle of community of goods around 1527 – at the very time the congregational order was upholding it. He held to the usual strict position on zins contracts, tithes and usury, but, he said, "I don't reject property. In the beginning of Christianity everything was common; but it is no command."[45] Hausmann's was not an isolated opinion

in Bern. In the same judicial interrogation in 1527 in which Hausmann made the above statement, Hans Treyer said that property
was all right so long as it was well used; the important thing was
that no Christian should allow a fellow Christian to be needy.[46]
Heinrich Seiler expressed himself in similar terms in 1529.[47] Hausmann returned to the subject in a statement he composed, also in
1529, while in prison:

Concerning temporal goods, how they should be common, and that a Christian should have no property, that is the opinion and point of the Scripture
in I John 3[:17]. I will abide by this passage, as it reads 'If anyone sees his
brother starving or in need but has no pity on him, how can the love of
God be in him?' It does not follow from that that one should make or has
made a command that all goods should be collected together, as some want
to understand it. It would also be contrary to the Scripture in Acts 5[:3-4],
where Peter says, 'Ananias, How is it that Satan has so filled your heart
that you have lied to the Holy Spirit and have kept for yourself some of the
money you received for the land? Didn't it belong to you before it was
sold?'[48]

This statement anticipates a future in which property-holding
Anabaptist groups would deemphasize their earlier position that
Christians have no absolute right of possession. Instead they would
insist that, just as Christian baptism must be voluntary, Christian
mutual aid must come about as the result of the voluntary decision
of property holders. Ananias had the right to keep some or all of
his property (although, of course, not to lie to the church about what
he did).

It has long been recognized that many elements of the Swiss
Anabaptists' social teaching were held by others as well. A broadly
approving attitude towards community of goods had been held by
Erasmus and Zwingli before the crisis point of the Reformation in
1524-25.[49] Fridolin Meyger's exchanges with Bucer on the subject
of usury were not antagonistic, and his essential point, that any
lending agreement in which the borrower bore the entire risk was
usurious, represented the prevalent opinion in late-medieval scho-
lasticism.[50] Nevertheless, the early Swiss Anabaptists assembled
these familiar elements into a new pattern, created by their ambition
to reconstruct what they believed to be the practice of the New
Testament church. Just as they wanted to practise baptism and the
Lord's Supper in the manner of the apostles, so did they wish to
replicate the apostolic practices described in Acts 2 and 4. By community of goods they meant the literal imitation of Acts 2 and 4;

they could not possibly have meant anything else. In sum, there is sufficient evidence to conclude that the governments of Zurich, Bern and St Gallen were correct in saying that the earliest Anabaptists rejected the taking of interest and living without labour. The Anabaptists soon clarified their position, explaining that they would pay what they owed, but they remained firm in their view that usury was a manifest evil.

The disputations of the early 1530s show that there were clear differences between the Swiss Anabaptists and the Reformed pastors that resulted directly from the institutionalization of the Reformation, even though the pastors tried to present these differences as the outcome of their more learned understanding of the Bible. From their first congregational ordinance, the Swiss Brethren had in their distinctive manner crystallized a rule from the German New Testament. It was a rule of sharing and a rule against exploitation, and it would be the Swiss contribution to the ongoing history of Anabaptist community of goods.

CHAPTER FIVE

The Anti-Materialistic Piety of Thomas Müntzer and Its Anabaptist Expressions

In the interrogation under torture of Thomas Müntzer the day following the battle of Frankenhausen, he declared that "he undertook the uprising so that all Christians should be equal, and to drive out or kill the princes and lords who would not support the Gospel." In response to the next question he divulged the names of prominent members of his League for the defence of the Allstedt Reformation, created during his pastorate there. Then, immediately thereafter, he said that the principle and goal of the Allstedt League was "Omnia sunt communia" and that goods should be distributed to everyone according to need. Whichever prince, count or lord was unwilling to do that, after being asked, should be beheaded or hanged."[1]

Skeptical historians have noted how the progression of the questioning turned a plausible statement about the aims of the Thuringian peasant uprising into an admission of the murderous intent of the earlier Allstedt League, whose overt acts of violence had not gone beyond an attack on a wonder-working statue of the Virgin. Instead of Christians merely being equal as in the first statement, in the second they were to share their goods; and the cause for killing rulers became socio-economic, instead of religious as in the earlier statement, while the description of how they were to be killed became more specific and threatening. This confession seemed to have one of the classic objectives of extorted confessions; it provided grounds for further arrests, interrogations under torture and executions.[2]

For historians who regarded Müntzer as a distant ancestor of the German Communist state, it was sometimes important to view the statement "omnia sunt communia" as authentic, despite the circumstances in which Müntzer said it. It was the "maximal program" of his Thuringian uprising, in contrast to his practical "minimal program," with which he was able to win the political cooperation of persons of social distinction.[3] If genuine, this statement would have been the one time Müntzer alluded explicitly to Acts 2 and 4 – the community of goods among the apostles in Jerusalem. The Vulgate text of Acts 2:44 was: *"Omnes etiam qui credebant, erant pariter et habebant omnia communia"* ("And all that believed were together and had all things common.")[4]. The questions of whether the statement "omnia sunt communia" was extorted and whether it was a slogan actually used by Müntzer at Allstedt seem unanswerable. More important was the concern in Müntzer's writings for equality among Christians. That equality had an economic side to it which was an integral part of a well-thought-out anti-materialistic piety. Müntzer did not expound a philosophical anti-materialism that made of matter an evil principle because it lacked spirit or was antagonistic to spirit, but he did denounce social materialism. His society's preoccupation with material things was, for Müntzer, the most prominent symptom of a disturbed relation among God, man and creatures in a corrupt, fallen world. Müntzer's anti-materialistic piety was best expressed in his last two polemical tracts of 1524, the *Ausgedrückte Entblössung* ("Manifest Exposé")[5] and the *Hochverursachte Schutzrede* ("Highly-provoked Vindication").[6] The latter work is less informative than the former about the social and economic applications of Müntzer's theology, because it was part of a malevolent exchange with Martin Luther; but the socio-economic viewpoint of both writings is the same.

Müntzer's attitude towards property was that it was the outcome of man's distorted relation to his fellow creatures, resulting from the fall of Adam and Eve. As a consequence of the original sin and the way it disturbed God's orginal order of creation, "all the joys of the body are an obstacle to the working of the Holy Spirit."[7] Selfishness, sexual pleasure and material accumulation stood in the way of salvation. In society as it actually existed, the very "business of keeping alive [*narung*]" brought it about that "everyone was obsessed with the collecting of material things [*creaturen*]."[8]

Both of Müntzer's last writings were directed against Luther, the *Vindication* more explicitly. Their polemical indictment was that Luther, like the "scribes" of Jesus's day, set a learned interpretation of the Bible against the voice of the Holy Spirit,[9] that he despised the Law, wanting it abolished rather than fulfilled,[10] and that, for all of his self-proclaimed bravery and independence, he attacked only helpless enemies such as priests and monks and merchants, while he flattered the feudal ruling class, the lords and princes.[11] Müntzer's *Exposé* was aimed particularly at the *grosse Hansen*,[12] the "Big Jacks," the ruling class which monopolized honour and possessions.

It is true that Müntzer did not idealize the poor or the commoners. As noted, his final dictum on the uprising of 1525 was that it had failed because of the commoners' selfishness.[13] The poor were hoodwinked by the clerics, both the old Roman clergy and the new "evangelical" clergy, to whom they passively entrusted their souls.[14] The people would have to be punished severely for "the disorderly pleasures with which they kill time."[15]

Nevertheless, Müntzer looked upon the commoners as the victims of a system created by clerics and aristocrats for their own purposes. His views were very much in the spirit of the great social upheaval of 1525. To the clergy, especially the learned biblical scholars whom Müntzer compared to the New Testament "scribes," he said that instead of educating the common man to be their equal, they wanted to monopolize authority over religion through their advantage in biblical knowledge and thus "to bring the testimony of the spirit of Jesus Christ to the university."[16] To the rulers he made the prediction which, even more than the statement "omnia sunt communia," has endeared him to subsequent revolutionary traditions: "the people will be free, and God alone will be their lord."[17]

A convincing interpretation of Müntzer's theology suggests that, for him, the people play the same role in the external world that faith performs in the heart and soul of the believer.[18] Both have a purgative function; faith destroys all creaturely attachments that contest the lordship of God within the individual; the people are destined to destroy the material lordship of creatures that opposes God's dominion over his creation. Müntzer was disposed to say that Luther's attack on merchants was a red herring dragged across the trail to throw the hounds off the scent. The real servants of mammon were elsewhere.[19] "The stinking puddle from which usury, thievery and robbery arises is our lords and princes. They make all creatures their property – the fish in the water, the bird in the air, the plant in the earth must all be theirs. Then they proclaim God's commandment among the poor and say, 'You shall not steal' ... They oppress everyone, the poor peasant, the craftsman ... are skinned and scraped."[20] The accomplices of the temporal lords were the clergy – most of all, new evangelical clerics such as Luther, who bribed the rulers both with their deference and with the confiscated properties of the papal church.[21]

Müntzer's message seethed with the imagery of social resentment and its substance was that the order of property was radically opposed to God's lordship, both in people's hearts and in the world. The special quality of the godless person was that, like the rich man in Luke 10, he thought that the very reason for his existence was "a long pleasurable life," which included a good conscience. "He works constantly at sensuality, avarice and pride."[22] The clerics and rulers were soft, self-indulgent: "big, fat bull-necks" who claim to monopolize religion[23]; "defenders of the faith" who "have passed their lives in beastly gluttony and drunkenness, brought up most tenderly from their earliest days, never had a bad day their whole life long and don't intend to have one … won't give up a penny of interest on their money."[24] Salvation came not with such pleasant, materially satisfied lives but through the inner turmoil of a struggle for faith that led to the renunciation of all material attachments.

The rich and powerful were not only closed off from genuine faith, they had closed the door to the salvation of the people. To the rich Müntzer quoted Matthew 6: "'You cannot serve God and riches.' Whoever accepts honour and goods as his masters, he is left eternally empty by God."[25] But also "because of the poison of the godless the poor people cannot come to repentance."[26] "The peasants are crushed by labour. Their whole life has been passed on a meagre living, so that they could fill the gullets of the arch-godless tyrants."[27] What could they be expected to know about the Christian faith? The hypocritical evangelicals tell the people to search the Scriptures to find their salvation, but at the same time they bless a social order which keeps the poor illiterate because of "anxiety about subsistence."[28] Müntzer's conclusion is that "in the face of usury, dues and rents no one can come to faith."[29]

The destruction of this wicked misordering of goods and power was the great providential task of the day. It was also the just and righteous fulfillment of the divine law, which Luther falsely claimed to be abolished.[30] Although Müntzer said he did not "love rebellion," neither was he opposed to "a justified uprising,"[31] particularly in circumstances in which "the lords themselves bring it about that the poor man is their enemy."[32] "It is the greatest abomination on earth that no one will care for the want of the needy."[33] Here the apocalyptic note entered Müntzer's reflections. The bad priests and rulers could not imagine that the biblical prophecy of the separation of the godless and the elect – "the godless will be cast down from the seat of judgment and the lowly and coarse raised up"[34] – would be fulfilled. He reminded his readers of the angels with the long spears: God would no longer merely look on, "He must shorten the day for his elect's sake (Matthew 24)."[35]

Using the language of the Reformation, but not the theology of Martin Luther, Thomas Müntzer attacked the priests and aristocrats on behalf of the common people. His denunciations tended toward a stripping away of the clerical monopoly on religion (which he thought Luther attacked only in words but not in deed) and the aristocratic monopoly on honour and possessions. His last two tracts in 1524 were a socially egalitarian religious manifesto of the commoners' resistance movement which he saw ripening.[36] Müntzer had a truly ascetic vision, according to which people would serve God by breaking their ties to a wickedly materialistic worldly social order. He believed this was possible because he saw signs of the end of things all around him. The failure of the uprising of 1525 taught him only that the commoners had sought their own selfish goals rather than the salvation of Christendom and that, in the language of John 7[:6], which he cited in his last letter to Mühlhausen: "My time has not yet come."[37]

As indicated, there is no way to be certain whether the statement "omnia sunt communia" was Müntzer's own principle or a projection of princely fears tortured out of him by an interrogator.[38] Recently Adolf Laube has argued strongly against the authenticity of the statement,[39] never denying Müntzer's anti-materialistic piety but holding that such a piety precluded Müntzer's working out a communist system. That would certainly be a sound argument, if we were to regard "omnia sunt communia" as a principle of a primitive social science, which it was not. The statement invokes Acts 2 and 4 as the objective of Müntzer's Allstedt covenant, which, Laube argues, is clearly nonsense in view of Müntzer's opposition to rebellion by subjects against their rulers, frequently expressed during his Allstedt pastorate. At first glance this seems a strong point. However, almost the whole population of Allstedt sided with Müntzer during the 1525 uprising. Is it farfetched to assume that the Allstedt covenant was revived during this later period?

Here we will briefly examine, in the context of Müntzer's entire theological outlook, the plausibility of his appealing to Acts 2 and 4. In his earliest known religious controversies, against Franciscans in Jüterbog and Zwickau in 1519 and 1520, Müntzer found particularly objectionable the proposition he attributed to the monk Tiburtius: "It is not absolutely necessary to live according to the Gospel."[40] Here, of course, he was challenging the fundamental monastic distinction, according to which poverty, chastity and obedience were a higher way, "counsels of perfection" to which only the "religious" were obligated, while the lesser "commands" were all that was required of the laity. The monks thought of themselves as putting Acts 2 and 4 into practice. In demanding that all Christians accept the whole Gospel as binding, Müntzer introduced the principle "omnia sunt communia" into the lives of the common laity.

For Müntzer, as was made clear in his "Prague Manifesto" of 1521, in which he first articulated an independent theology, the object of the Reformation was to set up a renewed church of the apostles. Because of his peculiar understanding of the ancient church historian Eusebius, Müntzer concluded that the church had lost the Holy Spirit in the late second century. As Müntzer paraphrased Eusebius, "after the death of the pupils of the apostles the unblemished Christian church became a whore through spiritual adultery."[41] Eusebius's picture of the apostolic church attributed to it renunciation of property and community of goods, characteristics that continued after the dispersion of the first Christians from Jerusalem."[42]

A similar reference to Acts 2 and 4, as the fruit of conversion by the Holy Spirit at Pentecost, appears in the writings of Augustine, which Müntzer said he had "reread"[43] in the year prior to his call to Zwickau. Ulrich Bubenheimer points out that Müntzer's debt to Augustine is an unstudied terrain in Müntzer scholarship.[44] Nevertheless, Abraham Friesen has recently made a strong argument that the interpretation of the parable of the tares (Matthew 13) in Augustine's anti-Donatist writings had a strong influence on Müntzer.[45] Müntzer repeatedly asserts that his own day is the harvest time when the tares, the weeds, must be separated from the good wheat.

To continue with Friesen's view of Müntzer's theological foundations, they consisted of a very personal combination of Eusebius's statements about the fall of the second-century church, Augustine's eschatological interpretation of the parable of the tares and Johannes Tauler's mystical spirituality. The last element, according to a near-consensus in Müntzer scholarship, was central to Müntzer's notions of individual spirituality, and it reinforced the interest in Acts 2 and 4 which Müntzer encountered in Eusebius and Augustine. In his printed sermons, which Müntzer read, Tauler devoted much attention to the descent of the Holy Spirit at Pentecost,[46] which had as its immediate consequence the practice of community of goods by the church of Jerusalem.

Müntzer's blending of Tauler, Eusebius and Augustine directed his attention to Acts 2 and 4, which described the practice of the apostolic church and thus set the norm for the restored church of the Reformation. Of course, the whole Reformation, from the salvation through tribulation of an individual elect Christian to the comprehensive transformation of the world, had to be led by the Holy Spirit. For this reason Müntzer never worked out a detailed picture of the new age; to have done so would have been tantamount to a blasphemous encroachment on God's prerogative.[47] Müntzer, it appears, held to Acts 2 and 4 by faith alone without the application of even primitive social-science reasoning. He was no utopian. The blankness of his social imagination, once the cataclysmic destruction of the present order was concluded, reminds one of Marx.

Again, this discussion does not *prove* that Müntzer taught the principle "omnia sunt communia", but Laube has, in my judgment, failed to demonstrate that it would have been implausible for him to do so.

Müntzer's anti-materialistic piety continued after the success of the princes' bloody war against the peasants. It was carried on by two survivors of the battle of Frankenhausen, Hans Hut and Melchior Rinck, who gave a distinctive tone to Anabaptism in Thuringia, Franconia, Hesse, the Tyrol and upper and lower Austria. Especially through Hans Hut's Anabaptism, there was a definite continuity between the uprising of the common man in 1525 and the grandest, most ambitious Anabaptist experiment with community of goods in Moravia. This debt was recognized by the Hutterite chroniclers, not only with respect to Hans Hut but also to Thomas Müntzer himself. One of the chronicles said of him: "Thomas Müntzer of Allstedt, in Thuringia, was a highly intelligent and eloquent man who proclaimed many a profitable doctrine based on the Sacred Scriptures against the Catholic and the Lutheran church."[48]

The Hutterite historical tradition connected the beginnings of communitarian Anabaptism in Moravia with the confrontation at Nikolsburg in 1527 between Hans Hut and Balthasar Hubmaier. The Great Chronicle identified with Hut's side of that controversy, going so far as to misrepresent Hut as a conventional non-resistant with beliefs like those of the Schleitheim Articles.[49] In fact, Hut had approved peasant militancy in 1525, eventually explained its failure in language similar to that of Thomas Müntzer, and in a sense continued Müntzer's work after he became an Anabaptist. He believed that Müntzer's mission in the Peasants' War began the apocalyptic tribulations of three and one-half years which would culminate in 1528 with the return of Christ and the punishment of the wicked. He maintained that Müntzer was the apocalyptic witness foretold in the Book of Revelation, that the wicked were Müntzer's old enemies, the priests and rulers, and that the covenanted people of God were those who received the sign of believers' baptism. He expected the Anabaptists to complete the punishment of the godless in 1528 after the tribulation of a Turkish invasion.[50]

A member of Müntzer's league during the Mühlhausen period,[51] Hut was visited by Müntzer in Bibra and entrusted with the publication of the *Manifest Exposé*, a responsibility he fulfilled at Hans

Hergot's press in Nuremburg in October 1524.[52] Thus the publication of the tract which best expressed the social implications of Müntzer's theology associated Hut and Hergot, who was executed in 1527 as the alleged author of the communist utopian work, *On the New Transformation of a Christian Life.*[53]

We know of Hut's beliefs from three sources: from his confessions after his arrest in Augsburg in September 1527, from his writings, and indirectly from the statements and writings of his followers. The confessions from the Augsburg interrogations, in which Hut proved a cunning and self-protective witness, partially conceal his hostility to property: "I never pressured anyone into selling his possessions, but I did teach that anyone who had more than enough should help the needy. Thereupon some people of means sold fields, vineyards or other properties and distributed the proceeds to the poorer brothers."[54] Here, of course, the allusion to Acts was clear enough, mingled, perhaps, with an echo of Müntzer's denunciation of the "abomination" that many so-called Christians did not attend to the wants of the needy.

This part of Hut's social message was the one that the rank and file of his converts absorbed. A typical view was that of an Anabaptist from Uttenreut in Franconia: "We didn't pledge ourselves to anything, beyond helping the poor according to our means for God's sake."[55] The blacksmith Hans Passauer of Rothenburg summed things up more cogently than most: "We have not made a league against the government. The new baptism is nothing other than the covenant of a good conscience with God. The Word of God binds us to love God and our neighbour, and requires that we should help the poor better than others."[56]

Yet these views expressed merely an interim ethic applying to the short time before the end of the world. Only the specially initiated among Hut's followers were told of his hopes for 1528. According to his lieutenant, Marx Maier, himself a refugee from the Peasants' War: "Hans Hut taught and prophesied that four years after the Peasants' War God will hand over the sword and vengeance to the Anabaptists in order to punish sin, stamp out all governments, kill everyone who has not received the new baptism and make all goods common. This article we do not reveal to everyone."[57] Similar associations between the final slaughtering of the ungodly and community of goods among covenanted Anabaptists appear in the statements of Georg Nespitzer and Hans Weischenfelder. They, too, made the point that Hut's eschatology was a secret teaching not revealed to everyone.[58]

Community of goods was a basic element of Hut's esoteric teaching, which he referred to as the "Seven Judgments." Specifically, it was an element of the sixth judgment, "the Kingdom of God," in which the just together with Christ would abolish rulership and private property.[59] The student Ambrosius Spittelmaier, an initiate into Hut's eschatology, describes with some elaboration Hut's views about "the kingdom of God, which God will give only to those who are poor in spirit." Since we lack a comparable discussion by Hut, Spittelmaier's statement provides the best access to Hut's anti-materialist eschatological piety.

No one can inherit this kingdom except those who on earth are poor with Christ. A Christian calls nothing his own, not even a place to lay his head. A real Christian should not own more on earth than he can cover with one foot. This does not mean that he should have no trade, or sleep in the woods, that he should have no fields or pastures, or that he should not work; rather that he should use nothing for himself alone, saying: 'this house is mine, this field is mine, this money is mine.' Instead, he should say, 'Everything is ours,' just as we pray: 'Our Father.'

In sum, a Christian should not call anything his own, but hold all things in common with his brother and not allow him to suffer want. I should not work so that my house be filled, and my bowl be full of meat, but rather I should see that my brother has enough. A Christian is more concerned about his neighbour than about himself (I Cor. 13) ... The kingdom of God will come here on earth (Matt. 5) but heaven and earth must first be renewed by fire (Isa. 66).[60]

Hut's own writings describe the first judgment, the baptismal covenant of God. His *Von dem geheimnus der tauf* ("On the Mystery of Baptism") was preserved by the Hutterites and rightly regarded as a part of their tradition. In it a digression shows how Hut, in Müntzer's footsteps, could connect anti-clericalism with a radical social critique: "Everyone says that each of us should stay in his vocation. If this is so, why didn't Peter remain a fisherman, Matthew a tax collector – and why did Christ tell the rich young man to sell what he had and give to the poor? If it's right that our preachers may have great possessions, then the rich young man would have been in the right to keep his possessions. Oh, Zacheus, why did you give up your property so frivolously, according to our preachers' rule you could have kept it and still been a good Christian!"[61]

Werner Packull has described how Augustin Bader, one of Hut's followers in Augsburg, responded to disappointment of the hopes for an end of the world in 1528 with a visionary exaggeration of Hut's apocalyptic beliefs. Bader's views have marked similarities to those of the *New Transformation* and Bader's closest associate was Oswald Leber, a veteran of the Peasants' War in the Odenwald. When arrested in 1530 by the Habsburg government of Württemberg, Bader and Leber expressed the characteristic anti-materialistic piety of Müntzer and Hut. Leber's ground for saying that "everything should be in common" was that the group wanted to "remove their hearts from everything external."[62]

Taking an opposite tack to Bader's, a number of Hut's articulate associates distanced themselves from his hopes for revenge for the Peasants' War and developed his social radicalism into forms appropriate to the political weakness and non-violent stance of most Anabaptists. The missionary conference of Anabaptist leaders in Augsburg in August 1527, while convinced that the end of the world was close, did not endorse the details of Hut's apocalyptic program.[63] At Regensburg late in 1527 representatives of Hut Anabaptism such as Leonhard Freisleben and Augustin Würzlburger reduced his ideas about community of goods to the view that everyone's needs should be attended to and no one should be forced to beg. Würzlburger also specified that "whoever can work and won't work because he counts on us providing for him, such a person we ban and regard as a heathen."[64] Packull's estimate was that "in these converts of Hut we find the beginning of a more sober, realistic Anabaptism concerned less with eschatology than with ethics."[65] Here Hut's interim ethic effaced his eschatological vision of the kingdom of God.

We find a more subtle adaptation of the piety of Müntzer and Hut in the career of Leonhard Schiemer, who spread a peaceful version of Hut's Anabaptism in Austria, Bavaria and the Tyrol. Schiemer held to Hut's apocalyptic hopes, but defused their violence and associated the beginning of the last three and one-half years of tribulation with the persecution of non-resistant Swiss Anabaptists rather than with the slaughter of the resisting commoners in the Peasants' War.[66] Hut's social anger still echoed in Schiemer's writings, which in their turn were preserved and honoured both by the Hutterites and the Marpeck brotherhood:

They pray: Give us this day our daily bread. But as soon as God gives it, it isn't *ours* anymore but *mine*. It isn't enough for them to concentrate on today – rather they are concerned about tomorrow contrary to God's command, since he commands that we should not take care for the morrow. They indeed take care not only for tomorrow but for the whole year; not only for one year but for ten, twenty, thirty years. They not only are concerned for themselves but for their children, not only when their children are young but also after they're grown up.[67]

If Thomas Müntzer and the Peasants' War no longer figured in Schiemer's eschatological chronology, Schiemer was, consciously or unconsciously, giving a classic statement of Müntzer's denunciation of material attachments – or, as Müntzer had expressed it, of "cleaving to the creatures."

Gottfried Seebass summed up Hut's position on community of goods as a loyal continuation of views he must have heard from Müntzer at Mühlhausen:

Even though he calls upon Acts 2:42–47 and 4:32–37, the insistence on community of goods in Hut's theology is not the expression of an arbitrary biblicism, which absolutizes a definite moment of primitive Christian congregational life. Rather, giving up property is the clearest outward sign of overcoming the sinful flesh, whose most characteristic sign is cleaving to the creatures, the will to have and possess, which shows that a person sets his hope on the world rather than on God. In this way the mystical idea of *Gelassenheit* becomes concrete in the demand for the abolition of all private property.[68]

A paler reflection of Müntzer's piety was left behind by another of his erstwhile followers, Melchior Rinck, who survived the battle of Frankenhausen to become the major Anabaptist leader in the border area of Hesse and Thuringia. For whatever reasons, Müntzer's apocalyptic violence did not maintain itself with Rinck as it did with Hut. Rinck worked in Müntzer's own region, but from 1528 to 1531, years in which the passions of 1525 had cooled somewhat.[69]

We can infer Rinck's views on wealth and possessions primarily from the central German Anabaptist congregations he left behind. Nevertheless, in one of his few extant writings he does express his attitudes toward property, at least indirectly. His main point, which connects such disparate figures as Thomas Müntzer and Pilgram Marpeck (and which is the burden of the *Aufdeckung der Babylonischen Hurn* ["The Uncovering of the Babylonian Whore"], to be discussed below), is the intolerable presumption of rulers who think that their worldly power gives them the right to dictate to their subjects in matters of religious faith. On the contrary, Rinck writes, anyone who has authority in the congregation of Christ must be the servant (*Diener*) of all, unlike worldly rulers who "own their subject as their slave (*Knecht*) and property, to dispose of like their inheritance according to their pleasure and arbitrary will." He continues that truly Christian princes should not behave in such a way with the Christian congregation and its possessions, even though the Lutheran "scribes" teach that there are different ethical principles for spiritual and for worldly rulers. After all, "everywhere we write, cry, sing and paint v.d.m.i.e." ["May the Word of God Remain in Eternity"] – the slogan emblazoned on Müntzer's rainbow banner at Frankenhausen in 1525."[70]

Within weeks of each other in July and August 1533 members of the Anabaptist congregations of Sorga and Berka in the centre of Rinck's sphere of activity were captured in large numbers and questioned, among other things about their views on community of goods. The Sorga group, consisting of twenty-five persons, was asked whether a Christian might have property and whether in time of need someone could seize the goods of another.[71] On the whole, they rejected taking from others. The minority that approved it did so only with reservations – "if someone is a proper Christian he will take nothing more than he needs."[72] The general view about property was to have it as if they did not have it: a Christian "may have it but in such a way that he has it not, and no one should have property."[73] Similarly ambivalent expressions were characteristic of the group: "property holding and propertyless, they have property only so long as it pleases God, but they abandon it when God or the neighbour requires"[74]; "they can have it, but should remain *gelassen*."[75] Having as not having, having with *Gelassenheit*, acting as stewards for the needy, is the common denominator of the apparent contradictions in statements of these Sorga Anabaptists. The group of nineteen from the Berka congregation[76] renounced property-holding: "Christians should hold and use all things in common, and in case of need one may well seize and use the goods of another"[77]; "all goods, with the exception of husbands and wives, should be common."[78] Still, their conception of community of goods was focused on sharing within the congregation: "everyone of my opinion and belief has just as much right to my goods as I do, but not the others who are outside the brotherhood"[79]; "one Christian is responsible to share with and help the other with his goods."[80]

The ideal of Christian community of goods was something stronger in Rinck's congregations than a mere conventional recognition of the duty to give alms, but, among the harassed Anabaptist villagers, sharing with needy fellow Anabaptists must have been its only positive expression. We know that these Anabaptists were already in contact with the Moravian missionary, Jörg Zaunring, before their hearings, and that shortly afterward they spent a troubled year-and-a-half among communitarian Anabaptists in Moravia.

In the early 1530s Philipp Ulhart in Augsburg published an anonymous tract, *The Uncovering of the Babylonian Whore*. The main purpose of the work was to expose and discredit any Christian, religious justification for the use of the sword of the *Obrigkeit*.[81] Clearly the recent about-face of the Lutheran theologians, now affirming the right of the German princes to resist the emperor, and the subsequent establishment of the Schmalkaldic League, provided an important background for the composition of the piece. The author predicted (wrongly, as it happened) that the outcome would be even more bloodshed than had been seen in the Peasants' War.[82]

No other writing of early Anabaptism made such a basic connection between the critique of the sword and the critique of property. "Selfishness, riches and glory" were the thorns that smothered the seed of the sower in Matthew 13, so that it perished without fruit.[83] The story of the Gadarene swine was used to expose the folly of people who drive away Christ because of a loss of temporal goods.[84] This was exactly what the "so-called Evangelical Christians" were doing when they dishonoured Christ with bloodshed by "abandoning imperial law under holy pretexts, in order to cover up their flesh and to protect their property."[85] They distorted Scripture "when necessary to serve their property and advantage."[86]

"The preservation of glory and property" was a favourite appeal of Satan.[87] Property and worldly lordship were fundamentally entangled: "Among the wicked belongs the sword of the wicked, and wicked rulers, of their own wicked fleshly type, in order out of selfishness to maintain physical peace among one another for the sake of their property. For Christ has nothing to do with Belial."[88] Nevertheless, temporal power was established out of God's mercy among people who did not accept the peace of God, "so that they would not totally destroy each other's lives and temporal goods." The peace of God "did not consist in any property"[89]; and worldly power would seem to be more or less as the Schleitheim Articles conceived it – ordained by God's mercy but outside his true peace.

Since the power of worldly government was so necessary for the protection of property, "This I would concede, that all who presume to have property and appeal and cry to the rulers to protect their property, that they are responsible to help the rulers to protect temporal property, both theirs and others', and to maintain it in temporal peace. For from worldly property comes the *Obrigkeit* and its subjects. But the congregations of Christ stem not from property but from Christ, and are subject to him, and everyone is responsible to his own kind of authority."[90] The author of *Uncovering* regarded the holding of property by Christians with the same disapproval as he did their participation in the *Obrigkeit*.

Walter Klaassen, whose research has furthered our knowledge of when *Uncovering* appeared and who printed it, believes that it was one of the early writings of Pilgram Marpeck.[91] If so, at that time Marpeck held a more dualistic view of the Christian and the *Obrigkeit* than he expressed at a later time in his long controversial exchange with Caspar Schwenckfeld. Still, both *Uncovering* and Marpeck's later writings on the *Obrigkeit* have the same primary point, that worldly power cannot be exercised for Christian purposes. At this time in his early career Marpeck was commissioned to baptize on the authority of the "church in the land of Moravia," the *Stäbler* ("staff bearers") of Austerlitz, who practised some form of institutionalized community of goods. In that sense his blending of the critiques of worldly authority and property would fit with this stage in his Anabaptist career, notwithstanding the later alienation between the Marpeck brotherhood and the Hutterites.[92] Klaassen, as a translator and editor of Marpeck's works, believes that he has discovered many expressions in *Uncovering* similar to those in Marpeck's authenticated writings.[93] Beyond this, and in my opinion more crucially, he argues that *Uncovering* is directed against Schwenckfeld's *Dass ein Obrer ein Christ / vnd ein Christ wol ein Obrer sein kan / welch Büchlen anfengklich vom vnderscheid des alten vnd neuwen Testaments ist geschrieben"* ("That a Ruler can be a Christian and a Christian a Ruler, a Booklet Originally Written about the Difference between the Old and New Testaments"), published in 1532 or 1533.[94] Provisionally, my opinion is that *Uncovering* is directed against the Lutheran theologians and their claim of a legitimate right to resist the emperor (a facet of the work of which Klaassen is well aware) rather than against Schwenckfeld. The one passage that Klaassen regards as conclusive says that, although "a small flock" is now revealing "the mighty power of God," the whore continues to try to dishonour them "through much seduction and error that stems from the midst of the blessed. 'But they were not of us' as John said" (I John 2:[19]).[95] Then the author moves into a polemic against Martin Luther and his followers that continues through the whole tract. Depending on the identity and experiences of the author, the first comments could refer to the Lutherans – the reference to "a small flock" notwithstanding. If the argument that *Uncovering* was directed against Schwenckfeld were stronger, Klaassen's case would be firm indeed – as it is, it rests more on textual similarities with Marpeck's writings, and that kind of claim is a good deal more difficult to prove.

The anti-materialistic piety just described was the most important thing south German-Austrian Anabaptists inherited from Thomas Müntzer. Balthasar Hubmaier accused Hut, with his predictions of an imminent end of the world, of leading simple folk to sell their property, and abandon their families in order to follow him.[96] Eukarius Binder, Hut's most faithful companion from the beginning of his baptizing mission in Franconia, sold a good deal of his property when he left his home to accompany Hut.[97] A peasant named Schmidt from the same region, as well as some vine growers, raised money from their properties to finance Hut's mission, in the confidence that the old world would last less than a year, "and before the year was up, they would have enough."[98]

Together with other leaders, Hut helped to create an unusually organized congregation among the Anabaptists in Augsburg. Discovered in late 1527 and early 1528, the Augsburg Anabaptists were investigated by the humanist city secretary, Conrad Peutinger, who, with Johannes Eck, was one of the few German intellectuals to defend the great companies, then under regular attack in the imperial diet.[99] Peutinger examined the mutual-aid practices of the Anabaptists thoroughly and suspiciously. In his eyes they violated the town's alms ordinance and posed the danger that the collected funds would be used to finance a military uprising.[100] Behind the mutual aid he sensed something still more radical. The Augsburg Anabaptists were said to have decided in 1528 that property holders were to be barred from the Lord's Supper.[101] Some of Hut's followers from Bamberg, now associated with the Augsburg Anabaptists, repeated his esoteric teaching that "goods should be held in common throughout all Christendom."[102]

The Augsburg hearings showed a general Anabaptist commitment to mutual aid, as well to the poor, to refugees and to travelling preachers. The members of the congregation were told that they would be treated by God as they treated the poor.[103] Their attempt to maintain a common purse administered by a deacon failed when relentless persecution produced an unwillingness to accept the diaconal office. Even after organized assistance broke down, however, individual, voluntary aid to the needy continued, sometimes anonymously.[104] In Augsburg, where various Anabaptist tendencies met, the piety of Hut supported mutual-aid practices like those of the Swiss Anabaptists, but it also contained a persistent radical undercurrent which rejected property absolutely.

Still another outcome of Hut's preaching about community of goods can be seen in the career of Wolfgang Brandhuber, a seamster who organized congregations in Austria and the Tyrol. Writing to the congregation of Rattenberg in the Tyrol from Linz in 1529, Brandhuber defended community of goods, by which he meant that all members had to make an open disclosure of their wealth and put it at the disposal of officers of the congregation responsible for the needy. Furthermore, Brandhuber specified that "each father of a household should work together in a common purse with those who share his faith, whether they be lord, servant, wife or maid." In many places the household, as the focus of production, was the largest practicable sphere of Christian community of goods. Brandhuber did not mean that it was "necessary to make a common collection of all possessions, for this is not appropriate everywhere." His basic point was that people who shared Christ – whatever their worldly status – should share their possessions: "For since we are constant in common possession of the greatest things – in Christ and the power of God, then why not in the smallest – in temporal goods?"[105]

The Anabaptists of south and central Germany and the Austrian lands, therefore, produced statements of piety in these early years that continued Thomas Müntzer's spiritual struggle for *Gelassenheit* and freedom from material trammels. So long as it could be applied only in congregations of scattered believers and in the economics of the household, this ideal assumed an outward form similar to the early practice of Swiss Brethren. Nevertheless, its renunciation of property and possession was more intense. For this reason the Hutterites judged rightly in particularly preserving the testimonies of the Hut Anabaptism tendency as sources of their communist spirituality.

CHAPTER SIX

Anabaptist Münster, 1534–1535: The War Communism of the Notables

Their learned teachers in Münster say that for fourteen hundred years there have been no Christians on Earth.[1]

– Jakob of Osnabrück

Since the 1960s Münster Anabaptism has been the object of new research that has made it less lurid and more intelligible by relating it more successfully to the rest of Melchiorite Anabaptism, the other urban communal reformations and the politics of the Holy Roman Empire. This research has more often than not concentrated on the preconditions that were essential to the Anabaptists' assumption of power in Münster, but in the process has added much to our grasp of the Anabaptist regime itself. Its approach has been analytical and it has generally avoided moralizing rhetoric and facile comparisons with the bizarre sects or totalitarian regimes of the twentieth century.[2] The outstanding recent historian of Anabaptist Münster is Karl-Heinz Kirchhoff. He has challenged both the traditional narrative and the traditional social stereotype about the Münster Anabaptists. Previously it was believed that the Anabaptists took power when a weak council lost control of lower-class rabble, stirred up by outside agitators, the Dutch prophets. Kirchhoff has argued that, instead, a body of civic-minded notables of high social standing reluctantly sided with the Anabaptists as the only means to preserve the endangered religious and political freedoms of their town.[3]

The Münster Anabaptists were genuine Anabaptists, not a corrupt sect misusing the Anabaptist name. The Anabaptist regime in Münster arose from a peaceful Anabaptist movement established in the town since the summer of 1533, and its survivors and successors became peaceful Anabaptists after the fall of Münster, except for a militant remnant. What was typically Anabaptist was not violence or non-violence but rejection of the wickedness of the world, as represented by the established church and government. The Swiss and south German Anabaptists, too, had oscillated between militance and social withdrawal when faced with the commoners' resistance movement in 1525.

Münster Anabaptism was unique because of its linkage to a civic, communal reformation led by Bernhard Rothmann, a non-Lutheran reformer, at a time and in a region in which the dominant political forces dictated a magisterial reformation and conformity to Lutheran theology. This unusual alliance between a communal reformation and Anabaptism gave Münster Anabaptism its special power, but also assured its ultimate failure. It also accounts for the prominence in Anabaptist Münster of political notables and for authoritarian, élitist traits which make it less the commoners' reformation than was the Anabaptism of 1525–26, with its many associations with the Peasants' War in south and central Germany and Switzerland.

Melchiorite Anabaptism was a different Anabaptism. If the original Swiss Anabaptism originated in 1525 in the midst of the Peasants' War, and south German-Austrian Anabaptism arose in 1526 in the immediate aftermath of the crushing of the commoners' resistance, Melchiorite Anabaptism began in 1530 in northern, Low German areas untouched by the events of 1525. Melchior Hoffman had been a radical lay preacher of the Reformation in the Baltic lands, shaped more by Wittenberg radicalism than by Luther.[4] In 1529 and 1530 he adopted the various forms of sacramental radicalism, including the commitment to believers' baptism. More fateful were other heterodox positions he worked out in interaction with radical and prophetic circles in Strasbourg: an idiosyncratic Christology one-sidedly focused on the divinity of Christ, a claim of personal charisma for himself as a messenger of the apocalypse, and the appointment of Strasbourg as a city of refuge at the end of the world, which Hoffman had long set for 1533. In 1531, in response to the execution of some Dutch followers, Hoffman decreed a two-year suspension of baptism. Imprisoned in Strasbourg in 1533, he predicted a theocratic interim kingdom in which a "revolution from above" would be conducted by a pious king instructed by a prophet. Together prophet and king would prepare the world for Christ's return, according to Hoffman's *Von der reinen Furcht Gottes* ("On the Pure Fear of God").[5] In the years before 1534 the Melchiorites were a significant sect but not a mass movement, chiefly centered in Strasbourg, Münster and the Netherlands. The focal importance of Melchior Hoffman for Anabaptism in Münster and the Netherlands is agreed upon by the contemporary histories of two Frisian Anabaptists, Obbe Philips and Nicolaas Blesdijk.[6]

The Reformation in Münster turned out to be a hothouse made to order for the expansion of Melchiorite Anabaptism. The political order in the city was legitimated by the communal will – the burghers regarded themselves as fellow citizens rather than subjects of the ruling council. In normal times the council ruled uncontested, but in times of popular excitement a long-established tradition gave the United Guild, a body that brought together the town's guild leaders, a right to veto actions of the council. Furthermore, each year ten electors, directly elected by the full citizens, chose the twenty-four-man council. Usually the electors reconfirmed the councilors in office but in times of public discontent they could replace them.[7] In early 1533, not only were twenty of the council members replaced at the time of the triumph of the Reformation, but a change of social caste occurred. The older group of political notables, whose families had traditionally sat in the council, were replaced by a new group, of equal wealth but lesser status, who had earlier dominated the United Guild.[8] Communal power was a reality in the Münster Reformation; correspondingly, the first Münster church ordinance of April 1533 made the radical proposal that preachers should be elected by their congregations.[9] But by the 1530s communal reformations, typical in the 1520s, were less frequent and carefully monitored by the dominant political estates of the empire. In the aftermath of the Peasants' War town councils were assigned legal responsibility to maintain the public peace of the empire. The Münster council was continually torn between the communal vitality of the town's Reformation and its assigned role in the power constellation of the Holy Roman Empire.[10]

Externally, Münster's Reformation was secured against the opposition of the town's overlord, the prince bishop, by the assistance of a powerful Lutheran neighbour, Philip of Hesse, the leader of the Schmalkaldic League. Due to the power of the league after its organization in 1531, the adherents of the Augsburg Confession enjoyed a *de facto* religious toleration. This was the basis of the political victory of the Münster Reformation, ratified by the Treaty of Dülmen on 14 February 1533.

It was Münster's ill fate, however, that its popular leading Reformer, Bernhard Rothmann, was an eclectic theologian, borrowing heavily from Swiss and south German sources.[11] The natural course of the Reformation in Münster, corresponding to its communal ethos and the theology of its leader, would have been Reformed.[12] At the time, however, the Swiss Reformed were suffering from the loss of Zwingli and Oecolampadius, while the Strasbourg theologians were working for a concord with Wittenberg. In the empire, as opposed to Switzerland, an official non-Lutheran Reformation was impossible. The theologians of Marburg and Wittenberg tried to whip Rothmann and Münster into Lutheran orthodoxy, to which Rothmann responded by opening himself and the city progressively to Melchiorite influence.[13] The spearhead of the Münster Melchiorite movement were the Wassenberg preachers, led by Heinrich Roll, who arrived from Jülich in September 1532. In April 1533 the north German Lutheran theologians rejected the church ordinance of the Münster Reformation, sniffing "sacramentarianism," and by the summer Rothmann had been won over by Wassenberger arguments in support of the Melchiorite principle of believers' baptism. Jan of Leyden, the future Anabaptist king, visited Münster in the summer of 1533 because he had heard "that the Word of God was preached there best and most forcefully."[14]

The Münster council and its Lutheran secretary, Johan von der Wieck, were appalled that Rothmann had set Münster on a course towards imperial outlawry by violating the terms of the anti-Anabaptist Mandate of Speyer of 1529.[15] But the Lutheranism of the Münster Reformation did not go much deeper than raison d'etat. When the council staged a debate on infant and adult baptism in August 1533 Rothmann was, in the public's eyes, the winner. Rothmann's radical religious development posed a dilemma for the "new notables" running the United Guild. The United Guild's communal role was to support Rothmann against the council's moves to suppress and silence him, in view of his broad popular support. Nevertheless, it hesitated to break ranks with the members of its own estate now in control of the council. A crisis in November 1533 led the Münster ruling elite in the council and the United Guild to fashion an unsatisfactory compromise, so as to avoid possible civil strife. Lutheran preachers from Hesse were called in to provide Münster with a respectable religious order, but Rothmann and his Melchiorite adherents continued to be tolerated in the town, in clear violation of imperial law and to the official displeasure of both the prince bishop and Philip of Hesse.[16]

At the end of 1533 Münster Anabaptism ignited Anabaptism in the Netherlands and set in motion the great religious, social and political crisis that temporarily made a mass movement of the Melchiorite sect. Rothmann's Bekenntnisse van beyden Sacramenten ("Confession of the Two Sacraments"), published in November, was a classic peaceful Anabaptist statement. The great eclectic Anabaptist theologian, Pilgram Marpeck, would recognize it as such when he made it the basis of his Vermahnung ("Admonition") of 1542, the

most important doctrinal expression of the Marpeck congregations.[17] Although the precise sequence of events is unclear, the
reinstitution of adult baptism among Netherlands Melchiorites in
late 1533 by the Haarlem baker Jan Matthijs was connected with
Heinrich Roll's bringing Rothmann's *Confession* to Amsterdam that
December. Now the Melchiorite sect was again unequivocally baptist, as it was to remain in its later Mennonite version (although not
in its Davidite variant).[18] Jan Matthijs demanded and received total
recognition and obedience as an apocalyptic messenger, moving the
end of the world by the apocalyptic number of three and one-half
months – from Hoffman's 1533 to Easter 1534.[19] Jan's baptizers introduced actual baptism of adult believers to Münster in January
1534; thus the adult baptisms marked a higher stage of the Melchiorite movement in Münster, not its beginning.[20]

Jan Matthijs's prediction of the end of the world gained mass
credibility through a "political miracle," the deliverance of Münster
to the Anabaptists in February. The council, unable to suppress
Rothmann's religious following, suffered a collapse of its own authority, so that the United Guild, especially one of the two aldermen,
Heinrich Redecker, became the real power in the town. An Anabaptist or Anabaptist sympathizer, Redecker organized burgher resistance in the face of rumours in late January and early February
that the bishop was about to attack the town, perhaps with the
treasonable complicity of the council. Redecker represented about
half the new ruling group of 1533, which now gradually sided with
the Anabaptists.[21] For them, religious sympathy with Rothmann
and his following was undoubtedly mixed with the motive of upholding civic independence and preserving the Münster Reformation against the bishop.

The events of 9–11 February, in which the previously non-violent
Anabaptists were instructed by their prophets to take arms, were
for the Münster Anabaptists an experience of God's intervention in
history, an otherwise inexplicable deliverance like that of the Isra-
elites crossing the Red Sea.[22] Confronted with the council's armed
supporters, as well as by a peasant military levy brought into Münster, and with the bishop on his way with an armed escort, the
outnumbered Anabaptists thought of themselves as sheep ready for
the slaughter.[23] The days of crisis, marked by unusual meteorolog-
ical phenomena,[24] ended with a compromise that secured power in
the hands of the pro-Anabaptist half of the ruling group. Redecker
and the United Guild organized the election of an Anabaptist council
on February 23. Jan Matthijs, accompanied by a number of his Dutch
followers, moved to Münster and proclaimed it the divinely ap-

pointed city of refuge in the final tribulations. Letters and emissaries from Münster to the Melchiorites in Westphalia and the Netherlands declared the political miracle of February 1534 to be a literal miracle.

Jan Matthijs, until his death on Easter 1534, enjoyed an uncontested charismatic authority that far surpassed Hoffman's and that of all later Melchiorite leaders.[25] In response to the events in Münster, a wave of apocalyptic excitement swept over all estates in Westphalia and the Netherlands. That the mighty had been cast down and the proscribed Anabaptists had become burgomasters and councilors in Münster was seen as a case of the world turned upside down and a certain sign of the end of days.

The apocalyptic mood reached a climax with attempts at mass immigration to Münster in March 1534. That prior conditions in the Netherlands in the 1530s contributed to a high level of social excitability is undeniable. This was a time of war, pestilence and unemployment,[26] just as the apocalyptic sections of the Bible had foretold that tribulations would be a sign of the last times. Yet the Münster Anabaptists' appeal, containing the promise that the immigrants' needs would be provided for, does not seem to have turned the journey to Münster into a poor people's crusade. Kirchhoff's studies of Anabaptism in Coesfeld and Warendorf, major sources of the Westphalian immigration, which unlike the Dutch trek of March 1534 successfully reached Münster, indicate that a social cross-section of the population participated.[27] Henrich Gresbeck, author of the major eyewitness account of Anabaptist Münster, wrote that the newcomers who arrived in Münster had left their possessions behind and that there were rich people among them.[28] Barend Dirks, a contemporary painter, depicting the migration of Netherlanders, described one of his paintings with the caption: "They sold jewels and clothes, land and property, in every nook and corner; hurrying on board ship with great desire, prophesying the quest for a new God."[29]

Most of the thousands of Netherlanders who set out for Münster in March 1534 did not get there, but submitted passively to disbandment with confiscation of their money and arms. Released by authorities horrified at their numbers, they became the object of later appeals from Münster and formed the rank and file of later militant actions in support of the beleaguered town, such as the seizure of Oldeklooster and the attack on the Amsterdam City Hall in the spring of 1535.[30] Blesdijk, like later historians, commented that the peaceful dispersion of the trekkers showed that they were moved more by apocalyptic excitement than genuine militancy.[31] On the other hand, there seems to have been no opposition to the trek within Melchiorite circles. Figures such as Jan Matthijs of Middelberg (an Anabaptist leader to be distinguished from his namesake, Jan Matthijs of Haarlem) and Jacob van Campen, who showed independence from the later Münster leadership, probably participated.[32] In fact, the trekkers of March 1534 provided the basic membership pool for Dutch Anabaptism until the end of its militant phase.

Yet Münster's unquestioned legitimacy among Melchiorites lasted only until Easter 1534, the predicted end of the world. During the first period of the siege, until Easter, Jan Matthijs of Haarlem exercised absolute authority in Münster, overawing the elected council and people such as Redecker who had put the Anabaptists in power.[33] When the prophesied supernatural deliverance did not come, Jan sallied out against the besieging army and, in effect, committed suicide on Easter, 5 April 1534.[34] His death left his followers trapped within Münster, doomed to cope with his failure as a prophet as best they could.

Jan of Leyden never enjoyed Jan Matthijs's legitimacy and authority. He called into question Münster's status as the New Jerusalem by toying with the idea of abandoning the town for an armed invasion of the Netherlands. Some militant Dutch Melchiorites, frustrated by King Jan's ineptness as a prophet, reacted to the failure of his prediction that Münster would be delivered before Easter 1535 by setting up a new promised David in the person Jan van Batenburg.[35] Now some voices, Obbe Philips and perhaps David Joris, questioned Münster's turn from the peaceful path of Melchior Hoffman. The doubtful legitimacy of King Jan's claim to be a prophet accounts for the weakness of the Netherlands uprisings of 1535 in support of Münster, especially the attack on the Amsterdam City Hall in May.

Certainly in the Netherlands the Münsterite movement was in decline after April 1534. In besieged Münster, in contrast to the appearance of absolute power vested in King Jan, a series of careful power-sharing arrangements were made between the immigrants and the local notables who had cooperated in the Anabaptists' taking power.[36] The result was an erosion of the strict community of goods instituted by Jan Matthijs. Community of goods and polygamy – the distinctive institutions of royal Anabaptist Münster – became chiefly responses to the siege and the associated problem of caring for Melchiorite refugees from Westphalia and the Netherlands. The reality of community of goods in Münster was nothing like the egalitarian transformation of patterns of life and work achieved by the Hutterites.[37] Although Münsterite polygamy reflected the broad interest among Reformation radicals in a regenerate sexuality, according to I Corinthians 7:29, it amounted in practice to nothing more than the regulating of the female majority according to the prescriptions of biblical misogyny.[38] There was a lot of desperate play-acting in Münster from the actor-king downward. These people must have recognized with one side of their minds after the failure of Jan Matthijs's prophecy that they were destined to violent death; as Rothmann put it in one of his last writings, if it were the will of God for them to be trampled under the feet of the beast they would bear it with patience.[39] In the meantime the hegemony of notables over commoners and of men over women continued.

Kirchhoff's prosopographical study of Anabaptist property-holders native to Münster, based on records of Anabaptist property confiscated following the bishop's conquest of the town, shows an astonishing normality in distribution of wealth among the Münster Anabaptists. The social structure of the Anabaptist property-holders turned out to be very similar both to that of post-Anabaptist Münster and to the comparable town of Hildesheim. In other words, a random sample of the Münster property-owners chose Anabaptism rather than Lutheranism or Catholicism in the Reformation crisis of 1532–35.[40] Kirchhoff arrived at a similar result by contrasting the Anabaptist ruling élite with the Anabaptist rank and file. Despite the introduction of community of goods, persons who had been rich property-owners in the old order were represented in disproportionate numbers among the political leaders of the new regime.[41] There was, indeed, a silent majority of the poor and of women in besieged Anabaptist Münster, but rather than being "the real carriers of Anabaptism,"[42] they were victims of the regime.

Anabaptist Münster was conquered in June 1535 after sixteen months of resistance, including the defeat of two assaults in May and late August 1534. The bishop was able to continue the costly siege only with extensive financial aid from the empire, justified by the threat that the Anabaptists allegedly posed to the public peace.[43] In the eyes of their enemies at least the Münster Anabaptists continued the commoners' rebellion of 1525.

Until the fall of Münster, internal Melchiorite criticisms of the Anabaptist state were scattered and muted. With the end of the Anabaptist resistance, however, such distinctive Münsterite principles as the militant pre-millenial kingdom and the polygamous marriage of the saints came quickly into dispute. At a conference of Melchiorite leaders held in Bocholt in August 1536 the victor's palm went to David Joris,[44] a new promised David who could appear to compromise the disputed issues by obscuring them. The Davidite sect became increasingly Nicodemite, eventually abandoning a distinctive baptismal practice. In the 1540s Menno Simons became the paramount leader of the Melchiorite remnant, now reduced from mass movement to sect, by radically toning down their apocalyptic expectations and focusing their "inner-worldly asceticism" on sober conduct, tempered only by the ecstasy of martyrdom. Yet Menno's Melchiorite Anabaptism contained sectarian distinctives, setting it apart from the groups in south Germany and Switzerland. It had more theological content, which expressed itself most prominently in Menno's preoccupation with the Christology of Melchior Hoffman, while the Swiss Brethren religion was almost exhausted in *Ordnungen*, rules of conduct.[45] The Swiss Brethren most radically expressed the levelling, laicizing impulse of the early Reformation, while the greater authority of Mennonite elders over their flock seems to have been a watered-down continuation of the charisma of the early Melchiorite prophets.

The reinterpretation of Münster Anabaptism set out here has decided relevance for our view of Münster's ambitious experiment with community of goods. Community of goods among Anabaptists in north Germany and the Netherlands was obviously not a direct and immediate result of the events of 1525, of the commoners' resistance and its suppression, and of the wave of believers' baptisms spreading from Zurich. Melchior Hoffman had contacts with various Strasbourg radicals, including Anabaptists, in the early 1530s,[46] but he was no mere transmitter of High German influences to the different milieux of Low Germany.

It now seems reasonable to distinguish three phases of the Melchiorite movement in Münster. The first extends from the summer of 1533, when Rothmann adopted the radical sacramental position of the Wassenbergers, to February 1534. During this period the Melchiorite movement was powerful, perhaps the most powerful religious current among the Münster commoners, but it still lacked official sanction and it still responded to its opponents with peaceful avoidance. From February 1534, with its "political miracles," to Easter of that year, Anabaptist Münster was at the focal point of an apocalyptic crisis which legitimated the prophetic authority of Jan Matthijs of Haarlem. Militancy and radical community of goods corresponded to this crisis. From April 1534 to the fall of the Anabaptist regime in June 1535 Münster's apocalyptic enthusiasm was in decline, but at the same time desperate efforts were made to preserve the energies and idealism of the earlier period under the inventive, institution-building leadership of Jan of Leyden. Rammstedt's concept of "the institutionalization of charisma" does, after all, despite its reserved reception by other scholars, seem a good description of what occurred in Münster after the disappointment with Jan Matthijs's prophecy.[47] Community of goods now was shaped increasingly by the military necessities of the siege and by the need to appease a leadership-group in which notables were prominent. Richard van Dülmen goes so far as to assert that, although community of goods was the declared goal of Münster's preachers and prophets, "it was only partially achieved and later even partially abolished."[48]

Community of goods was part of the stock of ideas of Bernhard Rothmann. In his first Anabaptist writing, *The Confession of the Two Sacraments*, Rothmann connected community of goods with the Christian solidarity of the Lord's Supper, in which the communicants are one body, one bread. Here Rothmann explicity cited Sebastian Franck's *Chronica*, where the apocryphal Fourth Epistle of Clement is used to show that property arose among Christians from the bishops' betrayal of their trust: "The bishop and his servants, the deacons, were common householders and stewards, not only in the spirit but for physical needs. They parcelled out all common goods according to everyone's needs. They then started to become avaricious, to turn common goods into private property and to appropriate it for themselves."[49] Franck, of course, was no Anabaptist, but his writings enjoyed great authority in the Netherlands among Melchiorites and later among Mennonites. His anti-authoritarian reflections on sacred and profane history conveyed among northerners the radicalism of the south German Reformation. In the section that Rothmann cited, Franck digressed from discussing the Lord's Supper to treat of the origins of property. "In justice everything should be common," wrote Franck. Property, like dominion, began with the usurpation of the wicked Nimrod after the Flood. Not only Acts 2 but Plato and Epicurus witnessed against it.

No doubt Sebastian Franck's ideal of a communist golden age in the past helped to shape Münster Anabaptists' reaction to the apocalyptic crisis which began in February 1534. But that crisis was dominated by another spirit less inclusive and tolerant than Franck's. Jan Matthijs called for the carrying out of God's will immediately and without compromise. The godless must be expelled from Münster without delay, leaving their property behind. Jan Matthijs personally commanded that, since property was abolished and all goods were now common to everyone, there should be an immediate conflagration of "letters and seals, as well as privileges, registers and all other books and accounts."[50] This wave of expulsion and destruction aimed at total purification. All things were to become new in the twinkling of an eye.

One of the few glimpses we have of the practice of the peaceful separatist congregation before the arrival of Jan Matthijs comes from Jakob Hufschmidt from Osnabrück, who left Münster about the time Jan arrived there, late in February 1534. Answering questions during an interrogation, he affirmed that the Anabaptists taught that usury and zins contracts were unchristian. They were not to be extracted by Anabaptists from others, nor were they to be paid by the Anabaptists themselves. The congregation had two officers concerned with the care of the poor. These reported cases of need, received voluntary contributions and administered poor relief.[51]

Certainly the significant exchange of populations that took place in Münster in February and March 1534, when about 2,000 non-Anabaptists were expelled and about 2,500 Anabaptists immigrated into the town,[52] was an important determining factor in the practice of community of goods. Both in Moravia and in Münster the radical practice of community of goods was connected with a refugee problem. The population exchange, of course, followed Jan Matthijs's prophetic script, which demanded both the extirpation of the godless and the gathering together of the regenerate in the few weeks of grace that remained before the end of the world. Something similar would have occurred anyhow, because no early modern town or city tolerated hostile elements during a siege, and because outside Münster persecution by the governments and flight by the Anabaptists were the predictable outcomes of the twist Jan Matthijs had given to the Melchiorite movement.

The appeal for Anabaptist immigration has usually been presented by historians as directed to the poor and unemployed – "There is sufficient provision for the saints," the trekkers were assured. Of course, in the next phrase the newcomers were instructed to bring money as well as food and clothing for the journey.[53] Rothmann's letter to Heinrich Slachtschaf, commanding him to bring the Anabaptist congregation in Coesfeld to Münster, shows how little the March appeals singled out the poor: "The Lord witnessed to us through his prophets that the saints are to be gathered into this town. Therefore they ordered me to write to you that you should tell the brothers to get here promptly, bringing with them the money, gold and silver that they have on hand; the rest of their goods they should hand over to the sisters, who should dispose of them and follow."[54] In the apocalyptic moment there were to be no rich or poor, no men or women; but in the provisional haven in Münster it appears that men with money were at a premium!

However that may be, it cannot be denied that, in the beginning of Anabaptist Münster, women and poor people responded with enthusiasm to its community of goods. A woman from Münster wrote to her sister outside, requesting that her daughter be sent to join her in Münster: "I'm not concerned whether she has clothes or not. Send her to me; she'll have enough here. For you should know that the Almighty has bestowed such grace upon us that I am able to go about in gold, velvet and silk clothes ... And the poorest have become as rich through God's grace as the burgomasters or magistrates of the town."[55]

The reordering of property arrangements seems to have begun with Jan Matthijs's preaching that the possessions of the emigrés should belong in common to those who remained. He organized the storage of household furnishings and clothing in appointed houses, as well as the destruction of deeds and the confiscation of valuables.[56] Jan Matthijs never changed Münster's institutional structure, unlike his successor Jan of Leyden. His authority was personal and indirect, so the actual promulgation of community of goods came from a consensus of the prophets, preachers and council.[57] Rothmann preached that "everything Christian brothers and sisters have belongs to one as well as the other. You will lack nothing – whether goods, clothing or house and home. You will receive whatever you need. God won't allow you to go wanting. Everything will be common. It belongs to all of us."[58]

Specifically, this decision of the council involved a call for all residents of Münster to surrender their money and precious metals. According to Gresbeck, there was a good deal of resistance and delay in compliance with this decree. The enforcement dragged on for two months, past Jan Matthijs's death, and involved some exemplary executions for non-compliance.[59]

Later in the year, writing his *Restitution*, Rothmann summed up the actual accomplishments of community of goods in Münster as the abolition of "buying and selling, working for money, and indebtedness and usury."[60] Here he equated community of goods with the abolition of a money economy. Gresbeck described the anti-money rhetoric of the Anabaptist leaders in the following terms: "They said that they were Christians, that a Christian should have no money, that it was totally unclean for Christians, that Christians should not buy and sell from each other but should barter, and that throughout the whole world the one town should barter with the other."[61] Enforcing a "natural" economy based on barter corresponded to the social idealism of the time, as we are reminded when we read Thomas More's description of how things were done in Utopia. Gresbeck's suggestion that there was talk about abolishing money everywhere in the world suits the temper of the end-time expectations aroused by Jan Matthijs. However, unlike documents of indebtedness, which were destroyed, money and precious metals were collected at the council's chancellery.[62] Again, the practice of the Münster government was like that in Utopia – the common store of money and valuables was used for dealing with outsiders, to pay for imports and to conduct military operations.

The executors of community of goods in Münster were the deacons. The meaning of community there was contained in, and circumscribed by, the tasks of these officers. The number of the deacons is one of many matters on which our sources conflict. Kerssenbroch refers to seven deacons, whom he mentions by name (four or five of whom Kirchhoff has identified as natives of Münster), while Gresbeck writes of three deacons in each parish, or eighteen all together.[63]

Deacons preserved and distributed the goods of emigrés, chiefly to assist immigrants but also, in principle, to aid all needy members of the community. The cloisters, emptied and plundered immediately after the election of the Anabaptist council, were used to accommodate newcomers, and so, apparently, were deserted houses.[64] The deacons also supervised common meals for the watch and for workers of both sexes repairing the walls and trenches. These meals were served at a community house, one located near each of the ten gates. One deacon supervised the procurement of food for each of the ten community houses.[65]

The deacon in each parish was commissioned to make an inventory of personal possessions, food, household goods and clothing, and to redistribute excess supplies to the needy poor. Gresbeck noted that after two or three visitations this practice fell into abeyance for a time, because in the early stages of the siege no one went hungry. He also observed that some people did not reveal everything they had to the deacons.[66]

Under Jan Matthijs a community of goods was introduced that variously affected different kinds of property. Money, precious metals and jewels were, in theory at least, removed from private possession and made into a public utility. All movable possessions, houses and property of emigrés were confiscated, some made available to immigrants, some preserved in public stores or otherwise kept in the control of the deacons and government. The movable and immovable property of Münster residents who did not flee in February 1534 (estimated by Kirchhoff as two-thirds of the population of Anabaptist Münster[67]) was only touched to the extent that it was inventoried and in principle made available for poor relief. For the time being there was no attempt to interfere with the Münster residents' possession of their houses. Such a state of affairs preserved many of the natural advantages of Münster residents, particularly the more prosperous of them centered among the "new notables" who had earlier helped the Anabaptists come to power.

Still, during the first prophet's six weeks of ascendancy a tremendous upheaval of property relations had occurred, money had been abolished as a medium of internal exchange and the principle of economic equality had been announced. Yet the patriarchal household continued as the primary unit of production and consumption – and was later confirmed in this function by household-centered polygamous marriage – and there was no practicable method to put all households on the same level of well-being. Both the absolute rigor of Jan Matthijs's acts and the hit-or-miss quality of the results were conditioned by his belief that the time was very short. For him it was.

Jan of Leyden had the unenviable job of trying to stabilize Anabaptist Münster on the morrow of the realization that the apocalypse had not come, at least not when and how it was expected. He played Niccolo Machiavelli's ultimate political role – that of the giver of laws and shaper of institutions, not once but twice, in creating the regime of the twelve elders and his own kingship. The theatrical effects of the career of the actor-tailor-prophet-king have often been noted, usually without appreciation of his necessary political tasks: the maintenance of apocalyptic enthusiasm among the rank and file of the besieged; and the integration of the two political élites of his realm, the Münster notables and the immigrant Melchiorites. Six of the twelve elders were former council members in Münster. Of the 148 members of King Jan's court, about half came from Münster and 25 of those had held office previously. Persons who had held office in Münster before the Anabaptists took power were more numerous in the higher than the lower positions at court, but they were not in the majority, holding one-third to one-half of the top positions.[68] Burgomaster Bernd Knipperdollinck acted, in effect, as vice-regent for Jan both under the elders and in the kingdom. How important he was considered to be is shown by his restoration to office after his thwarted attempt to gain popular support to set up his own, "spiritual" kingship.[69]

In one of the early decrees of the twelve elders, Jan of Leyden gave explicit recognition to a right of inheritance which had, presumably, never been interrupted in Anabaptist Münster. The adminstrator of inheritances was to be none other than Knipperdollinck.[70] The creation of the royal court gave rise to an ostentatious, privileged minority, especially offensive in the bitter, hungry last months of the siege.[71] Towards the end the rulers put women, children and old men who could not fight onto starvation rations, at the same time disingenuously permitting them to leave the town and expose themselves to the brutalities of the besieging mercenary army.[72] Gresbeck, who, we must remember, went over to the enemy at the end, insisted that community of goods in Anabaptist Münster was ultimately fraudulent: "But whoever was poor stayed poor. The person who had something was able to draw on it at the end, despite the fact that goods were supposed to be common. So hunger first afflicted the poor people, who suffered great misery."[73]

On the other hand, with the greater severity of the siege during the time of the kingdom, a kind of war-rationing was imposed. Both Gresbeck and Kerssenbroch describe a great collection of clothing and food from the houses shortly after the proclamation of the king-dom.[74] This collection was connected with an attempt to prescribe limits on the amount of clothing any individual was allowed. Gres-beck describes what occurred as more a collection of provisions for the Dutch newcomers and for the court than a genuine assistance of the needy. His bias, of course, was to present most of what occurred in Münster as a swindle for the benefit of the newly pow-erful Dutch immigrants. Such an interpretation has to be strongly modified by Kirchhoff's evidence of the continuing prominence of Münster residents in the Anabaptist ruling group[75] – but, in fact, perhaps half of the ruling group *were* outsiders newly raised to prominence in Münster, such as Jan of Leyden himself.

At this same time in the kingdom, official decrees instructed those with the more spacious houses to be prepared to accommodate guests from the outside. Münster's hopes for deliverance were fas-tened on a massive migration of militant Anabaptists from the sur-rounding territories. Gresbeck's account continued that the king and his councilors intended a general exchange of dwellings "so that the foreigners would have the best houses in the town." But "the com-mon people or burghers weren't willing. True, a part of the burghers were willing and moved out of their houses into better ones. Oth-erwise everyone who wanted to remained in his own house."[76] Here again King Jan was capable of acknowledging limits to his power in a way Jan Matthijs never did, except perhaps when he allowed himself to be talked out of an actual slaughter of non-Anabaptists in February 1534. The houses of the Münster residents, which the Anabaptist leadership sniffed at, then backed away from, were the chief remainder of unexpended wealth available to the bishop after the conquest.[77] The records of these confiscated houses and properties form the basis for Kirchhoff's study of the social composition of Anabaptist Münster.

Towards the end of the siege, war communism in Münster amounted not so much to confiscation of property, although house searches were frequent enough and vacant plots of ground were expropriated and put under cultivation,[78] as a dole to the hungry from government stores. The government used its treasure in the months before the town was entirely cut off from the outside to buy beer and flour and horses and cows. The last major task of the deacons was to visit the houses and distribute minimum rations according to the number of enumerated persons in each house.[79] The deacons' administration of community of goods, like everything else in the sixteen months of Anabaptist Münster, was determined by the siege.

Curiously, as the reality of Münster's communism was eroded, its dogmatic expression in Rothmann's writings was continually polished and sharpened. This same generalization applies to his apocalyptic writing.[80] When apocalyptic hopes were at their peak early in 1534 Rothmann composed a merely legalistic defence of the Münster government, presenting it as engaged in justified resistance to a tyrannical overlord. This was the substance of the *Bekentones des Globens und Lebens der Gemein Christe zu Monster* ("Confession of the Faith and Life of the Congregation of Christ in Münster"). By the time Rothmann hit the high apocalyptic pitch of *Van der Wrake* ("On Vengeance") in late 1534 genuine apocalyptic faith was on the wane, outside Münster anyhow, as the tract indirectly acknowledged. In his *Restitution* Rothmann proclaimed that the Anabaptist realm had abolished human exploitation: "the eating and drinking of the sweat of the poor, that is, to use our servants and our neighbours, so that they must work so that we may feast."[81]

In practice, Anabaptist communism in Münster fell far short of Rothmann's ideal. It reached its high point in the heady weeks following the "February miracle." Afterward it showed its tawdry reality as a dreary "war communism," modified and made still more unappealing by King Jan's responsiveness to the élite of notables who had put the Anabaptists in charge of Münster to begin with. The wheel of historical fashion has turned against the view that the peasants' and commoners' goals were unrealizable in 1525, but it still seems incontestable that the Münsterites were foredoomed to failure. Hardly a hundred years previously another apocalyptic trek to a place of refuge had generated a political and military power of substance at Tabor in southern Bohemia. Had Jan of Leyden's resistance somehow succeeded, communism in Anabaptist Münster would surely have been discarded, just as it was at Tabor.[82]

CHAPTER SEVEN

Anabaptist Moravia, 1526–1622: Communitarian Christianity in One Country

The united realms of Bohemia and Moravia were formally a part of the Holy Roman Empire but in practice they were an independent kingdom. Because of the legacy of the Hussite Wars, a century earlier than Anabaptist migration, Bohemia and Moravia were almost the only part of western Christendom with a legally secured tradition of tolerating a plurality of confessions.[1] Even before the Reformation Catholics, Utraquists and Bohemian Brothers had lived side by side, certainly not in amity but without religious warfare. In Moravia, particularly, Catholicism was very weak in the early sixteenth century. When Balthasar Hubmaier came to Nikolsburg (now Mikulov), Moravia, in the late spring or summer of 1526,[2] he was leaving the realms of his hated ruler, Archduke Ferdinand of Austria, for a land of religious toleration. Ironically, a few weeks later, on 29 August 1526, King Louis of Bohemia, Moravia and Hungary was killed in battle against the Turks at Mohács in Hungary. He was without direct heirs, and by virtue of a previous marriage treaty Archduke Ferdinand, married to Louis's sister, became King Ferdinand, ruler of Hungary, Bohemia and Moravia. This did not immediately change Moravia into a land of persecution. When the Moravian Estates recognized King Ferdinand in the fall of 1526, they required him to confirm their traditional rights, including freedom of religion. Despite intermittent Habsburg encroachment on Moravia's religious freedom, this constitutional shield protected Anabaptist settlement there for a century.

Hubmaier's arrival in Moravia was closely followed by the conversion and rebaptism of two persons of high rank, Martin Göschl, the coadjutor bishop of Olomouc, who dominated the Nikolsburg church, and Count Leonhart von Liechtenstein, the temporal lord of the town. The product of Hubmaier's first year at Nikolsburg was the creation of an Anabaptist version of the post-Peasants' War, socially conservative magisterial Reformation.[3] At the same time he secured a haven for persecuted Anabaptists. The Anabaptists of Hut's group, whose leaders were often Peasants' War veterans, and who expected that the world would end and the wicked ruling classes would be punished some time in 1528, were particularly hunted and persecuted. It was not mere paranoia that caused a ruler such as Georg of Ansbach-Bayreuth, who had a deservedly bad conscience about the way he suppressed the Peasants' War, to regard his local Franconian Anabaptism as a conspiracy to renew the rebellion.[4] When Hans Hut arrived in Nikolsburg around May 1527, a year later than Hubmaier, the scene was set for a dramatic confrontation.[5]

The clash between Hubmaier and Hut, remembered in Anabaptist history as the Nikolsburg Disputation, led to Hut's imprisonment by the Count of Liechstenstein. The Hutterites' *Chronicle* correctly judged that their tradition went back to Hut, not Hubmaier, despite all the fine things that Hubmaier wrote, and the Hutterites preserved, defending the baptism of adult believers.[6] Hubmaier declared that the baptism he taught and the one Hut taught were as different as heaven and hell, Orient and Occident, Christ and Belial.[7] Hut's close follower, Hans Schlaffer, recalled Hubmaier's adult baptisms at Nikolsburg as perfunctory mass affairs that gave little evidence of individual regeneration.[8] Hut's baptisms, on the other hand, bestowed an apocalyptic sign upon the elect in order to separate them from the wicked in anticipation of the imminent return of the Lord. It is hardly too much to call them an Anabaptist version of Thomas Müntzer's eternal covenant.[9]

The area of eschatology and apocalyptics was the one in which Hubmaier and Hut differed most abrasively at Nikolsburg. Hubmaier condescendingly recalled that he had tried to explain to Hut that each day in the three and one-half years or forty-two months with which Hut was trying to calculate the *parousia* stood for a full year; so Hut's calculations were off by a millennium and a few centuries.[10] It is hard to imagine a more pacifying eschatology, or one more disappointing to the vanquished suvivors of the Peasants' War, than Hubmaier's. In the confrontation of Hubmaier and Hut we are reminded of what diverse views there were about last things among the Reformers who were precursors of Anabaptism. Hubmaier's low eschatological temperature was reminiscent of Zwingli and Carlstadt; Hut's urgency continued the concerns of Müntzer.

Although Hubmaier voiced the universal Anabaptist view that property was but stewardship,[11] Hut's tradition carried a much more decisive affirmation of community of goods. The *Hutterite Chronicle* recorded that Hut and Hubmaier disagreed "on retaining the use of the sword," a dubious tradition since Hut shortly afterwards explicitly distanced himself from the non-resistant stipulations of the Schleitheim Articles.[12] In a broader sense, however, the *Chronicle* is correct. Even though Hut had not adopted the behaviour code of Anabaptist non-resistance, he agreed with the non-resistants about the impossibility of Anabaptism becoming a magisterial Reformation in which the ruler had a special place of honour in the church. Such an outcome would have made a mockery of the commoners' resistance of 1525, to whose values many or most of the Anabaptist refugees in Moravia remained committed.

Hubmaier's magisterial religious settlement in Nikolsburg and the tolerant constitution of Moravia afforded him no protection when King Ferdinand demanded that he be surrendered by Count Liechtenstein to answer for his rebellious activities at Waldshut during the Peasants' War.[13] Johannes Faber, the bishop of Vienna, presented Hubmaier's execution in March 1528 as punishment for rebellion rather than for heresy, although he believed that the two blended naturally. Jakob Hutter became an Anabaptist leader only after both Hubmaier and Hut were dead, and after 1528 had passed without divine deliverance. But the Hutterite eschatological mood was Hut's, not Hubmaier's. The community thought of itself as living in "these last dangerous times," and saw its Moravian home as a place of refuge for God's covenanted elect awaiting Christ's imminent return and as a prefiguration of the kingdom that he would perfect when he returned.[14] Their mission activities institutionalized for a century afterward Hut's ambition to assemble the elect of the last days. Their commoners' church and commoners' polity of craftsmen and peasants upheld Hut's legacy against Hubmaier's failed attempt to create a magisterial Anabaptism, much like the Reformed churches with their secured places for the learned and the powerful.

Although different views about the return of Christ and the place of the magistracy in the church provided a background for the division among the Nikolsburg Anabaptists in late 1527 or early 1528, the immediate issues were non-resistance and community of goods. The Anabaptist established church, led by pastor Hans Spittelmaier following Hubmaier's arrest, supported the Liechtensteins in armed protection of refugees from Anabaptist-hunting Habsburg officials, who threatened to cross the border from Austria into Moravia. Criticism arose among the refugees, based on the Schleitheim Articles' rule that Anabaptists should not employ arms under any circumstances whatever. Spittelmaier, following in the well-trodden path of Reformed leaders faced with Anabaptist minorities, told his congregation not to be led astray by the dissidents, led by Jakob Wie-demann, because they were creating a schism. The dissident group was nicknamed the *Stäbler* or "staff-bearers" and the others the *Schwertler* or "sword-bearers."[15]

The *Stäbler* also called themselves *Gemainschaffter*, "community people," because of their willingness to open their homes and share their property with the numerous homeless and destitute strangers pouring into the area.[16] Clearly, tensions between native Moravians who followed their pastors' lead to the Reformation and then to Anabaptism and the new population of refugee Anabaptists con-tributed to the separation of the *Gemainschaffter*.[17] In March 1528 Leonhart von Liechtenstein, after some good-humoured reluctance, expelled the schismatic Anabaptists, an action that led to the dra-matic beginning of communitarian Anabaptism the 22nd of that month. The banished group, which moved from Nikolsburg to nearby Austerlitz, chose two stewards (*Diener der Notdurft*). Accord-ing to the *Chronicle*: "These men then spread out a cloak in front of the people, and each one laid his possessions on it with a willing heart – without being forced – so that the needy might be supported in accordance with the teaching of the prophets and apostles. Isa. 23; Acts 2, 4 and 5."[18]

The first communitarian Anabaptists at Austerlitz numbered only two hundred adults, a small minority of the total Moravian Ana-baptist population. Non-communitarian Anabaptists – both Swiss Brethren and Marpeck congregations – continued to live in Moravia throughout the sixteenth century. However, within ten years there were twice as many communitarian Anabaptist settlements as non-communitarian congregations; by the end of the century the ratio was four to one.[19]

The great importance of what happened in 1528 is that it led, with twistings and turnings, to the Hutterite system. At the time it was just another Anabaptist schism. All Anabaptists were committed, after all, to the implementation of Acts 2, 4 and 5. It is only in retrospect (and falsely) that the Hutterites have become identified, to the exclusion of all other Anabaptist groups, with "community of goods." In the same year as the schism among the Nikolsburg Anabaptists and the establishment of the Austerlitz community, a group of Silesian Anabaptists led by Gabriel Ascherham settled in nearby Rossitz. They were joined before the end of 1528 by Swabian Anabaptists led by Philip Plener, who established their own settle-ment in 1529 at Auspitz.[20] Since these groups were affiliated with the *Gemainschaffter* until Jakob Hutter disfellowshiped them in 1533, presumably they met the higher standards of community of the

Stäbler. But, as a matter of fact, the implementation of Christian community of goods was a constant issue for contention and occasion for schism in the years from 1528 to 1533, and even afterward.

There was no total abolition of personal possessions in the Austerlitz community under Jakob Wiedemann, at least if Wilhelm Reublin's self-serving account of the next schism is to be credited. These quarrels were quarrels over leadership, but they concerned themselves on the surface with community of goods and failures to achieve that goal. Reublin reported that at Austerlitz the rich had their own houses, some of them living like nobles, that some of the elders' wives never appeared at the common table, and that the elders and their wives received preferential treatment with respect to food. He wrote of roasts, fine wines and furs among the leaders.[21] In his description of the quarrel that led to the secession of about half the Austerlitz settlement in January 1531 and the creation of a new group at Auspitz, Reublin underscored that the seceding group was given nothing to take with them, nothing more than the clothes on their backs. Even their bedding was taken from them.[22] This was in glaring contrast to the way the Nikolsburg rulers had treated the Wiedemann group in 1528, when the proceeds from property sales were given to them, and even sent to Austerlitz subsequent to their departure.[23] It became the norm, however. Those who came to the communitarian settlements were expected to turn over everything they had; but when individuals or groups left, these were acts of wickedness and so they left empty-handed. This background helps to explain the apparent hypocrisy of Reublin himself, who held back twenty-four gulden from the common store. Reublin had always been a canny survivor among the early Anabaptist leaders. When his savings were discovered while he was ill, as the *Chronicle* tells us, "He was excluded as an unfaithful, malicious Ananias."[24] In the final schism of 1533 which established Jakob Hutter's authority at Auspitz, he used a similar accusation of holding back personal wealth to depose his Tyrolean comrade, Simon Schützinger.[25]

The Hutterite *Chronicle* has preserved the bitterness of these quarrels in much unedifying detail. Although most of the principals ended up as Anabaptist martyrs, the contending groups paid no honour to each others' martyrs. The *Chronicle* contains no mention of the death of Jakob Wiedemann, the original *Gemainschaffter-Stäbler*, although he died in the same persecution and virtually at the same time as Jakob Hutter.[26] Hutter's deposing of Schützinger in 1533 ended two years in which the various communitarian brotherhoods had lived in loose harmony, recognizing Gabriel Ascherham as senior elder.[27] Ascherham, one of the few leaders to survive the

1535–36 persecutions, in which the Habsburgs tried to expel all Anabaptists from Moravia and the communities were thoroughly dis-
rupted, wrote a chronicle of his own which adamantly refused to
recognize Hutter as a martyr for the Gospel or to forgive him even
in death: "This Jakob Hutter was a puffed up, ambitious man. Therefore, he shoved aside Sigismund [sic] Schützinger and was chosen
as elder in his place ... Now people can sing songs and tell stories
about this Jakob Hutter however they like, I say that this Jakob
Hutter was a bad man."[28] Appendix B contains the text and translation of the only surviving fragment of Ascherham's lost chronicle.

It is difficult to know, given the damage to all the communities
in the persecution of 1535–36, how much Jakob Hutter actually had
to do with establishing the system of common life among the Hutterites. His name has survived in their tradition, and certainly he
began to organize the emigration from the Tyrol that provided such
a large part of the Anabaptist population in Moravia. It is easy to
understand the proprietary rage with which in 1535 Hutter reacted
to the news that, under the impression of contemporary events in
Münster, the Moravian Estates had acquiesced in King Ferdinand's
demand that the Anabaptists be expelled. "Oh, the bloodhound!
The murderer! Up in the Tyrol he drove us from house and home,
took what belonged to us and murdered us! And now he wants to
drive us out here, too!" It was this scolding rather than the Gospel
that cost Hutter his life, according to the one-sided judgment of
Gabriel Ascherham.[29] Be that as it may, after the abatement of persecution the more conciliatory, constructive leadership of the fourth
presiding elder, Peter Riedemann (1542–56) and that of his successor, Peter Walpot (1565–78), seem to have had a lot to do with
creating the Hutterite system of common life. Their writings institutionalized the charisma of Jacob Hutter.

The most distinctive hallmark of the Hutterites' system was also
what made them most offensive to their contemporary critics, their
systematic weakening of the family as a focus of productivity and
loyalty independent of the community. As long as economics
centred in extended family households engaged in crafts or agriculture, the Christian life modelled on the prescriptions of Acts 2,
4 and 5 could not mean a great deal more than living frugally in
order to share with the needy. The refugee experience certainly
weakened family-centred economics in Moravia, just as it did in the
comparable situation in Münster. In Moravia, unlike Münster, the
dead weight of the tradition-bound host community was shaken off
early and decisively after the exodus from Nikolsburg in 1528. The
more we learn about Münster the stronger the host community

appears in relation to the refugees – certainly, this difference in the two situations is one reason why the Moravian Anabaptists were the more successful in producing a new society.

The big houses of the Hutterite *Bruderhof* – about sixty-seven feet long, the ground floors for common work, meals and worship, the two-storey attics with small rooms, like monastic cells, for married couples – symbolized the victory of the community over the family.[30] For the Hutterites themselves, the *Bruderhof*, consisting of forty or more of these big houses, was "a big beehive where all the busy bees work together to a common end"[31]; their enemies regarded it as a "pigeon-coop" and made disparaging allusions to crowding and filth.[32]

What aroused the sincere or hypocritical horror of contemporaries was the removal of the children from their mothers as soon as they were weaned. Under the direction of nursery-school sisters they were cared for in groups of two or three hundred, which were sometimes swept by illness.[33] The Jesuit polemicist Christoph Fischer described the child-rearing practices of the community with great pathos: "Nature taught not only human beings but also un-reasoning animals to nourish, raise and protect the fruit of their bodies themselves, especially when they are young and tender … Only the perverse Anabaptists act against nature. They lack the understanding of the little bird or the compassion of the wild animal towards its young." He describes the children being driven around like geese, being treated without affection and as "for the most part unhealthy, bloated and swollen." After five years the mothers could no longer recognize their own flesh and blood, which, Fischer added salaciously, led to incestuous marriages.[34] Certainly an education system which removed infants from their parents when they were weaned, and turned them out as little adults apprenticed in a craft at age twelve, was designed to strengthen the community at the expense of the family. Although monastic life provided a general model, there was probably no other such radically integrated com-munity anywhere in sixteenth-century Europe.

Marriage practices tended in the same direction. When Hutterite missionaries convinced people to flee to Moravia, both men and women left "unbelieving" spouses behind. Remarriage in the lifetime of the abandoned spouse was officially not permitted. But the Hut-terites attached no special religious value to sexual continence (al-though sometimes acting severely against adultery within their own communities), and it is easy to believe contemporary anti-Hutterite writings which say that such remarriages did occur, naming specific cases.[35] Marriage among the young was supervised by the community elders in an offhand manner that seems to have paid even less attention to the feelings of the principals than the family-arranged marriages which were normal elsewhere at the time. Either a young man or a young woman, the descriptions differ, was told to choose among two or three persons of the opposite sex presented to him (or her) by the elders.[36] Marriage, child-rearing, living arrangements and work practices – all had the same result: the community was everything, and the family was as weak as it could be without disappearing entirely.

Each individual *Bruderhof* was run by cooperation between pastors and stewards, responsible respectively for the spiritual and temporal welfare of the community. The selection of the leaders has often been described in modern accounts as "democratic."[37] Actually the popular role seems to have been to accept or acclaim persons presented by the current leadership. When there was more than one candidate for an office, as sometimes occurred at least in the choice of pastors, the decision was made by lot, not by ballot. Riedemann's *Rechenschaft* ("Account") stressed that God is the source of authority in the community.[38] The stewards had several functions. A purchaser of supplies, foremen of the various crafts, and overseers of farming were coordinated by a general manager, who was responsible for organizing the economic life of the entire *Bruderhof* and for seeing to it that work, food and clothing were fairly distributed. Contractual agreements, called *Hausbriefe*, specified the privileges of each *Bruderhof* and its obligations to its Moravian landlord (or Hungarian landlord, as the Hutterite settlements expanded geographically).[39] The Hutterite communities were normally leasers, not buyers,[40] which suited their belief that they were pilgrims and sojourners awaiting the return of the Lord. The presiding elder of all the communities, by custom residing at Neumühl not far from Nikolsburg, was chosen by a selected leadership-group. The *Chronicle* refers to the 1619 election as being the product of deliberation by "all elders in the service of the Word and in the service for temporal affairs as well as all buyers and storekeepers and many other trusted brothers from all communities." In line with the theocratic self-understanding of the brotherhood, the resulting choice was a "joyful, unanimous decision."[41]

There was a definite oligarchical principle in the Hutterite system. In 1540, when the Hutterites were re-establishing themselves after the first great persecution, the issue was raised of whether the leaders should receive "double honour," and specifically whether they should be served "special food and drink."[42] Peter Riedemann, then in prison in Hesse, wrote a long epistle defending the "pillars of the house of God" against "slanderers."[43] The belief that those in authority should receive special treatment was well established in sixteenth-century common sense. It was reflected in the practice of most monasteries and in Thomas More's description of conditions in Utopia.[44] Yet to Hans Jedelshauser, who left the brotherhood during the late sixteenth century (in what Hutterite chroniclers called the "Golden Period"), the special treatment of the élite was proof of Hutterite hypocrisy and corruption. If community of goods was based on Paul's teaching that no Christian should enjoy abundance while others were needy, how could one justify the extra meals and fine food of the leaders, the silks and taffetas of their wives?[45] Even worse, he wrote, was unequal application of the ban, in which the ordinary members of the community lived under strict discipline, while the general manager of a *Bruderhof* or his assistant could be found drunk on the job or be known to commit adultery and have the matter hushed up.[46] Jedelshauser's tract breathes a disillusioned idealism, which is a good deal more credible than the learned anti-Hutterite polemics of Catholic clerics.

Christoph Fischer, the Jesuit, wrote scornfully of "Klaus Braidl, the Anabaptist king at Neumühl," suggesting a dangerous simile between Braidl, "the shoe-maker king,"[47] and Jan of Leyden, "the tailor king" of Münster. In fact, Braidl reigned for twenty-eight years over a kind of state, and a very extensive and prosperous one. Fischer claimed that in 1607 there were more than seventy settlements, in each of which four to six hundred people lived, not counting several centres such as Neumühl, in which the population probably numbered one thousand, or the Anabaptists outside the settlements working on contract for the nobility.[48] The number of settlements mentioned by Fischer corresponds to Jarold Zeman's historical topography of Hutterite settlements for the same period[49]; and his estimate of the number of Anabaptists in a *Bruderhof* fits with a contemporary Hutterite statement.[50] This could point to a total Hutterite population as high as forty thousand, although the scholars who have studied the subject most carefully, Frantisek Hrubý[51] and Hans-Dieter Plümper,[52] have arrived at the more restrained estimates of twenty and twenty-five thousand. In any event, it is necessary to revise earlier views that tended to regard the Moravian experience as only a marginal part of the Anabaptist story. The total number of non-communitarian Anabaptists in central Europe is really impossible to estimate, but after the statistical work of Claus-Peter Clasen[53] the notion that communitarian economic practices were "adopted by only a small minority of the Anabaptist movement"[54] is no longer credible. This seemed to be true centuries later only because Moravian Anabaptism was wiped out by the blood and iron of the Counter-reformation.

The strength of the Hutterite settlement in Moravia was based on regular emigration from the other parts of German-speaking central Europe. Fischer estimated an emigration of sixteen hundred people in 1587, eight hundred in 1604.[55] The Hutterite missions were certainly a major factor in the continuance of this flow of population, long after the Peasants' War was more or less forgotten and the persecution of Anabaptists had moderated.[56] Fischer's description of how the missionaries were instructed to avoid the main roads, to travel in the mountains and by night, is very believable, as is the summary of their message which he plagiarized from his fellow priest, Christoph Erhard:

They read to the people from the little Zwinglian Testament, printed at Zurich (which is just right for this devilish seduction), especially what is taught about external secular good works. Everyone should help his neighbour with gifts and loans; temporal goods should be enjoyed in common; no one should harm anyone but each should behave in a friendly and brotherly way to the other. No one should rule over the other, but all should be like brothers and sisters to each other (it pleases the poor admirably that the princes and lords should share with them) ... When they've stayed with them for a while, they tell them their purpose in the end ... Come to us in Moravia, to the promised land that is ours, and that God has given us. There you and your children don't have to suffer poverty and work hard as you do here. There you will certainly have food, clothing and shelter; your children will have training and schooling. You won't have to worry about anything. You women, when you're old you won't have anything to do but spin to avoid boredom and sit still. You men, you won't have to work hard anymore, only what you're able to do and as much as you want to.

The missionaries, moreover, were skilled in advising the emigrants how to get their money and property to Moravia without their rulers' knowledge.[57] As late as the 1580s one of the Hutterite missionaries said that in the Tyrol they had hundreds of sympathizers who were "not yet perfect," not yet ready to give up private property and depart permanently for Moravia. "From fear of the [Habsburg] tyrant," these people did not publicly confess their Anabaptist beliefs.[58] So in the Tyrol the Hutterite missionaries were fish who swam in a sea of Nicodemism. Likewise, they benefitted from the hunger and indebtedness of the Swabian vine-growing countryside in the 1570s. Claus-Peter Clasen has convincingly shown the correlation between economic factors and immigration to Moravia from this region.[59] In fact, Clasen has identified more Hutterite immigrants from Swabia than from the Tyrol, although he estimates that the Tyroleans were more numerous in the Hutterite leadership.[60]

Gathered by missions, organized by a self-confident élite into a close community that more than compensated for its lack of physical force by its total control of every aspect of its members' lives, the Hutterites presented a striking spectacle to outsiders. Hutterite overseers could command higher wages than non-Hutterites for running the landlords' estates.[61] Hutterite ceramics became so fashionable that they replaced pewter in all well-to-do Moravian homes, even those of zealous Catholics.[62] Hutterite doctors were regarded as the best, summoned to Prague to treat Emperor Rudolph II, despite their not having gone to university and learned about the four humours, as the ever indignant, incredulous Fischer reported.[63] "They live among us as free men, free from all labour services. They have the biggest farms, the best soil, the best meadows."[64]

Who were these people who had built such a prosperous and successful life in an adopted land? Again the Jesuit, who constantly demanded their expulsion if the governments lacked the fortitude to carry out the mandates for their execution, tells us more than the Hutterites themselves:

Are not the Anabaptists mostly vine growers, peasants, craftsmen, coarse, fleshly, ignorant, unlearned people, banded together from the common crowd? ... Don't they cast all higher schools to the wind? Don't they show contempt for the learned? Don't they reject the histories? ... They have no theologians or other learned people among them. Their ringleaders, elders and stewards are mostly craftsmen, coarse vine growers and peasants. The highest among them, whom they all obey and is now their king, namely Klaus Braidl, never studied anything better all his life than making and repairing shoes, and he is their oracle and idol! They look up to his high court at the Neumühl, and he doesn't understand a word of Latin![65]

Nor did these ignorant bumptious people use the honorific titles that were due to noblemen or rulers. Normally they just addressed their betters as "you"; and if they wanted to be particularly polite they said, "Herr." This was the practice not just of ordinary brothers, who perhaps did not know better, but of Klaus Braidl's "government" in its official correspondence.[66]

The Anabaptist exile community in Moravia, at least in its most prominent Hutterite manifestation, had created a realm of craftsmen and peasants living in a symbiotic relation with the tolerant, often non-Catholic Moravian aristocracy in the peaceful years between the Peace of Augsburg (1555) and the beginning of the Thirty Years' War (1618). Even Catholic nobles often had Hutterite nannies or, even worse, Hutterite wet-nurses, which, Fischer explained, applying his learning, made them biologically heretical (since they drank heresy with their nurses' milk).[67] When the Hutterites called them "mister" the noble lords only laughed. And the Hutterites referred to the friendly Hussite governor of Moravia, Friedrich von Žerotin, not by his distinguished title but as "our Fritz."[68] During the "golden period," despite their ritual denunciations of the wicked world, Hutterite society was tied to the surrounding aristocracy by ties of interest, and even, it seems, of some mutual affection. (On the other hand, there were undoubted economic tensions between the Hutterites and the Czech villagers in the regions they settled.)

Hutterite society was marked by what we may refer to as "the leading role of the artisanry." The major reason why the sixteenth-century settlements could average about five hundred persons while the twentieth-century Hutterites restrict their communities to one hundred and fifty to two hundred is the difference between the sixteenth-century economy based on the crafts and today's strictly agricultural economy. *Ordnungen*, guild-type regulations, were established to regularize practice and assure quality. Shoe-makers, millers, carpenters, dyers, potters, barber-surgeons, cutlers, watch-makers and smiths had such regulations.[69] Agriculture was an important part of Hutterite economic life, but the communities were not entirely self-sufficient. The living standard of the settlements was secured by profit from the crafts, which paid for the purchase of large quantities of grain, among other things for brewing beer.[70]

The prominence of craftsmen among the Hutterites is evident in the frequent mention of a person's craft in the *Chronicle*. All but one of the presiding elders from Jakob Hutter onward to the expulsion from Moravia in 1622 were craftsmen. This fact has led some interpreters to regard the Hutterites as primarily an urban immigration to Moravia,[71] which is clearly not the case. The biggest Hutterite recruitment in the Tyrol was from rural areas, the Puster, Eisack and lower Inn valleys; and 90 per cent of the Swabian immigrants identified by Clasen come, not from towns, but from villages.[72] The village craftsman was in fact the most typical Anabaptist leader in the later sixteenth century.[73] An interesting sample of the Hutterite leadership-group is provided by the forty-four missionaries identified by Clasen as either servants of the Word (pastors) or servants of temporal needs (stewards).[74] Among these missionaries appear the names of all but one of the Hutterite presiding elders from the time of Jakob Hutter to the early seventeenth century.[75] Missions were apparently regarded by the Hutterites as "the moral equivalent to war" and a test of worthiness for leadership. Only two intellectuals, a priest and a clerk of mines,[76] are included in this group, which bears out Fischer's comment about there being little room for the conventionally learned among the Hutterites. Twenty-two individuals are identified as craftsmen, including four future presiding elders, and the other twenty are of unspecified occupation, including Hans Kräl from Kitzbühel in the Tyrol, who was presiding elder from 1578 to 1583. Jedelshauser identifies Kräl as a peasant.[77] He distinguished himself by his endurance in prison during his 1557 mission and probably was judged worthy for advancement in the brotherhood on that basis.[78] The question is how many others of this group of Hutterite leaders with unspecified occupation were also peasants. Probably some of them were not peasants, given their apparently urban origin – Hans Arbeiter from Aachen, who crossed over from the Swiss Brethren,[79] or Christoph Gschäl from Rattenberg – and the fact that craftsmen were identified as such and peasants were not says something about order of rank among the Hutterites.

There was no specialized spiritual or intellectual estate among the Hutterites; the servants of the Word were craftsmen, and some peasants, who applied lay common sense to the message of their Zurich Bibles. Nor was there a merchant class. Peter Riedemann's *Account* laid down the law: "We allow none of our number to do the work of a trader or merchant, since this is a sinful business." The stewards in the communities bought raw material for the crafts and sold the products of the craftsmen's work; that was not being a merchant. Merchants, said Riedemann, were those who bought cheap to sell dear, their profit "making the ware dearer thereby for the poor, taking the bread from their very mouths and thus making the poor man nothing but the bondman of the rich."[80]

Legally, each *Bruderhof* was in a relation to its landowner similar to that of a town: that is, it had corporate obligations but its individuals were not personally subject to the lord, as were the peasants of a manor.[81] But the Hutterite communities had broken down the town-village distinction. They were seventy more or less equal settlements of about five hundred persons in which crafts and agriculture were practised side by side. There was none of the urban oppression that Gaismair had wanted to banish from the Tyrol when he called for the abolition of city walls and special privileges. The Hutterite community was a craftsman's and peasant's realm without clergy, aristocrats or merchants. The socially necessary tasks of offering spiritual direction, providing order and justice, and buying and selling had been taken over by craftsmen and peasants who remained craftsmen and peasants. They studied only the Bible, just as Gaismair had foreseen in the Tyrolean *Landesordnung* of 1526. Walter Klaassen summed up the purpose of Gaismair's *Landesordnung* as the creation of "an agrarian republic from which the clergy, the nobles and the financial moguls have been expelled." Christoph Fischer's angry complaint was that the shoe-maker Klaus Braidl at the Neumühl presided over just such a republic. Concessions had had to be made, of course, to the victory of the Habsburgs and the aristocracy in the Peasants' War, but the New Tyrol in Moravia ruled by Jakob Hutter's successors at Neumühl was very close in spirit to the new Tyrol envisaged in Michael Gaismair's *Landesordnung*.[82] The sword it lacked was not needed for internal control, although, as the Thirty Years' War would show, the lack of military strength did make the Hutterites vulnerable to outside aggression. The Hutterites, more radically than the medieval Swiss, had demonstrated the feasibility of creating a society of "masterless men."[83] They had realized most of the ambitions of the commoners of 1525, both the commoners who performed the first believers' baptisms and the commoners who resisted their social betters on behalf of the divine law in the Peasants' War.

Although Jedelshauser reports that the dictum of Riedemann's *Account* – "no Christian can be a ruler, and no ruler a Christian" – had become a proverb among the Hutterites,[84] there apparently was a Hutterite government at the Neumühl. Certainly there was a major assembly of the élite, as noted above, whenever it was necessary to choose a new presiding elder. There is nothing improbable about Erhard's statement that there was a council of twelve to advise the presiding elder on financial decisions or the policy to be followed towards a meeting of the Moravian Estates.[85] This was, of course, a government that did not wield the sword, whose ultimate sanction was exclusion from the community. It was a theocratic authority without instruments of violence at its disposal – like the Jewish Sanhedrin in first-century Roman Palestine, another of the several poignant parallels between Jews and Anabaptists.

The spiritual and intellectual underpinnings of Hutterite community of goods came, like the Anabaptist immigrants to Moravia, both from the Swiss and from the Müntzer-Hut Anabaptist traditions. A congregational *Ordnung*, obviously an adaptation of the Swiss congregational *Ordnung* of 1527, first appeared in a Hutterite manuscript codex that Robert Friedmann thinks was probably the work of Hut's lieutenant, Leonhard Schiemer, and was used in the Rattenberg congregation in the Tyrol. From there it was incorporated into the *Chronicle*, inserted at the year 1529. In the Rattenberg version the fourth article read, "every brother or sister shall yield himself in God to the brotherhood completely with body and life, and hold in common all gifts received of God, [and] contribute to the common need so that brothers and sisters will always be helped; needy members shall receive from the brotherhood as among the Christians at the time of the apostles."[86] The Swiss stress on *Ordnung* was always important in Hutterite religion: "it is by thorough organization alone that a good work may be established and maintained, especially in the House of God who himself is a God of order and a master-workman."[87]

A second, even more important, foundation of Hutterite piety was the identification of *Gemeinschaft* or community with *Gelassenheit* or surrender of self.[88] This is the strain of medieval piety that made the Hutterites collect the writings of Hans Hut and his followers, which in turn continue the traditions of Thomas Müntzer. Any clinging to material things indicated an inadequate surrender of self, a withholding of love from one's fellow Christians, potential fellow martyrs in the end-time church: "For love is a band of perfection; where she lives, she generates not a partial, but a perfect and complete community."[89] In the very modest place they gave marriage in their system the Hutterites showed their belief that "With all my worldly goods, I thee endow" was too important a vow to be wasted merely on the joining of a man and a woman. Müntzer and the Hutterites did not glorify poverty as did some powerful strains in medieval piety. They called for a modest sufficiency of material things as an interim stage on the way towards the true *vita apostolica*, which was not material poverty but a freedom from all material, creaturely attachments. Riedemann wrote: "The more the human being cleaves to the creature, commits to it and expects from it, the further he shows himself to be from the image of God and the community of Christ."[90]

The equation of community of goods with *Gelassenheit* was an important theme in the writings of Ulrich Stadler, in the Five Articles of 1547 and in Peter Walpot's elaboration of the Five Articles in the Great Articlebook (circa 1577).[91] Central to both the 1547 and the 1577 versions of the article on community of goods was the text from the Old Testament apocrypha, Ecclesiasticus 2:5: "Like gold in the fire, human beings are tested in the oven of *Gelassenheit*."[92] For Stadler, true love and the highest degree of *Gelassenheit* meant devoting oneself with all one's possessions to the community of saints.[93] Walpot embroidered this theme in the Great Articlebook. There, Adam's fall was portrayed as the result of his love of the creature and his contempt for the Creator. Salvation depended on presenting our hearts to God "empty and yielded" (*ledig und glassen*) and our hands washed of avarice[94]: "It is a great good, joy and liberation in the struggle of suffering and in *Gelassenheit* and community of temporal things, that from hope of eternal life the person generously puts the heavenly above everything earthly. This is a great and marvellous good, not to be driven down by any creaturely or human thing but to have overcome the inborn weakness of the body with the greatness of the heart."[95] Satan would soon trap anyone who pursued the desires of the body and the love of the creaturely, not to speak of possession of property, "for if poverty does not do the damage, he makes a snare out of riches."[96] Here, with explicit citing of the *Theologica Germanica* ("German Theology"),[97] Walpot drew on the anti-materialistic mystical piety that had been so important for Hut and Müntzer.

Yet in the transition from its use by Müntzer and Hut to its appearance in the writings of Peter Walpot, *Gelassenheit* underwent a certain impoverishment of content. If *Gelassenheit* gave a measure of spiritual depth to *Gütergemeinschaft*, which would have been lacking had it been merely an *Ordnung*, its close identification with community of goods drained *Gelassenheit* of much of its pathos. For Thomas Müntzer, the true surrender of *Gelassenheit* involved an identification with the sufferings of the "bitter Christ" as opposed to Luther's "honey-sweet Christ." Werner Packull has outlined the process by which Müntzer's and Hut's internal focus on Christ's sufferings in the believer's soul became for south German and Austrian Anabaptists an external identification with the sufferings of their own martyrs. Their position was that through these martyrs the body of Christ completed the sufferings of its head.[98] Against this background, the transformation of *Gelassenheit* from the obedient martyr's surrender of life to the obedient surrender of property in the *Bruderhof* could not help but amount to a further stage of externalization of the formerly mystical ideal. By the 1580s Hans Jedelshauser would complain about the dry objectivity of Hutterite piety, which had no place for the sufferings of Christ, in comparison to the revived Catholic piety of the Counter-reformation.[99]

Another trend in the Hutterite defence of community of goods was an increasingly aggressive and exclusive apologetic for the particular form of community practised in the *Bruderhof*. The Five Articles of 1547 contain a note of dualism between the church and the world reminiscent of the Schleitheim Articles: "Those who have withdrawn, foresaken and surrendered temporal things for the sake of Christ no longer have property. Whoever is driven by the Spirit into this poverty and *Gelassenheit* belongs to the spiritually poor, who can expect heavenly goods and salvation. Those who do the opposite will not be saved."[100]

At first Hutterite apologists recognized some of the difficulties in an absolute equation of Hutterite community of goods with Christianity. Certainly this was the case with Ulrich Stadler, who was initially affiliated with Jakob Wiedemann's Austerlitz community and joined the Hutterites only in 1537, three years before his death.[101] Answering the claim that in the New Testament community of goods had lasted merely for a brief period, from Pentecost to the dispersal of the apostles from Jerusalem, Stadler said that in the first century "people were left alone in their houses and not driven into miserable exile, but now the children of God have no place in the whole Roman Empire. For the Babylonian whore who sits on the dragon with the seven heads – I mean the Roman church, a synagogue of the living Devil – only spits out the children of God and drives them into the wilderness."[102] In this time of greater danger than ever before in history, the bride of the Lamb had been given a dwelling place in the wilderness in which to await the return of the Lord. Any believers who had not been driven from their houses should be loyal stewards of their goods just as the New Testament followers of Paul had been.[103] For Stadler, the Hutterite community of life was the outcome of the great persecution against the Anabaptists, which was in itself an apocalyptic sign. That Christians in earlier times might have expressed love and *Gelassenheit* in individual family dwellings was not denied: "The rules of living should be applied benefically according to conditions of time, place and the situation of the children of God."[104]

Later in the century Peter Walpot drew on the whole biblical record to establish that the world of the *Bruderhof* was the sole remnant of the early Christian church. The Hutterite order of life had been prophesied in the Old Testament and practised throughout the entire New Testament era, not merely for a short time in Jerusalem. Accordingly, the Hutterites alone had revived New Testament Christianity; in the sixteenth century their large multi-family settlements were the norm for the Christian life. In Walpot's eyes the Hutterites did indeed practise "Christianity in one country."

Walpot interpreted the Old Testament as a prefiguration of New Testament community, citing the remission of debts every seven years (Deut. 15), the Levites' lack of inheritance (Num. 18), and the miraculously equal distribution of the manna in the wilderness (Exodus 16) as foreshadowings of a property-less order.[105] The New Testament was interpreted as literally beginning the system of living continued by the Hutterites in Moravia. Jesus and the disciples established community of goods, with Judas as administrator of the common purse.[106] His betrayal, in which he avariciously sold his Lord for thirty pieces of silver, was an anticipation of the similar betrayals of Ananias and Sapphira,[107] Wilhelm Reublin and Simon Schützinger. As Walpot elaborated Matthew 5: "You have heard that it was said to the men of old, 'You shall not harden your heart against your poor brother but open your hand to him and lend to him according to his need, helping and supporting him from your property.' But in the New Testament Christ wants and commands that you give everything that you have to the poor and put everything into equal community."[108] Christ's advice to the rich young man to sell all he had (Matt. 19) was, then, no mere counsel of perfection but the literal requirement of the New Testament order. Jesus had had no place to lay his head (Matt. 8:20); his expulsion of the merchants and money-changers from the Temple (Matt. 21) was a sign for future ages "so that everyone may recognize the false church."[109] The command to choose between God and mammon (Luke 16:13) meant that Christians must renounce private property.[110] Jesus's comment that it is harder for a rich man to enter the kingdom of heaven than for a camel to go through the eye of a needle was not diluted in Walpot, as in Matthew 19, by the reflection that for God all things are possible: "For just as it is not possible for a camel to go through a needle's eye, so it is impossible for a rich man to be so small that he can enter [the narrow gate of] the kingdom of heaven."[111]

More important than his observations on the life of Christ and the disciples was Walpot's insistence that the order of community described in Acts 2 and 4, in which Christians shared their property in large groups, was continued throughout the New Testament. He cited Eusebius's church history to prove "that the faithful practised community not only at Jerusalem but at many places." He interpreted the Acts of the Apostles and the Pauline epistles to show that the community of goods begun at Jerusalem was continued at Antioch, in Macedonia, in Thessalonika, to which he added Alexandria, basing himself on Eusebius.[112] He conceded that sometimes the circumstances of a marriage outside the faith or the small number of believers at a particular place required living arrangements other than Hutterite-type settlements, but in small groups or in large New Testament Christians practised community of goods: "It was absolutely never at that time in Paul's opinion, heart or mind that a

Christian could possess and retain private property and use it as he wished. For his epistles testify to the contrary throughout."[113] Any advice that Paul or Peter gave, recommending proper and generous use of private property, must have been addressed not to Christians but to "the rich of this world." Anyone who interpreted Paul's letter to Philemon about the return of his slave, Onesimus, as indicating that the New Testament accepted a social order based on private property was surely, wrote Walpot, "blinded by the god of this world."

With a theological argument reminiscent of Marpeck's polemics against the Strasbourg spiritualists, and in that sense very much in the Anabaptist "mainstream," Walpot rejected any merely spiritual affirmation of the "communion of saints": "It should be realized that where there is a genuine spiritual communion, there is also external community of goods; the one cannot exist without the other and it does not endure without the other. Otherwise it would also follow that the interior baptism of the Spirit were sufficient and the external confirmation of water baptism unnecessary, although here, too, the one cannot exist without the other."[114]

In Walpot's Great Articlebook the stress on community of goods as the Hutterite "sectarian distinctive" receives its fullest expression. All religious communities, of course, develop a hermeneutical approach to their sacred literature that is relevant to their present condition. They could not do otherwise. But the Hutterites' rejection of professional biblical scholars, whom they saw as another privileged caste, deprived them of whatever sense they might otherwise have had of the historical distance between the New Testament and sixteenth-century Moravia. In crafting an absolute endorsement of their particular social and economic system from the study of their vernacular Zurich bibles, they peopled the New Testament with Hutterites.

By the late sixteenth century Hutterite missions were increasingly directed against other Anabaptists, Swiss Brethren, Marpeck Brethren and Sabbatarians.[115] These groups agreed with the Hutterites about adult baptism, but in the Hutterite view they lacked a proper Christian *Ordnung*, which meant a true community of goods.[116] The Hutterite attitude towards other Anabaptists had been steeled in the endemic sectarian controversies of Moravia, in which they were the big winners, as the populations and prosperity of their communities outstripped the Moravian Anabaptist groups who continued to live in single-family households and as remnants of their defeated competitors, the Gabrielites and Philippites, merged with them.[117] Writing to Philippites in upper Austria just a few years after the 1533 schism, Peter Riedemann illustrated how exclusive the Hutterite claims were: "When a brother leaves community and returns to private property, it is a sure sign that he has turned away from God and left the first love. This is enmity to God and loss of all God's gifts."[118] The Hutterite expression of Acts 2 and 4 was the only possible one; without community of goods there could be no Christianity; and Christianity could, pending the Lord's return, be practised only in Moravia and in the adjacent areas of Hungary.

If we are to talk about social revolutions, then, it is necessary to endorse Clasen's statement that "the Hutterites achieved the most radical and successful social revolution in sixteenth-century Germany." But the Hutterites were not "a movement of their own," to be set apart from other Anabaptists.[119] They were the institutionalized, flourishing culmination of the commoners' Reformation of 1525 and of Swiss and south German Anabaptism. For all of its ethos of martyrdom, Anabaptism flourished when and where the persecution stopped, and its brutalities could be sublimated into the literature and piety of martyrdom. So it was in the Hutterite golden period in Moravia, a land marked by a very unusual religious pluralism "in the calm and tolerant years after the Peace of Augsburg."[120] So it would be, too, for the Dutch Mennonites, a very different social expression of Anabaptism, in the years after they received toleration as a result of the successful Revolt of the Netherlands and the enlightened policy of the House of Orange.

Unfortunately, this world of "masterless men" (and women), which had built a functionally successful social and economic system without special castes of rulers, priests, intellectuals or merchants, which had created something different from the economy of landlordship (which the Marxists call "feudalism") and the economy of the market (which the Marxists call "capitalism"), was foredoomed to virtual extinction. Helpless against the material might and religious fanaticism of the early Thirty Years' War, the flourishing society described above was largely eradicated by the time of the official expulsion of the Hutterites from Moravia in 1622. The settlements in neighbouring Hungary (present Slovakia) did provide a base for a continuing half-life of a much smaller group of Hutterites in the seventeenth and eighteenth centuries, and the manuscripts carried to Hungary preserved the memory of the social world that the Counter-reformation had destroyed. But in the late seventeenth century the Hungarian Hutterites abandoned their distinctive community life, and in the second half of the eighteenth century, while the Enlightenment was sweeping France and England, Maria Theresa enforced the conversion to Catholicism of the last resisters among them.[121] When Austrian scholars began to study the Hutterite codices in their archives in the late nineteenth century, the first of them, Josef von Beck and Johann Loserth, thought that the Hutterites had disappeared into history.[122] Of course, the Hutterites did survive, through a small group in Transylvania which immigrated to Russia and, after 1874, to the United States and Canada.[123] Today the Hutterite colonies approach, or even surpass, the numbers of the Moravian golden age. For historians and sociologists they preserve the memory of an alternative possibility of social development. For themselves and the neo-Hutterite group that has worked since the First World War to copy their system, they are the beneficiaries of God's promise, through the Old Testament prophets, that a remnant of his people will always be preserved.

Epilogue

The Anabaptists' ideal of realizing the prescriptions of Acts 2 and 4 eventually took the form of Christian mutual aid instead of Christian community of goods. This change began very early among the Swiss Brethren, where mutual aid was a matter of assisting needy households in a congregation, as occurs even now among the Swiss Brethren's most literal descendants, the Old Order Mennonites and the Amish. We might call this the "barn-raising" type of mutual aid. Among the Dutch Mennonites, mutual aid took place in an economic context that can properly be called commercial capitalism; and there it assumed the form of international philanthropy.

One of the most poignant symbols of this change comes at the end of the *Hutterite Chronicle*. In the year 1665 the leaders of the battered and impoverished Hungarian Hutterites turned to the Dutch Mennonites for financial assistance. They had never had to ask for charity before, they wrote, and had turned it down once when Prussian Mennonites had offered it, but now they had no alternative. The letter sadly reviewed the good years in late sixteenth-century Moravia, fully aware of the tolerant protection the Hutterites had received from the Moravian aristocracy: "We had hoped and still hope, with God's grace, to live under a loved and respected government that is well disposed toward us. Zeal for God brought us together from many places in different lands – some of us by wonderful and amazing ways – and we found refuge under such a government. We gained our livelihood honestly by the sweat of our brow. Through toil and hard work we earned our daily bread, for which we praised and thanked God with all our hearts. But now we are completely at a loss." Gone was the condescension towards fellow Anabaptists; the propertied Mennonite benefactors were greeted in the Lord, "as those who also belong to the bride of Christ, fellow heirs of the promise of an eternal inheritance, heavenly glory, and the future kingdom of Christ."[1]

Even before the Hutterite appeal the prosperous Dutch Mennonites had organized collections to help persecuted brothers and sisters abroad. In the 1660s they assisted fellow Mennonites in Danzig and Poland as well as the Hutterites. After the revocation of the Edict of Nantes they were particularly generous in helping Huguenot refugees. In 1710 Dutch Mennonite philanthropy was institutionalized through the creation of the *Commissie voor Buitenlandsche Nooden* (the Commission for Foreign Needs). The commission's first task was to assist the Swiss Brethren, who were suffering a nasty persecution in Bern and were precariously tolerated in the Palatinate. The commission even, with considerable grumbling, paid for the passage to Pennsylvania of some impecunious Swiss Brethren from the Palatinate. Schwenckfelders, too, were helped, the uncomplimentary things the Silesian nobleman had written about the vulgar Anabaptists conveniently forgotten by the gentlemen in Amsterdam.[2]

Property had won appreciation only slowly and grudgingly among Anabaptists. The notoriety of community of goods as practised in Münster, as well as the claims of the Hutterites that the Christian church could be properly ordered only on the basis of their form of community, ultimately undermined the early Anabaptist consensus that community of goods was the Christian ideal.

Especially groups such as the Swiss Brethren and the Marpeck Brotherhood, who had continuously to defend themselves against aggressive Hutterite missionizing, could no longer afford to make vague affirmations of community of goods. In 1543 Cornelius Veh, on behalf of the Marpeck brotherhood in Moravia, condemned the Hutterites as a "harmful and pernicious" sect because they claimed to find Christ "in temporal goods, as community of goods."[3] The statement of the Swiss Brethren at the Frankenthal Disputation of 1571 is a good summation of the growing estrangement in the late sixteenth century between Anabaptists who accepted property and those who practised community of goods: "A Christian may have personal property and buy and sell. However, he must follow the teaching of Paul that he serve the poor with his property, and have it as though he had it not. That the people in Moravia practise community of goods, we wish neither to praise nor to defend."[4] In 1552 Menno Simons, constantly alert to wash the Münsterite stain from his brotherhood, listed as a "false accusation" the charge that the Mennonites had property in common. They had never taught or practised community of goods, he wrote. This was a practice discontinued by the early church, perhaps with good reason. However, unlike other groups and despite fierce persecution, none of their members or their orphaned children had ever had to beg.[5]

The Dutch Mennonites did not seek prosperity; it came to them. In the first century after toleration they were hard-working, anti-acquisitive people. As one recent scholar remarked, "it requires more than work to produce riches"[6]; and the tight community discipline of the ban always served to humble the aspiring. Nevertheless, it was a time of generally expanding prosperity in the Netherlands. The world commercial market inevitably exercised its pull on Mennonite merchants in Amsterdam or Hamburg, even if they insisted on doing irrational things, such as refusing to arm their merchant vessels against pirates and privateers. When representatives of the Commission for Foreign Needs greeted refugees from Bern in 1710, they recognized themselves as people of a different age from the Swiss mountaineers.[7] The equivocal blessings of toleration and capitalism would over a period of time make the Dutch Mennonites the most bourgeois of the confessions in the Netherlands.

The leading Anabaptist group of the late sixteenth century, the Hutterites, created a new society, neither "feudal" nor "capitalist," an authentic Moravian transmutation of Michael Gaismair's Tyrolean *Landesordnung*. In it the social radicalism of the early Reformation lived on unabated. The Dutch Mennonites of the seventeenth century, at least by the time they were engaging in international philanthropy and harnessing their country's diplomatic service to promote tolerance in less enlightened countries, had become a respected nonconformist minority, encapsulated in the early-modern capitalist world, and in no respect a threat to it.

Through the eighteenth and nineteenth centuries the world market expanded so as to become, what it had not yet been in the sixteenth century, an intimate, controlling factor in the lives of ordinary Europeans and North Americans. At the same time the Enlightenment articulated the vocabulary of non-religious, indeed anti-religious, social regeneration which had been lacking in the Reformation. When nineteenth-century humanitarian theorists attuned to the directions of social and technological change tried to build a society centred on community, they observed that the "leading role of the artisanry" would have to be replaced by the "leading role of the proletariat." They saw that if socialism were to come at all it could only be by way of the capitalism that had transformed their era. Reading the trends of their age, they fiercely asserted that the

development of socialism from capitalism was inevitable, and convinced themselves, although they were militant atheists, that it was
providential.

APPENDIX A

Anabaptists in the Peasants' War

ANABAPTISTS DURING THE WAR

SWITZERLAND-WALDSHUT

Aberli, Heini+	baker, Zurich		
Brötli, Johannes	priest, Zollikon and Hallau	leader	spiritual
Hubmaier, Balthasar	priest, Waldshut	leader	peasants' leader
Krüsi, Hans	monk, schoolmaster, weaver, rural St Gallen	leader	spiritual
Reublin, Wilhelm	priest, Witikon and Hallau	leader	spiritual
Rüeger, Hans	carpenter, Hallau		peasants' leader

FUTURE ANABAPTISTS

SWITZERLAND

Finsterbach, Arbogast	Upper Winterthur		
Girenbader, Hans	innkeeper, Grüningen	leader	peasants' leader
Maag, Hans+	miller, Grüningen		
Müller, Hans	Upper Winterthur		
Seiler, Uli (probably the "bad Uli")	peasant, Grüningen		
Soder, Heini	Liestal, Basel village		
Vontobel, Hans	shoe-maker, Grüningen		

BADEN, SWABIA

Feigenbutz, Hans	Esslingen	leader*
Jungmann, Michael	Kürnback, Württemberg condominium	
Leber, Oswald	priest	leader*
Spruer, Michel	Kirchberg, Württemberg	

TYROL

Brandenburger, Friedrich	Cologne	
Gasser, Anna	Ritten Plateau	
Gasser, Hans	Ritten Plateau	
Kobl, Ulrich	Ritten Plateau	
Lex, Christian	Eisack valley	peasants' leader
Messerschmied, Mathias	Klausen, Eisack valley	
Portz, Hans	Ritten Plateau	
Urscher, Erhard	peasant, Sarntheim, Sarn valley	
Wirt, Peter	Ritten Plateau	

FRANCONIA, HESSE, THURINGIA

Alexander N. +	schoolmaster, sexton, Einbeck	leader	
Andreas N.	master tailor, Meiningen		peasants' leader
Beck, Hans	Rosenbach/Uttenreuth		
Denck, Hans +	schoolmaster, humanist, Mühlhausen	leader	spiritual
Fry, Claus	furrier, Rothenburg		
Fuchs, Georg	Ilversgehofen/Erfurt		
Gilg N.	tailor, Sorga	leader*	
Grueber, Hans	peasant, Egenhof/ Uttenreuth	leader	
Grueber, Heinz	peasant, Egenhof/ Uttenreuth		
Grueber, Jörg	peasant, Egenhof/ Uttenreuth	leader*	
Harscher, Fritz	Reutles/Nuremberg		peasants' leader
Hartmann, Hans	tailor, Rothenburg		
Hen, Schmidt	Sorga		

Hut, Hans	sexton, Bibra/Henneberg	leader	
Hutter, Heinrich (Heinemann)	Ammern/Mühlhausen		peasants' leader
Hutter, Heinz	Sorga		
Kellermann, Eukarius+	carpenter, Coburg	leader	
Koch, Hans	Sorga		
Konz N.	brickmaker, Herzogenaurach/Bamberg		
Kraut, Heinz	tailor, Esperstedt	leader	
Lober, Endres	Sorga		
Lutz, Heinrich	Sorga		
Maier, Hans	Alterlangen, Herzogenaurach		
Maier, Marx	Alterlangen, Herzogenaurach	leader	
Maier, Michael	Alterlangen, Herzogenaurach		
Mansfeld, Dionysius	shoemaker, Eisleben		
Peter N.	wagoner, Herzogenaurach/ Bamberg		
Plat, Hans	Sorga		
Pretscher, Friedrich	monk, pastor, Nordheim		
Rinck, Melchior	pastor, Eckhartshausen	leader	peasants' leader
Römer, Hans	furrier, Eisenach	leader	
Schare, Heinz	linen weaver, Burglauer		
Scharf, Klaus	Mühlhausen	leader	
Schott, Hans	peasant, Frankenhausen village	leader*	peasants' leader
Stalf, Herman	Sorga		
Steus, Erhard	journeyman tanner, Mühlhausen		
Strigel, Hans	Rosenbach/Uttenreuth		
Tuchscherer, Philip	Rothenberg		peasants' leader
Volk, Georg	sexton, Haina/Henneberg	leader	
Ziese, Hans	Sorga		

(+) probably involved in Peasants' War
(*) not included in Clasen, "Anabaptist Leaders."

Fragment of the Lost Chronicle of Gabriel Ascherham

FOLGET DAS LEBEN DESS GROSSEN TAUBERS DAS IST.

Deß Jacobs Hutters (vonn welchen sich die Widertauffer Hutterisch nennen) beschriben von Gabriel Kirschner / von welchen die Gabrielischen Widertauffer herkommen / in seiner Croniken / welches tittel also lautet.

Was sich verloffen hat vnder den Brüdern / die auß aller teutschen Nation vertriben waren vmb deß Glaubens willen / die darumben zu derselbigen zeit in das Måhrernlandt kommen zu Auffenthalt ihres Lebens / von dem 1528. Jar biß auff das 1541 Jar. Ich wil schreiben (sagt er) was ich selbst gesehen / gehöret / vnd von warhafftigen Zeugen erfahren habe / vnnd nichts vber mein Gewissen anzeigen.

Auff das j. wz diser Jacob Hutter ein auffgeblasener ehrgeitziger Mensch / darumm verstach er den Sigismund Schitzinger / vnd wird an seiner statt zn einen Obristen erwehlet. Eh dz er aber erwehlet würde / mochte sich dz annemmen vnd Ehrgeitzigkeit nit verbergen / dann er mit grossen Zorn fur herauß / vnd sagte wider das Volck. Bin ich dann nit auch ein Apostel vnd Hirt / muß ich dan also von euch gestossen werden. Die gross Frucht aber die da

[56] folgete auß seinem Ampt / vnd seinen gemeinschafft auffrichten / was diese Liebe vnd Einigkeit zertrennet er / und die Völcker so vorhin einig waren / machet er vneinig.

Nun singe vnd sage man vonn disem Jacob Hutter was man wölle / so sage ich / daß diser Jacob Hutter ein böser Mensch gewesen ist / nachdem ich ihn wol erkennet habe / er habe sich gleich sieden vnd braten lassen / so weiß ich doch nichts vonn jhm zusagen / dann er hat solches in disem Land nicht beweiset. Ja er vbet Raach vber alle die / so dem Schützinger etwas geredt hetten / vnd mit seinem poltergeist vberfiel er die gemeine mit grossen drauen vnd sprach. Sehet jr jetzund / wenn jr gelobt habt / nemblich disen schalck habt jhr für from gehalten / vnnd habt mich verkleinert / vnd habt gesagt. Der Schützinger soll inn seinem Ampt fortfahren / alda habt jhr ein falsch Vrtheyl geben / darumb thut busse vmb solches.

Das heist ein rechter Poltergeist / ein Mensch der seine Ehre sucht / das ist nicht der Geist Pauli / es ist ein Geist Bileams Kinder / das heissen Narrenkinder. Als aber Jacob sein ruhm so hoch führet / vnnd rühmet er hätte den Geist Pauli / sagte ein Weib zu ihm. Du hast deß Teuffels Geist.

Zu der zeit aber / da der König die gemeinen wolt vertreiben auß Mährenland / da schicket die Ebtißin vonn Brinn jhre Diener auff Auspitz vnd trib den Jacob mit seinem Volck Auß dem Hauß. Da aber der Landshaubtman seine Diener zu ihm schickte / vnnd ihn den Königlichen Befehl fürhilt / da fieng der Jacob an vnd sprach. Ey der Bluthund der Mörder. Im Oberlandt hat er vns von Hauß vnd Hoff vertrieben / vnd das vnserig genommen / auch die vnserigen ermördet / nun will er vns auch hie vertreiben / vnd sagt zu den Diener deß Hauptmans / saget ewrem Herrn also. Wir wollen nindert hinziehen / hat der Bluthund ein Lust zu vnserm Blut / so last ihn kommen / da wöllen wir seyn warten. Die Die-

[57] ner aber sagten / wir können solche Bottschaft nicht mündtlich außrichten / denn es war deß redens vnd scheltens so vil von dem Jacob das sie solches nicht behalten kündten / darumb sagten sie. Schreibt solches auff einen Brieff mit vil schelten vnd lästern vber den König. Es war aber die Summa. Wir wollen hie des Königs warten. Da nun diser Brieff vberantwortet ward / suchet man disen Jacob / aber er macht sich bald davon vnnd wolt sich nicht finden lassen. Es wolt jhm villeicht der sach zu viel werden deß Königs da zuerharren. Darauß wol abzunemmen ist / das er nur ein Mensch von Wortten gewesen ist / vnd bey jhm nicht war. Solcher polterej aber müsten andere Leut entgelten in disem Land. Dieser Jacob aber floh hinauff in das Etschlandt / der König aber ließ Kundschafft vber jhn außgehen / da er jhn aber zu wegen bracht / ließ er jhn zu Innspruck verbrennen.

Also kam dieser Jacob vmb / vnter diesen Deckmäntlein / als so es vmb deß Evangelij willen geschehen wäre / welches aber auff diß mal nicht die vrsach was / sonder vmb seines schelten willen hat er müssen sterben / wann er zweintzig leben hätte gehabt.

Dieses ist trewlich vnd ohn alle verfelschung
von wort zu wort auß obgenannter Cro-
nicken deß Gabriels Kirschners ab-
geschrieben worden.

Text from Christoph Andrea Fischer, *Der Hutterischen Widertauffer Taubenkobel* ("The Pigeon-coop of the Hutterite Anabaptists") (Ingolstadt: 1607), 55–7.

TRANSLATION:

There follows the life of the big male pigeon, that is:

Of Jakob Hutter (after whom the Hutterite Anabaptists name themselves), as described by Gabriel the Furrier [Ascherham] from whom the Gabrielite Anabaptists originate, in his chronicle, which bears the title:

What took place among the brothers who were driven out of all German nations for the sake of the faith and who therefore came at the same time to Moravia to reside there from 1528 until 1541. I will write – he says – what I myself have seen, heard and learned from truthful witnesses and what I can state with a clear conscience.

First of all, this Jakob Hutter was a puffed up, ambitious man. Therefore, he shoved aside Sigismund [sic – really Simon] Schützinger and was chosen as elder in his place. But before he was chosen he was not able to disguise his presumption and ambition, for with great anger he stepped forth and said to the people: Am I, too, then not an apostle and shepherd; must I then be rejected by you in this way? But the great fruit that sprang forth from his office and his establishment of a fellowship was that he destroyed love and unity, and to the peoples who previously were united he brought disunity.

Now people can sing songs and tell stories about this Jakob Hutter however they like, I say that this Jakob Hutter was a bad man, since I saw through him well. If he was simmered and roasted, nevertheless I know nothing to say about him, for he did not pass the test in this country. Indeed, he took vengeance on all who spoke up for Schützinger, and with his raging spirit he attacked the congregation and said: See now whom you have praised, namely this villain, whom you regarded as pious, while you belittled me, in that you said that Schützinger should continue in his office. Here you gave a false judgment; therefore repent for that.

That is truly a raging spirit, a person who seeks his own honour; that is not the spirit of Paul; it is the spirit of the children of Bileam, which means fools' children. But when Jakob claimed so much for himself and bragged that he had the spirit of Paul, a woman said to him: You have the spirit of the devil.

At the time that the king [King Ferdinand] wanted to drive out the congregations from Moravia the abbess of Brünn sent her servants to Auspitz and drove Jakob with his people from the house. When, however, the captain of the province sent his servants to him and presented him with the royal command, then Jakob began to speak: Oh, the bloodhound, the murderer! Up [in the Tyrol] he drove us from house and home, took what belonged to us and murdered us! And now he wants to drive us out here, too! And he said to the servants of the captain: Tell your master as follows: We will not move away anywhere. If the bloodhound wishes to have our blood, let him come and we will wait for him. The servants, however, said: We cannot deliver such a message verbally, for they said this because it was so full of words and scolding from Jakob that they could not remember it all. So he wrote it all in a letter, with much scolding and slandering of the king. The sum of it, though, was: We will wait for the king here. Now, when this letter was delivered, this Jakob was sought for, but he quickly left the region and would not let himself be found. The whole business became too much for him to wait there for the king. From which it can be concluded that he was only a man of words and nothing more. Others in this land, however, had to pay the price for his raging. This Jakob fled up country to the Etsch region [the south Tyrol], but the king had notices sent out seeking him, and then he apprehended him and had him burned at Innsbruck.

In this way this Jakob perished, under the pretext that it happened for the sake of the Gospel, which however was not the real reason in this case. Rather, he would have had to die on account of his scolding, even if he had twenty lives.

This is transcribed word for word, faithfully, without any falsification, from the above mentioned chronicle of Gabriel the Furrier.

Notes

The following shortened references and abbreviations have been used throughout the notes:

LB	*Desiderii Erasmi Roterodami Opera omnia*, 10 vols. (Leyden: 1703–06), (Hildesheim: 1961–62).
Mennonite Encyclopedia	*The Mennonite Encyclopedia*, ed. Harold Bender, C. Henry Smith, 4 vols. (Scottdale: Mennonite Pub. House 1956–59).
Mennonitisches Lexikon	*Mennonitisches Lexikon*, ed. Christian Hege, Christian Neff, etc., 4 vols. (Frankfort, Weierhof, Karlsruhe: 1913–67).
Müntzer Schriften	*Thomas Müntzer. Schriften und Briefe*, ed. Günther Franz (Gütersloh: Gerd Mohn 1968).
QGT, 1, Württemberg	*Quellen zur Geschichte der Wiedertäufer*, 1: *Herzogtum Württemberg*, ed. Gustav Bossert, Sr, Gustav Bossert, Jr (Leipzig: Heinsius 1930).
QGT, 2, Bayern, 1	*Quellen zur Geschichte der Wiedertäufer*, 2: *Markgraftum Brandenberg (Bayern 1)*, ed. Karl Schornbaum (Leipzig: Heinsius 1934).
QGT, 3, Glaubenszeugnisse, 1	*Glaubenszeugnisse oberdeutscher Taufgesinnter*, 1, ed. Lydia Müller (Leipzig: Heinsius 1938).
QGT, 4, Baden-Pfalz	*Quellen zur Geschichte der Täufer*, 4: *Baden und Pfalz*, ed. Manfred Krebs (Gütersloh: Bertelsmann 1951).
QGT, 5, Bayern, 2	*Quellen zur Geschichte der Täufer*, 5: *Bayern 2*, ed. Karl Schornbaum (Gütersloh: Bertelsmann 1951).

QGT, 7, Elsass, 1	*Quellen zur Geschichte der Täufer, 7: Elsass 1 (Stadt Strassburg 1522–1532)*, ed. Manfred Krebs, Hans Georg Rott (Gütersloh: Gerd Mohn 1959).
QGT, 9, Hubmaier	*Quellen zur Geschichte der Täufer, 9: Balthasar Hubmaier Schriften*, ed. Gunnar Westin, Torsten Bergsten (Gütersloh: Gerd Mohn 1962).
QGT, 12, Glaubenszeugnisse, 2	*Quellen zur Geschichte der Täufer, 12: Glaubenszeugnisse oberdeutscher Taufgesinnter, 2*, ed. Robert Friedmann (Gütersloh: Gerd Mohn 1967).
QGT, 13, Österreich, 2	*Quellen zur Geschichte der Täufer, 13: Österreich, 2*, ed. Grete Mecenseffy (Gütersloh: Gerd Mohn 1972).
QGT, 14, Österreich, 3	*Quellen zur Geschichte der Täufer, 14: Österreich, 3*, ed. Grete Mecenseffy (Gütersloh: Gerd Mohn 1983).
QGTS, 1, Zürich	*Quellen zur Geschichte der Täufer in der Schweiz, 1: Zürich*, ed. Leonhard von Muralt and Walter Schmid (Zurich: Theologischer Verlag 1952).
QGTS, 2, Ostschweiz	*Quellen zur Geschichte der Täufer in der Schweiz, 2: Ostschweiz*, ed. Heinold Fast (Zurich: Theologischer Verlag 1973).
QGTS, 4, Täufergespräche	*Quellen zur Geschichte der Täufer in der Schweiz, 4: Drei Täufergespräche*, ed. Martin Haas (Zurich: Theologischer Verlag 1974).
Rothmann Schriften	*Die Schriften Bernhard Rothmanns*, ed. Robert Stupperich (Münster: Aschendorf 1970).
TQ Hessen	*Urkundliche Quellen zur hessischen Reformationsgeschichte, 4: Wiedertäuferakten 1527–1626*, ed. Günther Franz (Marburg: N.G. Elwert 1951).
WA	*D. Martin Luthers Werke, krit. Gesamtausgabe: Schriften* (Weimar: 1883ff.), 63 vols.
Z	*Huldrych Zwinglis sämtliche Werke* (Berlin: 1905; Leipzig: 1908; Zurich: 1961ff.), 14 vols.

INTRODUCTION

1 Claus-Peter Clasen, *Anabaptism. A Social History, 1525–1618. Switzerland, Austria, Moravia, and South and Central Germany* (Ithaca and London: Cornell University Press 1972), 152–7.

2 Günther Franz, *Der deutsche Bauernkrieg* (10th ed., Darmstadt: 1975). The first ed. was published in Munich and Berlin, 1933.

3 Peter Blickle, *The Revolution of 1525. The German Peasants' War from a New Perspective*, trans. by Thomas A. Brady, Jr and H.C. Erik Midelfort (Baltimore and London: Johns Hopkins 1981); *Gemeindereformation. Die Menschen des 16. Jahrhunderts auf dem Weg zum Heil* (Munich: 1985).

4 Paul Peachey, *Die soziale Herkunft der Schweizer Täufer in der Reformationszeit: Eine religionssoziologisch Untersuchung* (Karlsruhe: 1954).

5 Clasen, *Anabaptism*, 305–11.

6 Tom Scott, "The Peasants' War: A Historiographical Review," *Historical Journal* 22 (1979): 693–720, 953–74; *Freiburg and the Breisgau. Town-Country Relations in the Age of Reformation and Peasants' War* (Oxford: Oxford University Press 1986).

7 Henry J. Cohn, "Anticlericalism in the German Peasants' War 1525," *Past and Present* 83 (1979): 3–31; Justus Maurer, *Prediger im Bauernkrieg* (Stuttgart: Calwer 1979); Franziska Conrad, *Reformation in der bäuerlichen Gesellschaft. Zur Rezeption reformatorischer Theologie im Elsass* (Stuttgart: Steiner 1984).

8 Thomas A. Brady, Jr, *Ruling Class, Regime and Reformation at Strasbourg 1520–1555* (Leyden: Brill 1978), 1–3.

9 Heiko A. Oberman, "The Gospel of Social Unrest," in *The German Peasant War 1525. New Viewpoints*, ed. Robert W. Scribner and Gerhard Benecke (London: Allen and Unwin 1979), 50.

10 Ibid.; James M. Stayer, *Anabaptists and the Sword* (Lawrence: Coronado, 2d ed. 1976).

11 Peter James Klassen, *The Economics of Anabaptism, 1525–1560* (The Hague: Mouton 1964); Hans-Dieter Plümper, *Die Gütergemeinschaft bei den Täufer des 16. Jahrhunderts* (Göppingen: Alfred Kümmerle 1972).

12 Klassen, *Economics*, 64.

13 Acts 2: 44–45 (Revised Standard Version).

14 S. Groenveld, "'Sy laeten geenen Beedelaer onder haer zyn.' Diaconale zorg vóór 1900," in *Wederdopers, menisten, doopsgezinden in Nederland, 1530–1580*, ed. S. Groenveld, J.P. Jacobszoon and S.L. Verheus (Zutphen: Walburg 1981), 119–45; S. Groenveld, "Het 'doopsgezind eigene' in historische perspectief. Enkele opmerkingen," *Doopsgezinde Bijdragen* NR 7 (1981): 11–30; Donald F. Durnbaugh, ed., *Every Need Supplied. Mutual Aid and Christian Community in the Free Churches, 1525–1675 [Documents in Free Church History, 1]* (Philadelphia: Temple 1974).

15 Plümper, *Gütergemeinschaft*, 129–58, 201–4; Michael Mullett, *Radical Religious Movements in Early Modern Europe* (London: Allen and Unwin 1980), 33–54, esp. 38–9.

16 Otto Brunner, "Das 'Ganze Haus' and die Alteuropäische 'Okonomik'," in Otto Brunner, *Neue Wege der Sozialgeschichte* (Göttingen: Vandenhoeck 1956), 33–61.

17 *Gütergemeinschaft*, 146.

18 Paul S. Gross, *The Hutterite Way* (Saskatoon: Freeman 1965), xi.

19 *Anabaptism*, 209: "the historian, after thinking through their practical consequences, can only conclude that these doctrines would have resulted in disaster."

20 Thomas A. Brady, Jr, *Turning Swiss: Cities and Empire, 1450–1550* (Cambridge: Cambridge University Press 1985).

21 Wolfgang Lassmann, "Projektbeschreibung: Ketzerei und Täufertum in Sudtirol im 16. Jahrhundert (24 Aug. 1982)," 11.

22 Hans-Jürgen Goertz, *Pfaffenhass und gross Geschrei. Die reformatorischen Bewegungen in Deutschland 1517–1529* (Munich: Beck 1987). It might be added that a book on the Reformation whose final chapter is entitled "die Ambivalenz einer Epoch" is hardly an ideological statement.

23 Brady, *Ruling Class*, 46: "The leading ideas of Reformation Germany were chiefly theological ideas, without a firm grasp of which the culture and self-consciousness of the age simply cannot be understood."

24 Bernd Moeller, "Problems of Reformation Research," in Bernd Moeller, *Imperial Cities and the Reformation*, trans. by H.C. Erik Midelfort and Mark U. Edwards, Jr (Philadelphia: Fortress 1972), 6–7.

25 Conrad, *Reformation*, 14.

CHAPTER ONE

1 Friedrich Engels, *Der deutsche Bauernkrieg*, in *Marx-Engels, Werke*, 39 vols. (Berlin: Dietz 1973), 7:409: "Der grossartigste Revolutionsversuch des deutschen Volks."

2 Max Steinmetz, "Theses on the Early Bourgeois Revolution in Germany, 1476–1535," in *The German Peasant War 1525. New Viewpoints*, ed. Robert W. Scribner and Gerhard Benecke (London: Allen and Unwin 1979), 9.

3 Hajo Holborn, *A History of Modern Germany*, 3 vols. (New York: Knopf 1964) 1:173–4: "It was estimated that by late April, 1525, 300,000 peasants were under arms ... It is estimated that 100,000 peasants lost their lives in the course of the war ..."

4 Peter Blickle, *The Revolution of 1525. The German Peasants' War from a New Perspective*, trans. by Thomas A. Brady, Jr and H.C. Erik Midelfort (Baltimore and London: Johns Hopkins 1981), 124. Blickle's argument for using the term "Revolution of 1525" is developed in his conclusion, 190–3. He says, finally, that the point of his employing "revolution," a modern scholarly concept, together with "common man," which originates in sixteenth-century sources, is to underscore his conviction that "what happened in 1525 was a deliberate movement, proceeding on a rational course and with challenging ethical

claims, for human self-realization." See also the careful discussion of three contrasting approaches to the "revolutionary dynamic of the Reformation movements" in Hans-Jürgen Goertz, *Pfaffenhass und gross Geschrei. Die reformatorischen Bewegungen in Deutschland 1517–1529* (Munich: Beck 1987), 235–50; and the thoughtful and nuanced East German approach to many of the same themes in Adolf Laube, "Radicalism as a Research Problem in the History of Early Reformation," in *Radical Tendencies in the Reformation: Divergent Perspectives*, ed. Hans J. Hillerbrand (Kirksville, Mo.: Sixteenth Century Journal 1988), 9–23.

5 One of the best short English narratives of the Peasants' War is still A.F. Pollard, "Social Revolution and Catholic Reaction in Germany," *The Cambridge Modern History*, 12 vols. (Cambridge: 1902–1910), 2: 174–95. The indispensable long narrative, despite a partially dated interpretation, is Günther Franz, *Der deutsche Bauernkrieg* (Munich and Berlin: 1933), republished in many successive editions. Another narrative, up to date with current research both in the Soviet bloc and the West, is Günter Vogler, *Die Gewalt soll gegeben werden dem gemeinen Volk. Der deutsche Bauernkrieg 1525* (Berlin: Dietz 1983).

6 Blickle, *Revolution of 1525*, 189.

7 Jean Wirth, *Luther: Etude d'Histoire Religieuse* (Geneva: Droz 1981), 58–9.

8 Adolf Waas, "Die grosse Wende im deutschen Bauernkrieg," *Historische Zeitschrift* 158 (1938): 473–91.

9 Vogler, *Bauernkrieg*, 51.

10 Wirth, *Luther*, 58: "… ce qui n'est probablement qu'un mensonge par ommission."

11 Thomas A. Brady, Jr, *Turning Swiss. Cities and Empire, 1450–1550* (Cambridge: Cambridge University Press 1985), 10–11.

12 Henry J. Cohn, "Anticlericalism in the German Peasants' War 1525," *Past and Present* 83 (1979): 12; Francis Rapp, "The Social and Economic Prehistory of the Peasant War in Lower Alsace," in Scribner and Benecke, *Peasant War*, 52–4.

13 Tom Scott, *Freiburg and the Breisgau. Town-Country Relations in the Age of Reformation and Peasants' War* (Oxford: Oxford University Press 1986); Tom Scott, "Reformation and Peasants' War in Waldshut and Environs: A Structural Analysis," *Archiv für Reformationsgeschichte* 69 (1978): 82–102, 70 (1979): 140–69; Peter Blickle, "Nochmals zur Entstehung der Zwölf Artikel im Bauernkrieg," in *Bauer, Reich und Reformation. Festschrift für Günther Franz*, ed. Peter Blickle (Stuttgart: Eugen Ulmer 1982), 286–308.

14 Justus Maurer, *Prediger in Bauernkrieg* (Stuttgart: Calwer 1979), 161; Heiko A. Oberman, "The Gospel of Social Unrest," in Scribner and Benecke, *Peasant War*, 50.

15 Tom Scott, "The Peasants' War: A Historiographical Review," *Historical Journal* 22 (1979): 693–720, 953–74: "… Blickle, whose analysis although vastly more profound and differentiated … essentially perpetuates the view of the Peasants' War as a political struggle which was first put forward over forty years ago by Franz …" (953) Scott's book on Freiburg and the Breisgau undergirds the critique in the historiographical review (see n. 13).

16 Ibid., 964.

17 John U. Nef, "Industrial Europe on the Eve of the Reformation," *Journal of Political Economy* 49 (1941): 1–40, 183–224.

18 Friedrich Engels, *Marx-Engels, Werke*, 39 vols. (Berlin: Dietz 1973), 20: 312.

19 Brady, *Turning Swiss*, 119–33.

20 Scott, "Historiographical Review," 953: "The unspoken assumption behind most analysis of the political programmes and consciousness in the Peasants' War is that its unprecedented compass and virulence can adequately and ought properly to be explained in terms of ideology."

21 Ibid., 961.

22 Robert S. Lopez and Harry A. Miskimin, "The Economic Depression of the Renaissance," *The Economic History Review* 14 (1962): 408–26.

23 Crane Brinton, *The Anatomy of Revolution* (New York: Prentice-Hall 1965), 64: "Social antagonisms seem to be at their strongest when a class has attained to wealth, but is, or feels itself, shut out from the highest social distinction, and from positions of evident and open political power."

24 John C. Stalnaker, "Towards a Social Interpretation of the German Peasant War," in Scribner and Benecke, *Peasant War*, 36–7.

25 Blickle, *Revolution of 1525*, 15.

26 Ibid., 51.

27 Ibid., 29–35, 68–71.

28 Ibid., 26–7.

29 Ibid., 47–9; Scott, *Freiburg*, 77–98; see also Scott, "Historiographical Review," 697, n. 14.

30 Blickle, *Revolution of 1525*, 70–1.

31 David Sabean, *Landbesitz und Gesellschaft am Vorabend des Bauernkriegs* (Stuttgart: 1972), esp. 100–20; David Sabean, "Family and Land Tenure: A Case Study of Conflict in the German Peasant War 1525," in Scribner and Benecke, *Peasant War*, 174–89.

32 Sabean, "Family," in Scribner and Benecke, *Peasant War*, 175.

33 Ibid., 174–83.

34 Blickle, *Revolution of 1525*, 109; Vogler, *Bauernkrieg*, 72.

35 Sabean, "Family," in Scribner and Benecke, *Peasant War*, 179–80.

36 Scott, "Historiographical Review," 699–700; Scott, *Freiburg*, 114–62.
37 David Herlihy, "Population, Plague and Social Change," in *Social and Economic Foundations of the Italian Renaissance*, ed. Anthony Molho (New York: Wiley 1969), 77–90.
38 Tom Scott, "Peasant Revolts in Early Modern Germany," *Historical Journal* 28 (1985): 462.
39 Peter Blickle, "Peasant Revolts in the German Empire in the Late Middle Ages," *Social History* 4 (1979): 235–7.
40 Blickle, *Revolution of 1525*, 81–3; see Franziska Conrad, *Reformation in der bäuerlichen Gesellschaft. Zur Rezeption reformatorischer Theologie im Elsass* (Stuttgart: Steiner 1984), 37–41, for an excellent short statement on the organization and functions of the village communes in Alsace.
41 Bernd Moeller, *Imperial Cities and the Reformation*, trans. by H.C. Erik Midelfort and Mark U. Edwards, Jr (Philadelphia: Fortress 1972), 41–115. Hans-Christoph Rublack, "Martin Luther and the Urban Social Experience," *The Sixteenth Century Journal* 16 (1985): 16: "Recently, a more ambitious attempt to revitalize Moeller's approach has been developed by Peter Blickle."
42 Ernst Walder, "Der politische Gehalt der Zwölf Artikel der deutschen Bauernschaft von 1525," *Schweizer Beiträge zur Algemeinen Geschichte* 12 (1954): 5–22.
43 Brady, *Turning Swiss*, 154, n. 13: "... the sacral commune [was] both a leading idea, in the Marxian sense, and a shared value, which at times could be defended by the commons against their rulers ..."
44 Scott, "Peasant Revolts," 463.
45 Horst Buszello, *Der deutsche Bauernkrieg von 1525 als politische Bewegung* (Berlin: Colloquium 1969), 19–67.
46 Brady, *Turning Swiss*, 28–32.
47 Peter Blickle, "Die Zwölf Artikel der Schwarzwälder Bauern von 1525," in *Reformation und Revolution ... Festschrift für Rainer Wohlfeil*, ed. Rainer Postel (Stuttgart: Steiner 1989), 100; Gottfried Seebass, *Artikelbrief, Bundesordnung und Verfassungsentwurf. Studien zu drei zentralen Dokumenten des sudwestdeutschen Bauernkrieges* (Heidelberg: Carl Winter 1988), 87.
48 Brady, *Turning Swiss*, 57–72.
49 Ibid., 39; Buszello, *Bauernkrieg als politische Bewegung*, 152–3.
50 Blickle, *Revolution of 1525*, 84–6; Robert Howard Lord, "The Parliaments of the Middle Ages and Early Modern Period," *Catholic Historical Review* 16 (1930): 125–44.
51 Blickle, *Revolution of 1525*, 105–24, 137–45; Buszello, *Bauernkrieg als politische Bewegung*, 19–34.
52 The Marxist historians, because of their excessive reverence for the nineteenth-century Marxist classics, have been slowest to abandon the

myth of the national objectives of the Peasants' War. See Steinmetz, "Theses on the Early Bourgeois Revolution," in Scribner and Benecke, *Peasant War*, 17: "The early bourgeois revolution, which culminated in the Peasant War, represented the first attempt of the popular masses to create a unified national state from below."

53 Blickle, *Revolution of 1525*, 105–54.

54 Brady, *Turning Swiss*, 58.

55 Scott, "Historiographical Review," 966, expresses both the empirical reality and his interpretation of it: "The war was not simply a peasants' struggle; it was the reaction of the countryside as a whole – peasants, craftsmen, local preachers – to the massive shifts in the structure of the rural economy and society in late medieval Germany."

56 Horst Buszello, "The Common Man's View of the State in the German Peasant War," in Scribner and Benecke, *Peasant War*, 115; Vogler, *Bauernkrieg*, 102, regarding the propertied status of the "serf," Jäcklein Rohrbach, the peasant leader at Weinsberg; Günther Franz, "Die Führer im Bauernkrieg," in *Bäuerliche Führungsschichten in der Neuzeit*, ed. Günther Franz (Büdingen: 1974), 1–15.

57 Blickle, *Revolution of 1525*, 113–16; Thomas F. Sea, "Imperial Cities and the Peasants' War in Germany," *Central European History* 12 (1979): 3–37.

58 Brady, *Turning Swiss*, 186–93.

59 Blickle, *Revolution of 1525*, 116–22; Marion Kobelt-Groch, "Von 'armen frowen' und 'bösen wibern' – Frauen im Bauernkrieg zwischen Anpassung und Auflehnung," *Archiv für Reformationsgeschichte* 79 (1988): 119–53; Franz, *Bauernkrieg*, 189–90.

60 Scott, *Freiburg*, 155–62; Scott, "Historiographical Review," 957–65.

61 Scott, "Historiographical Review," 957, 962; see also Scott, *Freiburg*, 229–35.

62 Blickle, *Revolution of 1525*, 155–61; Goertz, *Pfaffenhass*, 103–8, 163–83.

63 Oberman, "Gospel of Social Unrest," in Scribner and Benecke, *Peasant War*, 45; Conrad, *Reformation*, 117–24.

64 Cohn, "Anticlericalism," 16.

65 Ibid., 15–16: "Wir moegen vor den Pfaffen nicht genesen"; for the most recent discussion of the Bundschuh conspiracies, see Scott, *Freiburg*, 165–89.

66 Cohn, "Anticlericalism," 8; Brunfels's pamphlet is published in *Flugschriften der Bauernkriegszeit*, ed. Adolf Laube and Hans Werner Seiffert (Cologne and Vienna: Böhlau 1978), 158–77.

67 Cohn, "Anticlericalism," 7–8; Maurer, *Prediger*, 65–71.

68 Cohn, "Anticlericalism," 20–4.

69 Ibid., 26–7.

70 Ibid., 17–20.

71 Scott, "Historiographical Review," 711; Heide Wunder, "'Altes Recht' und 'Göttliches Recht' im Deutschen Bauernkrieg," *Zeitschrift für Agrargeschichte und Agrarsoziologie* 24 (1976): 54–66.

72 Blickle, *Revolution of 1525*, 86–93; Gerald Strauss, *Law, Resistance and the State. The Opposition to Roman Law in Reformation Germany* (Princeton: Princeton University Press 1986), 126–35.

73 Franz, *Bauernkrieg*, 108.

74 Buszello, *Bauernkrieg als politische Bewegung*, 51–2.

75 Paul Herzog, *Die Bauernunruhen im Schaffhauser Gebiet 1524/25* (Fribourg, Switz. dissertation: Aarau 1965).

76 Peter Blickle, etc., "Zürichs Anteil am deutschen Bauernkrieg. Die Vorstellung des göttlichen Rechts im Klettgau," *Zeitschrift für die Geschichte des Oberrheins* 133 (1985): 81–101.

77 Ibid., 83–4.

78 Ibid., 85–7, 99–100.

79 Ibid., 88–9, 93–4, 101.

80 Herzog, *Bauernunruhen*, 37: "Ohne die reformatorischen Ideen, verbunden mit dem Radikalismus der Täufer, wäre ein allgemeiner Aufstand undenkbar." From a somewhat different standpoint, with specific reference to Alsace, Conrad, *Reformation*, 139: "Erst das Bewusstsein, im göttlichen Auftrag zu handeln, gab den Bauern den Mut, den Aufstand zu initiieren und voranzutreiben. Erst die neue religiöse Selbsterfahrung gab der Erhebung eine Dimension, die die Beschränkung vorheriger Bauernaufstände sprengte."

81 Blickle, "Zürichs Anteil," 95: "Dass die bäuerliche Argumentation das Evangelium missbräuchlich verwende, ja verständnislos, wird schwerlich auf die Dauer halten lassen, auch wenn es eine heute noch verbreitete Auffassung ist."

82 Walter Elliger, *Thomas Müntzer. Leben und Werk* (Göttingen: Vandenhoeck 1975), 643–8; Scott, *Freiburg*, 233–4, uses the same kind of argument, but with much greater caution.

83 Blickle, "Zwölf Artikel der Schwarzwälder," in Postel, *Reformation und Revolution*, 98: "soll allein ... das gotlich wort, one allen menschlichen zusatz gepredigt werden."

84 Heiko A. Oberman, *Masters of the Reformation. The Emergence of a New Intellectual Climate in Europe*, trans. by Dennis Martin (Cambridge: Cambridge University Press 1981), 187–209.

85 Blickle, *Revolution of 1525*, 195–6.

86 Günther Franz, ed., *Quellen zur Geschichte des Bauernkrieges* (Munich: Oldenbourg 1963), 174: "und uns da ainhelligklichen entschlossen, allain zu handeln nach Lut und Inhalt des gotlichen Worts, welches man durch gelert, christenlich Manner erfaren und erlernen sell."

87 Blickle, *Revolution of 1525*, 99; Vogler, *Bauernkrieg*, 85.

88 Wirth, *Luther*, 53–7; in summary, 57: "Les saints quittent les ban-
    nières, le Verbe de Dieu s'y installe, mais le soulier à lacet (*Bundschuh*
    en allemand), symbole de la révolte, devient une tradition."
89 Scott, *Freiburg*, 234; Conrad, *Reformation*, 133.
90 Short narratives of the military phase of the peasant movement of
    1525 are to be found in the translator's introduction to Blickle, *Revolu-
    tion of 1525*, xv–xxii, and in A.F. Pollard, "Social Revolution," 181–91.
    The most complete account is in Franz, *Bauernkrieg*, 92–300.
91 Rudolf Endres, "The Peasant War in Franconia," in Scribner and Ben-
    ecke, *Peasant War*, 77–8.
92 Scott, "Peasant Revolts," 456–7.
93 Friedrich Engels, *The German Revolutions*, ed. Leonard Krieger (Chi-
    cago and London: University of Chicago Press 1967), 116–17: "... only
    the princes could gain by the ending of the Peasant War. This hap-
    pened in reality. They gained not only relatively, through the weak-
    ening of their opponents, the clergy, the nobility and the cities, but
    also absolutely through the prizes of war which they collected. The
    church estates were secularized in their favour; part of the nobility,
    fully or partly ruined, was obliged gradually to place itself in their
    vassalage; the indemnities of the cities and peasantry swelled their
    treasuries, which, with the abolition of so many city privileges, had
    now obtained a much more extended field for financial operations."
94 J.H. Hexter, *Reappraisals in History: New Views on History and Society
    in Early Modern Europe* (New York and London: 1961), 26–49; J. Rus-
    sell Major, "The Renaissance Monarch: A Contribution to the Period-
    ization of History," *Emory University Quarterly* (1957), 112–24.
95 Blickle, *Revolution of 1525*, 170–82: "The evidence for Upper Germany
    thus refutes the thesis that the lost Revolution of 1525 was linked
    causally to the structure of the absolute state; and it is doubtful that
    this thesis is valid for any part of the entire area of the revolution."
96 Franz Lau, "Der Bauernkrieg und das angebliche Ende der luther-
    ischen Reformation als spontaner Volksbewegung," *Luther-Jahrbuch* 26
    (1959): 109–34. Excerpted in *Reformation and Authority*, ed. Kyle Ses-
    sions (Lexington: Heath 1968), 94–101.
97 Blickle, *Revolution of 1525*, 185.
98 Moeller, *Imperial Cities and the Reformation*, 103–15.

CHAPTER TWO

1 *WA*, 11: 229–81.
2 Wenzeslaus Link, "Ob die Geistlichen auch schuldig sind, Zins zu geben," in *Flugschriften der Bauernkriegszeit*, ed. Adolf Laube and Hans
   Werner Seiffert (Cologne and Vienna: Böhlau 1978), 152–3.

3 Paul A. Russell, *Lay Theology in the Reformation* (Cambridge: Cambridge University Press 1986), 92, 132, 139, 173–4.

4 Gunter Zimmermann, *Die Antwort der Reformatoren auf die Zehntenfrage* (Frankfort, Bern: Peter Lang 1982), 55–64.

5 Otto Brunfels, "Vom Pfaffenzehnten," in Laube and Seiffert, *Flugschriften*, 158.

6 Ibid., 159.

7 Ibid., 163.

8 Ibid., 176.

9 Ibid., 169–70.

10 Ibid., 160.

11 Ibid., 167.

12 Ibid., 170, 176.

13 Ibid., 173.

14 "Die Memminger (Allgäuer) Bundesordnung," in Laube and Seiffert, *Flugschriften*, 33.

15 Laube and Seiffert, *Flugschriften*, 589.

16 Jakob Strauss, "Dass Wucher zu nehmen und zu geben unserem christlichen Glauben entgegen ist," in Laube and Seiffert, *Flugschriften*, 178.

17 Ibid., 180–1.

18 Ibid., 181–3.

19 Thomas A. Brady, Jr, *Turning Swiss: Cities and Empire, 1450–1550* (Cambridge: Cambridge University Press 1985), 119–27.

20 Strauss, "Wucher," 187.

21 Ibid., 189.

22 *WA*, 11: 277–8.

23 Link, "Ob die Geistlichen," 156–7.

24 Peter Blickle, *The Revolution of 1525. The German Peasants' War from a New Perspective*, trans. by Thomas A. Brady, Jr and H.C. Erik Midelfort (Baltimore and London: Johns Hopkins 1981), 18.

25 Gottfried Seebass, *Artikelbrief, Bundesordnung und Verfassungsentwurf. Studien zu drei zentralen Dokumenten des sudwestdeutschen Bauernkrieges* (Heidelberg: Carl Winter 1988), 55–148.

26 "Memminger Bundesordnung," 32–4.

27 "Die Zwölf Artikel," in Laube and Seiffert, *Flugschriften*, 26–7.

28 Ibid., 31.

29 Walter Elliger, *Thomas Müntzer. Leben und Werk* (Göttingen: Vandenhoeck 1975), 643–8.

30 Peter Blickle, etc., "Zürichs Anteil am deutschen Bauernkrieg. Die Vorstellung des göttlichen Rechts im Klettgau," *Zeitschrift für die Geschichte des Oberrheins* 133 (1985): 83–4; "Die Artikel der Annaberger Bergarbeiter," in Laube and Seiffert, *Flugschriften*, 135–6.

31 Laube and Seiffert, *Flugschriften*, 59, 65, 80.
32 Ibid., 139–43.
33 "Artikel der fränkischen Bauernschaft (Taubertaler Programm)," ibid., 109; see also "Feldordnung der fränkischen Bauern (Ochsenfurter Neue Ordnung)," in *Flugschriften des Bauernkrieges*, ed. Klaus Kaczerowsky (Reinbek: Rowohlt 1970), 63.
34 Laube and Seiffert, *Flugschriften*, 109.
35 Günther Franz, ed., *Quellen zur Geschichte des Bauernkrieges* (Darmstadt: Wiss. Buchgesellschaft 1963), 536.
36 Friedrich Weigant, "Der Reichsreformentwurf (Heilbronner Programm)," in Laube and Seiffert, *Flugschriften*, 73–9.
37 Günter Vogler, "Tendenzen der sozialen und politischen Programmatik im deutschen Bauernkrieg. Ein Vergleich mit Gaismairs Tiroler Landesordnung," in *Die Bauernkrieg und Michael Gaismair*, ed. Fridolin Dörrer (Innsbruck: Tiroler Landesarchiv 1982), 101–2, 110.
38 Brunfels, "Pfaffenzehnten," 174–5.
39 "Zwölf Artikel," 29–30. The demand in article 6 to order labour services "wie unser eltern gedient haben allain nach laut des wort Gots," and the contrast in article 9 of "alter geschribner straff" and "new satzung" exemplify the undercurrent of appeal to the old law in the Twelve Articles.
40 Ibid., 28.
41 Blickle, *Revolution of 1525*, 26–7.
42 "Die Ortenauer Vertrag," in Laube and Seiffert, *Flugschriften*, 50–1.
43 "Zwölf Artikel," 28–9.
44 "An die Versammlung gemeiner Bauernschaft," in Laube and Seiffert, *Flugschriften*, 123–8.
45 Siegfried Hoyer, "Karlstadt: Verfasser der Flugschrift 'An die Versammlung gemeiner Bauernschaft'?," *Zeitschrift für Geschichtswissenschaft* 35 (1987): 128–9, 137.
46 "Zugeständnisse an die Bamberger Stiftsuntertanen," in Laube and Seiffert, *Flugschriften*, 43.
47 "Ortenauer Vertrag," 51–3.
48 *Müntzer Schriften*, 473.
49 "Zwölf Artikel," 27–8.
50 Ibid., 30.
51 "Ortenauer Vertrag," 52–3.
52 "Die Erfurter Artikel," in Laube and Seiffert, *Flugschriften*, 65; Kaczerowsky, *Flugschriften*, 45–51.
53 "Ortenauer Vertrag," 45.
54 "Memminger Bundesordnung," 32.
55 "Der Artikelbrief der Schwarzwälder Bauern," in Laube and Seiffert, *Flugschriften*, 111.

56 Laube and Seiffert, *Flugschriften*, 20–1.

57 M.M. Smirin, *Die Volksreformation des Thomas Münzer und der grosse Bauernkrieg* (Berlin: Dietz 1952), 372–83. In its attempt to establish an improbable interpretation based on the Marxist classics by the sheer weight of diligent scholarship, Smirin's book is a monument of Stalinist historiography.

58 "Taubertaler Programm," 109.

59 "Tiroler Landesordnung," 139; trans. from Walter Klaassen, *Michael Gaismair. Revolutionary and Reformer* (Leyden: Brill 1978), 131.

60 Laube and Seiffert, *Flugschriften*, 583.

61 "An die Versammlung," 133–4.

62 Jürgen Bücking, *Michael Gaismair: Reformer-Sozialrebell-Revolutionär. Seine Rolle im Tiroler "Bauernkrieg" (1525/32)* (Stuttgart: Klett-Cota 1978), 58–92, 96–104. Bücking analyzes the radicalization process between Gaismair's first *Landesordnung* of May 1525 and the second *Landesordnung* discussed here.

63 Ibid., 97–8, citing Z 3: 563, shows that a "new Switzerland" in the south Tyrol (Etschland, the region around Meran and Bozen), affiliated with old Switzerland and with the new Switzerland in Graubünden, was precisely the object of Ulrich Zwingli at the time: "Und allem Etschland (soll) von stund an fryheit und ein eigen regiment verheissen (werden) one alle der Pünden (Graubünden) und unser beschwerd, usgenommen ein zimmlich järlich täll (Abgabe), damit man inen hilff tuon mög, die inen ghein beschwerd sye. Ouch früntlich pündtnussen mit inen ze machen, das man sy nimmer me(r) verlassen well etc."

64 "Tiroler Landesordnung," 139; trans. Klaassen, *Gaismair*, 131.

65 "Tiroler Landesordnung," 139–40, 142.

66 Ibid., 142–3.

67 Ibid., 140–2.

68 Vogler, "Tendenzen," 106; Bücking, *Gaismair*, 85.

69 "Hans Hergot," "Von der neuen Wandlung eines christlichen Lebens," in Laube and Seiffert, *Flugschriften*, 547–57. See also Gerhard Zschäbitz, "'Von der newen wandlung eynes Christlichen Lebens' – eine oft misdeutete Schrift aus der Zeit nach dem Grossen Deutschen Bauernkrieg," *Zeitschrift für Geschichtswissenschaft* 8 (1960), 908–18.

70 Laube and Seiffert, *Flugschriften*, 546, 642.

71 "Hergot," "Von der neuen Wandlung," 554.

72 Ibid., 555.

73 Ibid., 553.

74 Ibid., 557.

75 Ibid., 547.

76 Ibid., 557.

77 Ibid., 551.

78 Ibid., 552.

79 Ibid., 549.

80 Ibid., 547–9.

81 Ibid., 549.

82 Ibid., 547.

83 Ibid., 548.

84 Ibid., 550.

85 Ibid., 548.

86 Ibid.: "... derselbigen menschen behawsung wird beyeynander seyn ynn eyner vorsamlung nach Cartheusers weys."

CHAPTER THREE

1 *Anabaptism. A Social History, 1525–1618. Switzerland, Austria, Moravia, and South and Central Germany* (Ithaca and London: Cornell University Press 1972), 152–7.

2 Ibid., 458–9.

3 Ibid., 21. The number of converts to Anabaptism for that period was increased to 4,356 in Claus-Peter Clasen, *The Anabaptists in South and Central Germany, Switzerland and Austria. Their Names, Occupations, Places of Residence and Dates of Conversion: 1525–1618* ([Goshen, Indiana]: The Mennonite Quarterly Review for the Mennonite Historical Society 1978), 9.

4 John Oyer, *Lutheran Reformers against Anabaptists: Luther, Melanchthon and Menius and the Anabaptists of Central Germany* (The Hague: Nijhoff 1964); Walter Klaassen, *Michael Gaismair. Revolutionary and Reformer* (Leyden: Brill 1978); Gottfried Seebass, "Bauernkrieg und Täufertum in Franken," *Zeitschrift für Kirchengeschichte* 85 (1974): 284–300; C. Arnold Snyder, *The Life and Thought of Michael Sattler* (Scottdale and Kitchener: Herald 1984); Hans-Jürgen Goertz, *Die Täufer. Geschichte und Deutung* (Munich: Beck 1980); Martin Haas, "Der Weg der Täufer in die Absonderung," in *Umstrittenes Täufertum, 1525–1975. Neue Forschungen*, ed. Hans-Jürgen Goertz (Göttingen: Vandenhoeck 1975), 50–78; Werner O. Packull, *Mysticism and the Early South German-Austrian Anabaptist Movement, 1525–1531* (Scottdale: Herald 1977); James M. Stayer, "Reublin and Brötli: The Revolutionary Beginnings of Swiss Anabaptism," in *The Origins and Characteristics of Anabaptism*, ed. Marc Lienhard (The Hague: Nijhoff 1977), 83–102; James M. Stayer, "Radical Early Zwinglianism: Balthasar Hubmaier, Faber's *Ursach* and the Peasant Programmes," in *Huldrych Zwingli, 1484–1531: A Legacy of Radical Reform*, ed. E.J. Furcha (Montreal: Faculty of Religious Studies, McGill University 1985), 62–82. A precursor of this trend of interpreta-

tion connecting Anabaptism and the Peasants' War is Gerhard Zschäbitz, *Zur mitteldeutschen Wiedertäuferbewegung nach den grossen
Bauernkrieg* (Berlin: Rütten and Loening 1958). Recent corroboration
has been supplied by Hans-Peter Jecker, "Die Basler Täufer," *Basler
Zeitschrift für Geschichte und Altertumskunde* 80 (1980): 6–131;
Heinrich Beulshausen, *Die Geschichte der osthessischen Täufergemeinden*,
2 vols. (Giessen: Wilhelm Schmitz 1981); and Matthias Hui, "Die andere Reformation im Grüningen Amt. Die revolutionäre Bewegung
der aufständischen Bauern, radikalen Prädikanten und streitbaren
TäuferInnen in einem Zürcher Untertanengebiet von 1525 bis 1530,"
Akzessarbeit, Theology Faculty, Bern University 1988.

5 Emil Egli, ed., *Actensammlung zur Geschichte der Zürcher Reformation in
den Jahren 1519–1533* (Zurich: 1879), 93, 899; Robert Hoppeler, "Zur
Charakteristik des Leutpriesters Simon Stumpf von Höngg," *Zwingliana* 4 (1926): 321–9.

6 *Actensammlung*, 81, 132–3; QGTS, 1, Zürich: 2–4.

7 *Actensammlung*, 137.

8 Z, 2: 458–525. See Hans Nabholz, *Die Bauernbewegung in der Ostschweiz, 1524–25* (Bülach: 1898), 52–6, for Zwingli's views on the tithe
and related matters.

9 QGTS, 1, Zürich: 2–4. The leader among modern interpreters in pin-
pointing the significance of the tithe controversy in the "prehistory" of
Anabaptism is J.F.G. Goeters, *Ludwig Hätzer (ca. 1500 bis 1529) Spiritu-
alist und Antitrinitarier* (Gütersloh: Bertelsmann 1957), 34–5, and "Die
Vorgeschichte des Täufertums in Zürich," in *Studien zur Geschichte und
Theologie der Reformation. Festschrift für Ernst Bizer*, ed. L. Abramowski
and J.F.G. Goeters (Neukirchen-Vluyn: Neukirchner Verlag 1969),
255–9.

10 Calvin Augustine Pater, *Karlstadt as the Father of the Baptist Movements:
The Emergence of Lay Protestantism* (Toronto: University of Toronto
Press 1984), 134–59.

11 QGTS, 1, Zürich: 16.

12 James M. Stayer, "Die Anfänge des schweizerischen Täufertums im
reformierten Kongregationalismus," in *Umstrittenes Täufertum*, 39–46.

13 J.J. Hottinger and H.H. Vögeli, eds., *Heinrich Bullingers Reformationsgeschichte*, 2 vols. (Frauenfeld: 1838), 1: 238; QGTS, 1, Zürich: 35–6.

14 Stayer, "Reublin and Brötli," 89–99; see Peter Bierbrauer, "Die Refor-
mation in den Schaffhauser Gemeinden Hallau und Thayngen," in
Bauer und Reformation, 1: Zugänge zur bäuerlichen Reformation, ed. Peter
Blickle (Zurich: Chronos 1987), 21–53.

15 QGTS, 2, Ostschweiz: 22, n. 3; Staatsarchiv Schaffhausen, Justiz, B1
1527 [sic – although the date of the document is 16 May 1525], 27–30,
Ratsprotokolle, 6 (1522–26), 256, 264.

16 *QGTS, 1, Zürich*: 45–6, 54–5, 391–2; *QGTS, 2, Ostschweiz*: 48–9.

17 Johann Loserth, "Die Stadt Waldshut und die vorderösterreichische Regierung in den Jahren 1523–1526," *Archiv für österreichische Geschichte* 77 (1891): 6–149; Stayer, "Reublin and Brötli," 90–2.

18 *QGTS, 2, Ostschweiz*: 49.

19 *QGTS, 1, Zürich*, 391–2.

20 Karl Schib, *Geschichte der Stadt und Landschaft Schaffhausen* (Schaffhausen: 1972), 267–8; Stayer, "Reublin and Brötli," 97–8.

21 *QGTS, 2, Ostschweiz*: 23–4, 48–9.

22 A.J.F. Zieglschmid, ed., *Die älteste Chronik der Hutterischen Brüder* (Ithaca: Cayuga 1943), 50–2, 91–8; Heinold Fast, "Wie doopte Konrad Grebel? Overwegingen bij Meihuizens uitleg van de bronnen," *Doopsgezinde Bijdragen* NR 4 (1978): 22–31.

23 Karl Schib, ed., *Hans Stockars Jerusalemfahrt 1519 und Chronik 1520–1529* (Basel: 1949), 114, 116; Karl Schib, ed., *Quellen zur neueren Geschichte Schaffhausens* (Thayngen-Schaff. 1948), 24–5; J. Huber, ed., "Heinrich Küssenbergs Chronik," *Archiv für schweizerische Reformations-Geschichte* 3 (1876): 423.

24 Clasen, *Anabaptism*, 459, renders the name incorrectly as "Hans Füeger."

25 *QGTS, 2, Ostschweiz*: 42–6.

26 Ibid., 23, n. 1.

27 Staatsarchiv Schaffhausen, Justiz, B1 1527, 27, 28.

28 Caspar Wirz, ed., *Akten über die diplomatischen Beziehungen der römischen Curie zu der Schweiz, 1512–1552* (Basel: 1895), 178: "pensioni private in Scafusa."

29 *QGTS, 2, Ostschweiz*: 251–3, 256–73, 393, 583, 607–8; Heinold Fast, "Hans Krüsis Büchlein über Glauben und Taufe, ein Täuferdruck von 1525," *Zwingliana* 11 (1962): 456–75.

30 Vienna, 1528; reprinted in Johann Loserth, *Doctor Balthasar Hubmaier und die Anfänge der Wiedertaufe in Mähren* (Brünn: 1893), 210–16.

31 Stayer, "Radical Early Zwinglianism," 62–82.

32 *Ursach*, 213.

33 *Ibid.*, 213–14.

34 Torsten Bergsten, *Balthasar Hubmaier: Seine Stellung zu Reformation und Täufertum, 1521–1528* (Kassel: Oncken 1961), 277–301.

35 *Ursach*, 211–12.

36 Ibid., 215: "er bekhennt, wie er der pawrn artigkel, so jm von jnen aus dem heer zukhummen sein, dyselbigen jnen erweytert und aussgelegt ..." Gottfried Seebass, *Artikelbrief, Bundesordnung und Verfassungsentwurf. Studien zu drei zentralen Dokumenten des südwestdeutschen Bauernkrieges* (Heidelberg: Carl Winter 1988), 28, gives the reading

"aus dem Höre," which he says could indeed refer to the peasant army, but which he thinks more likely refers to an Upper Swabian territory, "das Gebiet um den Schiener Berg zwischen dem Zeller und dem Unteren See am Westende des Bodensees, das Höre oder Höri."

37 *Ursach*, 212.

38 Johannes Faber, *Doctoris Joannis Fabri adversus Doctorem Balthasarum Pacimontanum ... orthodoxae Fidei Catholica Defensio* (Leipzig: 1528), fol. G4^{vo}.

39 Gunther Franz, ed., *Quellen zur Geschichte des Bauernkrieges* (Munich: Oldenbourg 1963), 235, 1.9 — 236, 1.25; see Seebass, *Artikelbrief*, 17–54.

40 *Ursach*, 212–13.

41 *Ursach*, 213.

42 Peter Blickle, "Nochmals zur Entstehung der Zwölf Artikel im Bauernkrieg," in *Bauer, Reich und Reformation. Festschrift für Günther Franz*, ed. Peter Blickle (Stuttgart: Eugen Ulmer 1982), 306, n. 101.

43 Alfred Stern, *Über die zwölf Artikel der Bauern* (Leipzig: 1868); Wilhelm Mau, *Balthasar Hubmaier* (Berlin and Leipzig: 1912).

44 Günther Franz, "Die Entstehung der 'Zwölf Artikel' der deutschen Bauernschaft," *Archiv für Reformationsgeschichte* 36 (1939): 193–213.

45 Blickle, "Nochmals zur Entstehung," 286–308; Scott's ms. discovery is published as an appendix to Peter Blickle, "Die Zwölf Artikel der Schwarzwalder Bauern von 1525," in *Reformation und Revolution ... Festschrift für Rainer Wohlfeil*, ed. Rainer Postel (Stuttgart: Steiner 1989), 96–100.

46 "Radical Early Zwinglianism," 48–9; "Neue Modelle eines gemeinsamen Lebens. Gütergemeinschaft in Täufertum," in *Alles gehört allen. Das Experiment Gütergemeinschaft vom 16. Jahrhundert bis heute*, ed. Hans-Jürgen Goertz (Munich: Beck 1984), 27.

47 Seebass, *Artikelbrief*, 55–148.

48 Ibid., 87.

49 Bergsten, *Hubmaier*, 246–7; Thomas A. Brady, Jr, *Turning Swiss. Cities and Empire, 1450–1550* (Cambridge: Cambridge University Press 1985), 57–72.

50 Carl Sachsse, *D. Balthasar Hubmaier als Theologe* (Berlin: 1914), 108–9.

51 *Ursach*, 212.

52 Ibid., 213.

53 Bergsten, *Hubmaier*, 296–8; Justus Maurer, *Prediger im Bauernkrieg* (Stuttgart: Calwer 1979), 337–9, 560–2; Walter Elliger, *Thomas Müntzer: Leben und Werk* (Göttingen: Vandenhoeck 1975), 651–72; Tom Scott, "Reformation and Peasants' War in Waldshut and Environs: A Structural Analysis," Part 2, *Archiv für Reformationsgeschichte* 70 (1979): 147–8. Scott has more recently repeated the same position in "The 'Volks-

reformation' of Thomas Müntzer in Allstedt and Mühlhausen," *Journal of Ecclesiastical History* 34 (1983): 205: "Despite certain reservations the provisions of the draft clearly reflect Müntzer's thinking ..."

54 Seebass, *Artikelbrief*, 165–70.

55 Ibid., 155–9.

56 My argument follows Peter Blickle, "Thomas Müntzer und der Bauernkrieg in Südwestdeutschland," *Zeitschrift für Agrargeschichte und Agrarsoziologie* 24 (1976): 79–80. Curiously, in *The Revolution of 1525*, trans. Thomas A. Brady, Jr and H.C. Erik Midelfort (Baltimore: Johns Hopkins University Press 1981), 148, Blickle seems to change his view: "the Draft of a Constitution ... borrowed heavily from Thomas Müntzer."

57 *Ursach*, 212–13.

58 Ibid., 213: "so verwilige sy in den obern laster."

59 *QGT, 9, Hubmaier*: 455; Z, 2: 343–6.

60 *Müntzer Schriften*, 544.

61 Seebass, *Artikelbrief*, 158–9, 177–9.

62 Ibid., 155–9.

63 Scott, "Reformation and Peasants' War," 147: "... the invocation of the secular ban as the penalty for refusal to join the Black Foresters' Christian Union so strongly resembles Hubmaier's doctrine of the spiritual ban that Bergsten's description of them as no more than simultaneous phenomena deriving from a common New Testament source looks like special pleading. Who else was supposed to have instructed the peasants in the meaning and application of such passages from the Scriptures?"; Maurer, *Prediger*, 335: "Der 'weltliche Bann' im Artikelbrief ist ja eine wörtliche Übertragung des kirchlichen Banns Hubmaiers."

64 Franz, *Quellen*, 235, 1. 11: "dem armen gemeinen Man in Stetten und uf dem Land."

65 Ibid., 235, 11. 18–19: "on alle Schwertschlag und Blutvergiessung."

66 Ibid., 236, 11. 11–20.

67 Ibid., 235, 11. 38–41: "... mit denen, so sich sperren und widern, brüderliche Verainigung inzugon und gemainen cristenlichen Nutz zu fürdern, ganz und gar kain Gemainschaft halten noch bruchen söllen, und das weder essen, trinken, baden, malen, bachen, agkern, mäyen."

68 *QGT, 9, Hubmaier*: 316: "... die Christen kain gemainschafft mit einem solhen menschen, weder in worten, essen, trincken, malen, bachenn oder annderlay gestalt haben sollen."

69 The text of the letter from Collin to Aberli appears in Loserth, "Stadt Waldshut," 102–3; Bergsten, *Hubmaier*, 205, 319, n. 91; *QGTS, 1, Zürich*: 161, 196–7.

70 John H. Yoder, "Die Kristallisationspunkt des Täufertums," *Mennonitische Geschichtsblätter* 24 (1972): 35–47.

71 Paul Herzog, *Die Bauernunruhen in Schaffhauser Gebiet 1524/25* (Fribourg, Switz. dissertation: Aarau 1965), 55, 135.

72 Ibid., 55, classes Schleitheim as a community "unter starkem Einfluss der täuferischen Lehren von Johannes Brötli." See *QGTS*, 2, *Ostschweiz*: 48–9, where a Schaffhausen government report of November 1528 says that Reublin baptized "vil von Hallow und an ander orten unser oberkeit."

73 Snyder, *Sattler*, 97–104.

74 Goertz, *Die Täufer*, 20–3; C. Arnold Snyder, "The Schleitheim Articles in Light of the Revolution of the Common Man: Continuation or Departure?," *Sixteenth Century Journal* 16 (1985): 419–30.

75 Snyder, *Sattler*, 60–5.

76 Heinold Fast, "Michael Sattler's Baptism: Some Comments," *Mennonite Quarterly Review* 60 (1986): 364–73; C. Arnold Snyder, "Michael Sattler's Baptism: Some Comments in Reply to Heinold Fast," *Mennonite Quarterly Review* 62 (1988): 496–506.

77 Franziska Conrad, *Reformation in der bäuerlichen Gesellschaft. Zur Rezeption reformatorischer Theologie in Elsass* (Stuttgart: Steiner 1984), 138.

78 Gerhard Zschäbitz, "Die Stellung der Täuferbewegung im Spannungsbogen der deutschen frühbürgerlichen Revolution," in *Die frühbürgerliche Revolution in Deutschland*, ed. Gerhard Brendler (Berlin: Akademie-Verlag 1961), 152–62; Blickle, *Revolution of 1525*, 185: "[The Anabaptists] sought to save a remnant of the communal Reformation by withdrawing from the realm of this world ..."

79 Clasen, *Anabaptists ... Names*, 48.

80 Jecker, "Basler Täufer," 92–4.

81 Emil Dürr and Paul Roth, eds., *Aktensammlung zur Geschichte der Basler Reformation in den Jahren 1519–1534*, 6 vols. (Basel: 1921–1950), 1: 391; 2: 302.

82 Ibid., 2: 245–7, 302.

83 Ibid., 1: 381, 391; 2: 638–9; 6: 292, 294.

84 Gustav Strickler, *Geschichte der Herrschaft Grüningen. Das ist Geschichte des Züricher Oberlandes und seiner Beziehungen zur Stadt Zürich und dem See* (Zurich: Art. Institut Orell Füssli 1908), 139–54, contains an archivally based text of the twenty-seven articles (144–5), which, Strickler explains, is superior to the version in Bullinger's *Reformationsgeschichte*. Martin Haas, "Täufertum und Revolution," in *Festgabe für Leonhard von Muralt* (Zurich: Berichthaus 1970), 293–5, shows the potential of the Grüningen *Fründschaften*, networks based on extended families, to bring Zurich's authority to a standstill over the treatment of Anabaptists. Many Grüningen non-Anabaptists found their loyalties to Ana-

baptists in their *Fründschaften* more pressing than their obligations to the Zurich government to maintain its religious order, particularly at a time when the Rüti uprising had called into question the whole relation between Grüningen and Zurich. This accounts for the caution with which the Zurich government dealt with the Grüningen Anabaptists, but also shows that the threat posed by rural Anabaptism was real. Hui, "Andere Reformation," 18–33, 112–14, rejects any attempt to distinguish Peasants' War and Anabaptism in the Grüningen situation. Without wanting to detract from the worth of his study, which has thoroughly mastered the Grüningen scene, I must insist that the Peasants' War and Anabaptism have to be distinguished in scale. While virtually the whole Grüningen community was involved in the commoners' resistance, only a small minority subsequently became Anabaptists. See also Matthias Hui, "Von Bauernaufstand zur Täuferbewegung," *Mennonitische Geschichtsblätter* 46 (1989): 113–44.

85 *QGTS, 1, Zürich*: 172; Clasen, *Anabaptists ... Names*, 69; Clasen, *Anabaptism*, 459, listed as a Peasants' War participant. Claus-Peter Clasen, "The Anabaptist Leaders: Their Numbers and Background. Switzerland, Austria, South and Central Germany, 1525–1618," *Mennonite Quarterly Review* 49 (1975), 127, counts Girenbader among seventy-one Swiss Anabaptist leaders whom he names for the 1525–29 period. Hui, "Andere Reformation," 65–7, 117–18.

86 *QGTS, 1, Zürich*: 145, 150, 172; Clasen, *Anabaptists ... Names*, 68. Not listed as a Peasants' War participant by Clasen. Paul Peachey, *Die soziale Herkunft der Schweizer Täufer in der Reformationszeit* (Karlsruhe: Heinrich Schneider 1954), 60–1, denies that Hans Vontobel was an Anabaptist. He has obviously been misled by faulty indexing in *QGTS, 1, Zürich*: 411. See Hui, "Andere Reformation," 67, 118, esp. n. 25.

87 *QGTS, 1, Zürich*: 172–3; see Strickler, *Grüningen*, 144–5.

88 *QGTS, 1, Zürich*: 158.

89 Ibid., 396–7; Hui, "Andere Reformation," 68, 118–19, esp. n. 48.

90 *QGTS, 1, Zürich*: 173; Hui, "Andere Reformation," 67–8, 118; Clasen, *Anabaptists ... Names*, 68. Not listed as Peasants' War participant by Clasen, although so identified in earlier literature; see Peachey, *Soziale Herkunft*, 61.

91 *QGTS, 1, Zürich*: 171–2.

92 I also include Arbogast Finsterbach and Hans Müller from Oberwinterthur among Zurich Anabaptists with a background in the peasant uprisings of 1525. They are not included in Clasen, *Anabaptists ... Names*, 67–73; and Peachey, *Herkunft*, 56–8, argues against considering them to be Anabaptists. The sources in *QGTS, 1, Zürich*: 96, 100–1, show that both were in the peasant assembly at Töss and that they

attended a meeting of Anabaptists. Finsterbach, moreover, was visited by Grebel and discussed adult baptism with him. Neither went so far as to accept adult baptism before the government called them to account, but that seems an overly rigid criterion to apply in identifying Anabaptists and, moreover, is one that Clasen himself does not use consistently.

93 Harold S. Bender, *Conrad Grebel (c. 1498–1526): The Founder of the Swiss Brethren* (Goshen: Mennonite Historical Soc. 1950), 136–62; Heinold Fast, "Conrad Grebel: The Covenant on the Cross," in *Profiles of Radical Reformers: Biographical Sketches from Thomas Müntzer to Paracelsus*, ed. Hans-Jürgen Goertz (Scottdale: Herald 1982), 118–31. Bender's concern was to show that Grebel was in no way "responsible for the peasants' revolt" (155), a matter on which no one is going to challenge him, but his description of Grebel's movements following January 1525 shows Grebel active almost exclusively in areas where the commoners' upheaval was either in progress or very recently suppressed. This did not appear significant from Bender's standpoint because Grebel addressed himself in his travels exclusively to religious issues.

94 Hui, "Andere Reformation," 74–89, 119–21.

95 *QGTS, 1, Zürich:* 109; *QGT, 7, Elsass,* 1: 63–4; Christian Neff, "Jakob Gross," *Mennonite Encyclopedia,* 2: 598–9.

96 Clasen, *Anabaptists ... Names,* 9, 17, 21.

97 Gustav Bossert, "Augustin Bader von Augsburg, der Prophet und König," *Archiv für Reformationsgeschichte* 10 (1913): 141–3; 11 (1914): 110–11.

98 *QGT, 1, Württemberg:* 528–33; *QGT, 4, Baden/Pfalz:* 348–60; Claus-Peter Clasen, *Die Wiedertäufer im Herzogtum Württemberg und in benachbarten Herrschaften: Ausbreitung, Geisteswelt und Soziologie* (Stuttgart: W. Kohlhammer 1965), 168, n. 81; Clasen, *Anabaptism,* 459.

99 Clasen, *Anabaptism,* 459; Clasen, *Wiedertäufer im Württemberg,* 168, n. 81.

100 Clasen, *Anabaptism,* 459; Clasen, *Anabaptists ... Names,* 126; Clasen, *Wiedertäufer im Württemberg,* 168, n. 81. See *QGT, 1, Württemberg,* 71–3, 1,003, n. 4. Clasen's list should be corrected: Michel Spruer, not Sporer, is the Anabaptist from Kirchberg who participated in the Peasants' War. It is an open question whether he was the Michel Sporer to whom Schwenckfeld wrote a letter, *QGT, 1, Württemberg:* 1,003–7.

101 Clasen, *Anabaptism,* 459; Clasen, *Wiedertäufer im Württemberg,* 168, n. 81; James M. Stayer, *Anabaptists and the Sword* (Lawrence: Coronado, 2d ed. 1976), 160, n. 74.

102 Jean Rott, "Guerre des paysans et anabaptisme: le cas de Boersch en Basse-Alsace," in *Investigationes Historicae. Eglises et Societe au*

XVIe Siecle, 2 vols., ed. Jean Rott (Strasbourg: Librairie Oberlin 1986), 2: 93–8.

103 Clasen, *Anabaptists ... Names*, 92, lists the gardener Clemens Ziegler as an Anabaptist, a doubtful judgment in view of Ziegler's profile in Strasbourg as an independent religious maverick. But if Clemens Ziegler is to be classed as an Anabaptist at all, he must be numbered among the Anabaptists who participated in the peasants' uprising, albeit in its earlier, non-violent phase: Robert Friedmann, "Clemens Ziegler," *Mennonitisches Lexikon*, 4: 600–1.

104 Klaus Deppermann, Werner O. Packull and James M. Stayer, "From Monogenesis to Polygenesis: The Historical Discussion of Anabaptist Origins," *Mennonite Quarterly Review* 49 (1975): 86.

105 Packull, *Mysticism*, 64–5.

106 *QGTS*, 2, *Ostschweiz*: 274; Werner O. Packull, "Denck's Alleged Baptism by Hubmaier. Its Significance for the Origin of South German-Austrian Anabaptism," *Mennonite Quarterly Review* 47 (1973): 327–38.

107 Gottfried Seebass, "Müntzers Erbe. Werk, Leben und Theologie des Hans Hut," unpub. Habilitationsschrift, U. Erlangen-Nuremberg, 1972, 2 vols., 1: 566: "es sich hier um ein völlig anderes Täufertum handelt."

108 Harold S. Bender, "The Zwickau Prophets, Thomas Müntzer and the Anabaptists," *Mennonite Quarterly Review* 27 (1953): 16.

109 The work of Packull and Seebass has highlighted Hut's importance; on Rinck, see Oyer, *Lutheran Reformers*, 41–113; Erich Geldbach, "Toward a more Ample Biography of the Hessian Anabaptist Leader Melchior Rinck," *Mennonite Quarterly Review* 48 (1974): 371–84.

110 Beulshausen, *Osthessische Täufergemeinden*, 1: 89–97; 2: 51–6.

111 Of course, the importance of the Peasants' War experience for Hut's tie to Denck can be exaggerated. Hut and Denck were in contact in Nuremberg before the Peasants' War; see Packull, *Mysticism*, 38.

112 Heinold Fast, in *QGTS*, 2, *Ostschweiz*: 403, n. 5: "Durch Thomas Müntzer hatte er einen Ruf als Schulmeister nach Mühlhausen in Thüringen empfangen und wandte sich wahrscheinlich zuerst dorthin." Georg Baring, "Hans Denck und Thomas Müntzer in Nürnberg 1524," *Archiv für Reformationsgeschichte* 50 (1959): 145–81. The source is Ernst Staehlin, ed., *Briefe und Akten zum Leben Oekolampads* (Leipzig: Heinsius 1927), 1: 365.

113 *QGTS*, 2, *Ostschweiz*: 274; Franz, *Quellen*, 536.

114 Packull, *Mysticism*, 62; Scott, "Volksreformation," 200–1, 207, corrects the view that this took place in the fall of 1524. Rather it occurred in the spring of 1525, when the Peasants' War was at full flood: "The league was, from the outset, intended as more than a defensive alliance: Müntzer conceived it as the vanguard of true believers."

115 Otto Merx, Günther Franz and Walther Peter Fuchs, eds., *Akten zur*

Geschichte des Bauernkrieges in Mitteldeutschland, 2 vols. (Aalen: Scientia 1964), 2: 897–8.

116 Beulshausen, *Osthessische Täufergemeinden*, 1: 47–59; 2: 25–33.

117 Ibid., 1: 85–8; 2: 49–50; see *TQ Hessen*, 31, 49–50.

118 Paul Wappler, *Die Täuferbewegung in Thüringen von 1526–1584* (Jena: Gustav Fischer 1913), 38, calls him the "Haupttäufer in Nordthüringen"; Clasen, "Anabaptist Leaders," 158.

119 Clasen, "Anabaptist Leaders," 158; Beulshausen, *Osthessische Täufergemeinden*, 1: 234: "Sein Bekenntnis ... gibt nicht nur Aufschluss über das umfangreiche Wirken und die Tätigkeit dieses Mannes, sondern lässt in ihm zugleich einen der edelsten Vertreter des gesamten Täufertums erkennen." Oyer, *Lutheran Reformers*, 71: "Alexander, the most influential of the northern Thuringian leaders."

120 Clasen, "Anabaptist Leaders," 158; Clasen, *Anabaptism*, 205: "Scharf and his followers were even called 'Scharf's sect.'"

121 Clasen, "Anabaptist Leaders," 158; Oyer, *Lutheran Reformers*, 71–2, lists Kraut – together with Georg Köhler, Alexander, Hans Both and Ludwig Spon – as one of the most important leaders in his region.

122 This is the view of Seebass, *Müntzers Erbe*, 1: 386–94, 405–6. Seebass's statement, 1: 406; 2: 325–6 – "Römer selbst war etwa in Juni 1527 von einem Anhänger Huts getauft worden" – is a tempting hypothesis based on the similarity of apocalyptic ideas rather than direct source evidence.

123 Wappler, *Täuferbewegung*, 287.

124 Seebass, *Müntzers Erbe*, 182–3. Seebass quotes the contemporary Peasants' War chronicle of Lorenz Fries: "Nun kame derselbigen zeit ain kursner aus Thuringen, so des Thoman Muntzers junger ainer was in das läger (of the Bildhäuser band). Der fing auch an zu predigen, und was sein predig dahin gericht, man solte die obrickait mit dem schwert vertilgen und das blut darumb vergiesen."

125 Wappler, *Täuferbewegung*, 270.

126 Ibid., 256, 257.

127 Ibid., 270.

128 Clasen, "Anabaptist Leaders," 158; see n. 196 below.

129 Clasen, "Anabaptist Leaders," 157. Wappler, *Täuferbewegung*, 41, n. 8, suggests that Christoph from Meissen or Mühlhausen may have been identical with the Anabaptist Christoph Rudolf from Oberdola (a village in the Mühlhausen area). See n. 196 below.

130 See the account of the conspiracy against Erfurt in Stayer, *Anabaptists*, 190–3; this should be supplemented by Frank Boblenz, "Die Hinrichtung Hans Römers am 18.5.1535 in Göttingen," *Wissenschaftliche Zeitschrift Univ. Halle* 38 (1989), 133–5, which presents new evidence.

131 *TQ Hessen*, 55.

132 Beulshausen, *Osthessische Täufergemeinden*, 1: 7–10, 251–3; 2: 2–4, 145–7.
133 *TQ Hessen*, 64–71, the source for the data of the following paragraph; also, Beulshausen, *Osthessische Täufergemeinden*, 1: 276–8; 2: 160–2. Werner Packull shared with me an early version of his current research on Peter Riedemann. When published, that study will discuss the Anabaptist congregation in Sorga in some detail. Thanks are due to Packull for clarifying my understanding of the relations between resident tenants and refugees in the Sorga congregation.
134 Ulrich Bubenheimer, "Thomas Müntzer," in *Protestantische Profile. Lebensbilder aus fünf Jahrhunderten*, ed. Klaus Scholder and Dieter Kleinmann (Frankfort: Athenäum 1983), 45–6.
135 Beulshausen, *Osthessische Täufergemeinden*, 1: 216–25; 2: 121–6.
136 Ibid., 1: 227–34; 2: 128–34.
137 *TQ Hessen*, 55, 56, statements of Ludwig Spon and Hans Ringleb. Beulshausen, *Osthessische Täufergemeinden*, 1: 228: "Alexanders Weg zum Täufertum führte gleich dem Melchior Rincks und zahlreicher anderer Täuferführer der Frühzeit über Bauernbewegung und Bauernkrieg, obwohl das nicht mit letzter Sicherheit nachzuweisen ist." Clasen, *Anabaptism*, 458–9, does not include Alexander as a Peasants' War participant.
138 Wappler, *Täuferbewegung*, 376; *TQ Hessen*, 57.
139 Merx, Franz and Fuchs, *Akten*, 2: 758, 803, 925. Hutter was in Alexander's group, which was not baptized, "der ursachen, das sie noch nicht volkomen weren wurden in dem worte" (Wappler, *Täuferbewegung*, 377); and unlike some of the others he probably did not receive adult baptism. He appears as Heinemann Hutter in Clasen, *Anabaptists ... Names*, 200, and is not to be confused with Heinz Hutter, one of the leaders at Sorga and another Peasants' War survivor (Clasen, *Anabaptists ... Names*, 208). The two are confused in the index to *TQ Hessen*, 539.
140 Clasen, *Anabaptism*, 204–5; Oyer, *Lutheran Reformers*, 162, n. 3; the schism on the marriage issue is clear in the documents published in Wappler, *Täuferbewegung*, 423–46.
141 Oyer, *Lutheran Reformers*, 97, 162–8; Wappler, *Täuferbewegung*, 410, 417.
142 Wappler, *Täuferbewegung*, 433–4.
143 Ibid., 430, 432.
144 Ibid., 429.
145 Ibid., 442.
146 *TQ Hessen*, 58, 71, 79–80; Wappler, *Täuferbewegung*, 358; *The Chronicle of the Hutterian Brethren*, 2 vols. (Rifton, N.Y.: Plough 1987), 1: 110–29, 163; Beulshausen, *Osthessische Taufergemeinden*, 1: 279–81; 2: 163–

7. Packull's research (see n. 133) corrects Beulshausen's impression that the Sorga congregation was expelled from Moravia after a mere two months in late 1533. Packull shows that this error goes back to Wappler's misreading of one of his sources (*Täuferbewegung*, 104, 358).

147 Wappler, *Täuferbewegung*, 461–7.

148 *TQ Hessen*, 71–3; Wappler, *Täuferbewegung*, 155–6; Stayer, *Anabaptists*, 197–8, 339–41, where a version of the Krug confession is reproduced from Stadtarchiv Augsburg, Urgichten 1533.

149 Stayer, *Anabaptists*, 341.

150 Ibid., 339.

151 Seebass, "Bauernkrieg," 284–300.

152 On the identity of Volk and Volkhaimer, I am indebted to the suggestion of Werner O. Packull, "Thomas Müntzer und das Hutsche Täufertum," *Mennonitische Geschichtsblätter* 46 (1989): 33.

153 Georg Berbig, "Die Wiedertäufer im Amt Königsberg in Franken 1527/1528," *Deutsche Zeitschrift für Kirchenrecht* 35 (1903): 312. Volk continued, "Bekennt darneben das er auch gepredigt hab, es sei unrecht, das sie in der entperung aufrürisch gewesen sein." See Packull, *Mysticism*, 63–4, for the view of Hut and his followers that in 1525 "the peasants had failed because they sought their own rather than God's honour"; Clasen, "Anabaptist Leaders," 157; but not included as a Peasants' War participant in Clasen, *Anabaptism*, 458–9.

154 Georg Berbig, "Die Wiedertäuferei im Ortslande Franken, im Zusammenhang mit dem Bauernkrieg," *Deutsche Zeitschrift für Kirchenrecht* 35 (1903): 397.

155 Seebass, *Müntzers Erbe*, 1: 224; Joseph Edmund Jörg, *Deutschland in der Revolutions-Periode von 1522–1526* (Freiburg: Herder 1851), 671, n. 14; Marx Maier in Clasen, "Anabaptist Leaders," 156; only Michael Maier appears among Peasants' War participants in Clasen, *Anabaptism*, 459.

156 Packull, *Mysticism*, 211; Clasen, "Anabaptist Leaders," 156; not included by Clasen as a Peasants' War participant.

157 Berbig, "Königsberg," 310–11.

158 Seebass, *Müntzers Erbe*, 1: 225; Jörg, *Revolutions-Periode*, 671, n. 14; Hermann Clauss, "Kleine Beiträge zur Geschichte der Wiedertäufer in Franken," *Zeitschrift für bayerische Kirchengeschichte* 16 (1941): 168–9; Clasen, *Anabaptism*, 459, includes Peter but not Konz in his list of Anabaptist Peasants' War participants.

159 Seebass, *Müntzers Erbe*, 1: 210–11; included as an Anabaptist Peasants' War participant in Clasen, *Anabaptism*, 459.

160 Seebass, *Müntzers Erbe*, 1: 230; QGT, 2, *Bayern*, 1: 61, not included by Clasen as a Peasants' War participant.

161 Seebass, *Müntzers Erbe*, 1: 235, 239; *QGT, 2, Bayern*, 1: 80, 88; Clasen, *Anabaptists ... Names*, 189. None of them is included by Clasen as an Anabaptist who participated in the Peasants' War. Possibly Hans Strigel from Rosenbach should be included in this group. He was active in the Peasants' War and may have been identical with the Fritz Strigel from Uttenreuth whom Hut baptized; Seebass, *Müntzers Erbe*, 2: 243, n. 257; *QGT, 2, Bayern*, 1: 80, 94.

162 Seebass, "Bauernkrieg," 298.

163 Günther Franz, *Der deutsche Bauernkrieg*, (Munich: Oldenbourg 1933), 287–92; Seebass, *Müntzers Erbe*, 1: 285–304.

164 Seebass, *Müntzers Erbe*, 1: 304–6.

165 *QGT, 2, Bayern*, 1: 186–8; Seebass, *Müntzers Erbe*, 1: 248; Seebass, "Bauernkrieg," 298.

166 Seebass, *Müntzers Erbe*, 1: 216–19.

167 *QGT, 2, Bayern*, 1: 188.

168 Beulshausen, *Osthessische Täufergemeinden*, 1: 176–80; 2: 98–100.

169 Above all, the disqualifying of a hitherto accepted source: *QGT, 2, Bayern*, 1: 196.

170 Seebass, "Bauernkrieg," 298; *QGT, 2, Bayern*, 1: 126, 180, 219; not included by Clasen as a Peasants' War participant.

171 Seebass, "Bauernkrieg," 298; *QGT, 5, Bayern*, 2: 167, 223; included in Clasen, *Anabaptism*, 459, as a Peasants' War participant.

172 Clasen, *Anabaptism*, 459.

173 Clauss, "Kleine Beitrage," 174; Wilhelm Wiswedel, "Friedrich Pretscher," *Mennonitisches Lexikon*, 3: 394, contributes an article entirely dependent on Clauss but with the information about Pretscher's participation in the Peasants' War carefully edited out. Apparently Wiswedel considers it justifiable to create Anabaptist non-resistant martyrs in this way.

174 Jürgen Bücking, *Michael Gaismair: Reformer-Sozialrebell-Revolutionär. Seine Rolle im Tiroler "Bauernkrieg" (1525/32)* (Stuttgart: Klett-Cota 1978), 58–105, esp. 98.

175 Besides Bücking (n. 174) and Wolfgang Lassmann (n. 186), also important for my understanding of the Tyrolean situation is Werner O. Packull, "Die Anfänge des Täufertums im Tirol," as yet unpublished (originally written for a volume based on the 1989 Müntzer anniversary in East Germany). Packull connects the Anabaptists mentioned by name with a wider group of associates whom he regards as likely Gaismair supporters (n. 34, 83). Particularly, he regards N. Mairhofer, who had close connections with Hans Gasser on the Ritten Plateau in the late 1520s, as a likely partisan of the commoners' cause in 1525.

176 Bücking, *Gaismair*, 92–3.

177 Ibid., 85, 93–4; *QGT, 13, Österreich,* 2: 39, 493–4; Jürgen Bücking, "Mathias Messerschmieds 'reformatorische' Agitation in Klausen (1527)," *Der Schlern* 46 (1972): 342–4.

178 *QGT, 13, Österreich,* 2: 78–9, 81, 148–9, 175; Clasen, *Anabaptists ... Names,* 149; not included by Clasen as Peasants' War participants.

179 Packull, "Anfänge."

180 Karl-Franz Zani, "Urfehde des Malers Bartlmä Dill," *Der Schlern* 49 (1975): 170–1.

181 *QGT, 14, Österreich,* 3: 92–3; Clasen, *Anabaptists ... Names,* 149; not included by Clasen as a Peasants' War participant.

182 *QGT, 14, Österreich,* 3: 75–7.

183 Ibid., 77–8; *QGT, 13, Österreich,* 2: 81; Hans Fischer, *Jakob Huter. Leben, Froemmigkeit, Briefe* (Newton, Mennonite Publication Office 1956), 20.

184 Zieglschmid, *Älteste Chronik,* 77.

185 Karl Kuppelwieser, "Die Wiedertäufer in Eisacktal," unpub. Ph.D. diss., Innsbruck University 1949, 281; identified as a Peasants' War participant in Clasen, *Anabaptism,* 459.

186 Wolfgang Lassmann, "Möglichkeiten einer Modellbildung zur Verlaufsstruktur des tirolischen Anabaptismus," in *Anabaptistes et dissidents au XVIe siècle,* ed. Jean-Georges Rott and Simon L. Verheus (Baden-Baden and Bouxwiller: Valentin Koerner 1987), 297–309.

187 Haas, "Täufertum und Revolution," 293–5; *QGTS, 1, Zürich:* 156.

188 Lassmann, "Möglichkeiten einer Modellbildung," 304. A similar view in Bücking, *Gaismair,* 105: "Für die Mehrzahl der besiegten tirolischen Bauern schlagen nach 1526 die unklaren pro-reformatorischen Emotionen um in das Täufertum, das sich auf die Laienauslegung der Bibel stützt ... und der mit den Siegern verbundenen katholischen Priesterkirche eine deutliche Absage erteilt."

189 For example, Clasen, *Wiedertäufer in Württemberg,* 168; a summary in Maurer, *Prediger,* 221–39.

190 Zschäbitz, "Stellung der Täuferbewegung," 152–62.

191 Clasen, *Anabaptism,* 152–72. One is struck by the ingenuousness with which in the chapter "The Anabaptists and Society" Clasen argues – in his section on "Revolution," 152–7 – that there is no evidence for a link between the peasant uprising and Anabaptism. Immediately afterward – in the section "Revolutionary Anabaptists," 157–72 – he produces evidence of such a link.

192 Wappler, *Täuferbewegung,* 363–4.

193 Packull, *Mysticism,* 106–13.

194 Clasen, *Anabaptism,* 154.

195 Clasen, *Anabaptists ... Names,* 9, 15, 97.

196 Volkmar Fischer, who I, too, believe must have been involved in the

Peasants' War; but Clasen's source – Wappler, *Täuferbewegung*, 258 – does not establish this, and I have not found other evidence to confirm it. Claus Steinmetz from Mühlhausen and Christoph Rudolph from Merxleben participated in the Peasants' War (Merx, Franz and Fuchs, *Akten*, 2: 595–6, 649–50, 828). It seems doubtful if they are the same as the Claus Steinmetz from the Mühlhausen village of Felchta, who only appears as an Anabaptist in 1545, or the Christoph Rudolf who turns up as an Anabaptist in 1533 in Oberdola, a village about twenty kilometers from Merxleben. (Clasen, *Anabaptists ... Names*, 200, 204.)

197 Lienhart Wenig from Esslingen is a "perhaps" in Clasen, *Wiedertäufer in Württemberg*, 168, n. 81, on the basis of unpublished evidence.

198 Seebass, "Bauernkrieg," 297, refers to Jörg Neuendorf as among those who "wegen Beteiligung am Bauernkrieg verborgen bleiben mussten," but his evidence (Wappler, *Täuferbewegung*, 249) establishes Neuendorf's prominence as an Anabaptist, nothing more. Packull, *Mysticism*, 90, 206, n. 13, repeats the contention of earlier research that Wolfgang Vogel, an important follower of Hut, "may have been implicated in the peasants' revolution." The treatment of Vogel in Maurer, *Prediger*, 444, 611, does not confirm this. Klaassen, *Michael Gaismair*, 113, says that the preacher Hans Vischer whom Gaismair brought into the Tyrol in 1525 "is almost certainly identical with Hans Bünderlin, later Anabaptist leader and spiritualizer." Ulrich Gäbler, however, has written a thorough account of Bünderlin/Vischer's movements, "Johannes Bünderlin von Linz (vor 1500 bis nach 1540). Eine biographische Skizze," *Jahrbuch für die Geschichte des Protestantismus in Österreich* 96 (1980): 355–70. In a letter to me Gäbler expressed the view that it was probably a case of two Hans Vischers.

199 Maurer, *Prediger*, 233, summarizing the participation of preachers in the Peasants' War: "Schreiben, Verhandeln und Vermitteln waren beliebte Tätigkeiten."

200 Basing their supposition on reports of Jakob Hutter carrying a gun (*QGT, 14, Österreich*, 3: 37), the editors of the new English *Chronicle of the Hutterian Brethren*, 1: 83, n. 1, say, "It is probable that he was a partisan of Michael Gaismair."

201 Stephen Blake Boyd, "Pilgram Marpeck and the Justice of Christ," unpublished Th.D. thesis, Harvard University 1984, 26–41.

202 Clasen, *Wiedertäufer in Württemberg*, 168–9.

CHAPTER FOUR

1 James M. Stayer, "The Swiss Brethren: An Exercise in Historical Definition," *Church History* 47 (1978): 174–95.

2 John H. Yoder, "Der Kristallisationspunkt des Täufertums," *Mennonitische Geschichtsblätter* 24 (1972): 35–47.

3 Fritz Blanke, *Brüder in Christo; die Geschichte der ältesten Täufergemeinde (Zollikon: 1525)* (Zurich: Zwingli 1955); John Horsch, "The Rise and Early History of the Swiss Brethren Church," *Mennonite Quarterly Review* 6 (1932): 243.

4 Harold S. Bender, *Conrad Grebel, c. 1498–1526. The Founder of the Swiss Brethren* (Goshen: Mennonite Historical Society 1950), xi-xii; for example, QGTS, 2, Ostschweiz: 225–8: Marpeck "an die, so man schweitzer brueder nennth etc. jm 1543."

5 QGTS, 2, Ostschweiz: 601; my translation is a freer version of the one in Leland Harder, ed., *The Sources of Swiss Anabaptism. The Grebel Letters and Related Documents* (Scottdale: Herald 1985), 345.

6 QGT, 4, Baden-Pfalz: 117.

7 Besides the instances mentioned below, see Z, 6-1: 82–5; Eng. trans., Samuel Macauley Jackson, ed., *Ulrich Zwingli (1484–1531). Selected Works* (Philadelphia: University of Pennsylvania Press 1972 paper ed.), 168–9. This is probably an elaboration of the Heini Frei story.

8 QGTS, 2, Ostschweiz: 3–4; see trans. in Harder, *Swiss Sources*, 509.

9 Bender, *Grebel*, 205: "Brethren must be ready to give of their money and goods to aid those who are in need, to the extent of acknowledging the claim of the church upon their possessions, although community of goods is rejected."

10 John H. Yoder, ed., *The Legacy of Michael Sattler* (Scottdale: Herald 1973), 45, 53, n. 99; Staatsarchiv Bern, UP, vol. 80, 5: "Zum fünften. Alle bruder und schwester diser gemein soll keiner nütt eigens haben sunder wie die christen zur zit der apostel alle ding gemein hieltend, und in sunderheit ein gmein guot hinderlegten, da von den armen, nach dem einem yecklichen nott syn wirt, darvon handreiche gescheche und wie zu der zit der apostel keinen bruoder lassen mangel han," in Ernst Müller, *Geschichte der Bernischen Täufer* (Nieuwkoop: de Graaf 1972, repr. of Frauenfeld, 1895 ed.), 37. Dr. Heinold Fast, Emden, has most recently verified previous judgments that this congregational ordinance was written by the same hand as the earliest copy of the Schleitheim Articles (QGTS, 2, Ostschweiz: 35, n. 32). In a letter to W.O. Packull, 10 August 1988, he adds that the two documents were not written by a professional scribe. This leads him to conclude that the documents in the Bern archives were most likely the ones confiscated from the Anabaptists, and that in that case the congregational ordinance and the Schleitheim Articles circulated together. This inference would permit a dating of the ordinance as before April 25, 1527, when the Bern Reformer Berchtold Haller sent a copy of the Schleitheim Articles to Zwingli (Z, 9: 104f.).

11 *QGTS, 1, Zürich*: 48.

12 Ibid., 49–50.

13 Ibid., 216–17.

14 *Z*, 1: 309; trans. in Samuel Macauley Jackson and Clarence Nevin Heller, eds., *The Latin Works and the Correspondence of Huldrych Zwingli*, 3 vols. (New York and Philadelphia: Putnam and Heidelberg 1912–29), 1: 267.

15 *Z*, 4: 432; trans., Harder, *Swiss Sources*, 409.

16 Walter Jacob, *Politische Führungsschicht und Reformation. Untersuchungen zur Reformation in Zürich 1519–1528* (Zurich: Zwingli 1970), 73–83.

17 For my previous comments on this subject, see James M. Stayer, *Anabaptists and the Sword* (Lawrence: Coronado, 2nd ed., 1976), 98–9.

18 Blanke, *Brüder*, 68–75.

19 *Z*, 6-1: 43; trans., Harder, *Swiss Sources*, 410.

20 *QGTS, 2, Ostschweiz*: 265; trans., Harder, *Swiss Sources*, 425.

21 Heinold Fast, "Wie doopte Konrad Grebel?," *Doopsgezinde Bijdragen* NR 4 (1978): 26–7; *QGTS, 2, Ostschweiz*: 636.

22 James M. Stayer, "Reublin and Brötli: The Revolutionary Beginnings of Swiss Anabaptism," in *The Origins and Characteristics of Anabaptism*, ed. Marc Lienhard (The Hague: Nijhoff 1977), 83–102; Harder, *Swiss Sources*, 707, n. 14.

23 *QGTS, 1, Zürich*: 54.

24 Otto Brunner, "Das 'ganze Haus' und die alteuropäische 'Okonomik,'" in *Neue Wege der Sozialgeschichte* (Göttingen: Vandenhoeck 1956), 33–61.

25 Martin Haas, "Die Weg der Täufer in die Absonderung. Zur Interdependenz von Theologie und sozialem Verhalten," in *Umstrittenes Täufertum, 1525–1975. Neue Forschungen*, ed. Hans-Jürgen Goertz (Göttingen: Vandenhoeck 1975), 50–78.

26 *QGTS, 1, Zürich*: 121, 124: "Item er wil nit bekantlich sin, das er je glert habe, das man jemandts nüdts umb das sin gen sölte"; trans., Harder, *Swiss Sources*, 439.

27 *QGT, 9, Hubmaier*: 178; see *Z*, 2: 451.

28 *QGTS, 4, Täufergespräche*: 227–8.

29 Ibid., 29, 32, esp. 25: "den zinss sol man geben, aber nit nemen."

30 *QGTS, 1, Zürich*: 126; Haas, "Weg," 72.

31 Martin Haas, ed., Täuferquellen: Aargau, Bern, Solothurn, ms., #281, Hans Hausmann (1527), Hans Treyer (1527); #306, Heinrich Seiler (1529), Vyt Ottli (1529): "Zins und zenden ze geben: Ein christ werde geben was man im anvordre. Aber kein christ werde weder zins, zenden, übernutz noch wůcher nemen, dann sölichs verboten."

32 *QGTS, 4, Täufergespräche*: 20–9.

33 Ibid., 23.

34 Brunner, "ganze Hause," 49–51, 56–7.

35 *QGTS, 4, Täufergespräche*: 25.

36 Walther Köhler, *Huldrych Zwingli* (Leipzig: Koehler and Amelang 1943), 262–76.

37 *QGTS, 4, Täufergespräche*: 24–31.

38 Ibid., 31.

39 Ibid., 32.

40 Ibid., 229.

41 *QGT, 7, Elsass, 1*: 235–6.

42 Ibid., 218–24.

43 Ibid., 63.

44 Haas, TQ: Aargau, Bern, Solothurn, ms., #306.

45 Ibid., #281.

46 Ibid.

47 Ibid., #306.

48 Nelson P. Springer & Joe Springer, eds., "The Testimony of a Bernese Anabaptist," *Mennonite Quarterly Review* 60 (1986): 302–3 (I have departed slightly from the Springers' translation). Haas and Clasen, *Anabaptists ... Names*, 49, use Hausmann instead of the Springers' "Hansmann."

49 Erasmus, *Enchiridion, LB*, 5: 31A: "Si nihil amas nisi in Christo, si omnia tua bona putas omnibus esse communia." For Zwingli, see n. 14 above.

50 John T. Noonan, *The Scholastic Analysis of Usury* (Cambridge: Harvard University Press 1957).

CHAPTER FIVE

1 *Müntzer Schriften*, 548.

2 Walter Elliger, *Thomas Müntzer. Leben und Werk* (Göttingen: Vandenhoeck 1975), 795–6.

3 Manfred Bensing, *Thomas Müntzer und der Thüringer Aufstand 1525* (Berlin: Deutscher Verlag der Wissenschaften 1966), 138–9; Manfred Bensing, "Idee und Praxis des 'Christlichen Verbündnisses' bei Thomas Müntzer," in *Thomas Müntzer* (*Wege der Forschung*, CDXCI), ed. Abraham Friesen and Hans-Jürgen Goertz (Darmstadt: Wissenschaftliche Buchgesellschaft 1978), 324–5: "Dieser vielfach in Zweifel gestellte Kommunismus Müntzers war die Quintessenz seiner ganzen religiös-philosophischen Weltauffassung."

4 This allusion to the Vulgate convinced some non-Marxist historians of the veracity of Müntzer's statement. See Carl Hinrichs, *Luther und Müntzer. Ihre Auseinandersetzung über Obrigkeit und Widerstandsrecht* (Berlin: de Gruyter 1952), 20–2.

5 *Müntzer Schriften*, 266–319. The now standard English translation is Peter Matheson, ed., *The Collected Works of Thomas Müntzer* (Edinburgh: T. & T. Clark 1988), 253–323. I have used my own translations but have benefitted by consulting Matheson.

6 *Müntzer Schriften*, 321–43; Matheson, *Collected Works*, 324–50.

7 *Müntzer Schriften*, 305; see 334.

8 Ibid., 293–4.

9 Ibid., 297, 303.

10 Ibid., 324, 325, 326, 327.

11 Ibid., 336–7, 340.

12 Ibid., 267.

13 Ibid., 473: "ein yder seyn eygen nutz mehr gesucht dan dye rechtfertigung der christenheyt."

14 Ibid., 293, 295.

15 Ibid., 300.

16 Ibid., 270.

17 Ibid., 343.

18 Hans-Jürgen Goertz, "Der Mystiker mit dem Hammer. Die Theologische Begründung der Revolution bei Thomas Müntzer," in Friesen & Goertz, *Müntzer*, 422.

19 *Müntzer Schriften*, 336–7.

20 Ibid., 329.

21 Ibid., 337, 341.

22 Ibid., 291.

23 Ibid., 299.

24 Ibid., 299–300.

25 Ibid., 282.

26 Ibid., 293.

27 Ibid., 294.

28 Ibid., 275.

29 Ibid., 303.

30 Ibid., 328.

31 Ibid., 335.

32 Ibid., 329.

33 Ibid.

34 Ibid., 289.

35 Ibid., 283.

36 Ibid., 337.

37 Ulrich Bubenheimer, "Thomas Müntzer," in *Protestantische Profile. Lebensbilder aus fünf Jahrhunderten*, ed. Klaus Scholder and Dieter Kleinmann (Frankfort: Athenäum 1983), 45–6.

38 For the princes' fears about Müntzer's communist plans, see Abraham

Friesen, *Thomas Muentzer, a Destroyer of the Godless: The Making of a Sixteenth-Century Religious Revolutionary* (Berkeley: University of California Press 1990), 232.

39 Adolf Laube, "Thomas Müntzer und die frühbürgerliche Revolution," *Zeitschrift für Geschichtswissenschaft* 38 (1990): 128–41, esp. 136–40.

40 Müntzer to Luther, 13 July 1520, *Müntzer Schriften*, 359: "Non est iugiter secundum evangelium vivendum." See the discussion in Gerhard Brendler, *Thomas Müntzer. Geist und Faust* (Berlin: Deutscher Verlag der Wissenschaften 1989), 55–6.

41 *Müntzer Schriften*, 494.

42 Friesen, *Thomas Muentzer*, 49.

43 *Müntzer Schriften*, 353; Friesen, *Thomas Muentzer*, 69.

44 Ulrich Bubenheimer, *Thomas Müntzer. Herkunft und Bildung* (Leyden: Brill 1989), 233.

45 Friesen, *Thomas Muentzer*, 53–72.

46 Ibid., 22–5.

47 See Tom Scott, *Thomas Müntzer. Theology and Revolution in the German Reformation* (New York: St. Martin's 1989), 171–2.

48 Joseph Beck, ed., *Die Geschichtsbücher der Wiedertäufer in Oesterreich-Ungarn* (Vienna: 1883), 12; Eng. trans. in Hans J. Hillerbrand, *A Fellowship of Discontent* (New York: Harper 1967), 27.

49 James M. Stayer, "Hans Hut's Doctrine of the Sword: An Attempted Solution," *Mennonite Quarterly Review* 39 (1965): 181–91.

50 Hans-Dieter Schmid, "Das Hutsche Täufertum. Ein Beitrag zur Charakterisierung einer täuferischen Richtung aus der Frühzeit der Täuferbewegung," *Historisches Jahrbuch* 91 (1971): 327–44; Gottfried Seebass, "Müntzers Erbe. Werk, Leben und Theologie des Hans Hut," unpub. Habilitationsschrift, U. Erlangen-Nuremberg, 1972, 2 vols.; Werner O. Packull, *Mysticism and the Early South German-Austrian Anabaptist Movement* (Scottdale: Herald 1977), 62–117. These works represent the current consensus about Hut; in contrast, see, for example, Herbert Klassen, "The Life and Teachings of Hans Hut," *Mennonite Quarterly Review* 33 (1959): 171–205, 267–304.

51 Seebass, "Müntzers Erbe," 1: 167–8.

52 *Müntzer Schriften*, 265–6; Hinrichs, *Luther und Müntzer*, 135–6.

53 Ferdinand Seibt, "Johannes Hergot. Die Reformation des 'Armen Mannes'," in *Radikale Reformatoren*, ed. Hans-Jürgen Goertz (Munich: Beck 1978), 84–92; Eng. trans., *Profiles of Radical Reformers* (Scottdale: Herald 1982), 97–106; Gerhard Zschäbitz, "'Von der newen wandlung eynes Christlichen Lebens' – eine oft misdeutete Schrift aus der Zeit nach dem Grossen Deutschen Bauernkrieg," *Zeitschrift für Geschichtswissenschaft* 8 (1960): 908–18.

54 *QGT, 2, Bayern, 1*: 44; confession of 5 October 1527, in Christian
   Meyer, "Die Anfänge des Wiedertauferthums in Augsburg," *Zeitschrift
   des Historischen Vereins für Schwaben und Neuburg* 1 (1874): 231.
55 Gerhaus Ottin, confession of 1528, in *QGT, 2, Bayern, 1*: 92.
56 Confession of 12 March 1529, in *QGT, 5, Bayern, 2*: 170–1.
57 Confession of 1529, in ibid., 178–9. Gottfried Seebass, "Bauernkrieg
   und Täufertum in Franken," *Zeitschrift für Kirchengeschichte* 85 (1974):
   298; Eng. trans. in Werner O. Packull and James M. Stayer, eds., *The
   Anabaptists and Thomas Müntzer* (Dubuque: Kendall/Hunt 1980), 162.
   Despite Maier's clear identification of the godless as not only the rulers but all others "welcher sich nit wider hab taufen lassen," Hut's
   enmity was, like Müntzer's, specifically directed against priests and
   rulers: "Alda wurden dann die heiligen straffen die andern, nemlich
   die sunder, die nit puss gethan hetten, da muessten die pfaffen, so
   falsch geprediget antwurt geben irer leere und die gewaltigen irs regi-
   ments." (Meyer, "Anfänge," 242).
58 Nespitzer, confession of 12 July 1530, in *QGT, 2, Bayern, 1*: 188; Weischenfelder, confession of January 1528, in Paul Wappler, *Die Täuferbewegung in Thüringen von 1526–1584* (Jena: Fischer 1913), 280: "die
   guter solten unter inen, den taufern, allein gemein sein ... Die
   Taufer wissen ir puntnus des Turken halben nit alle, allein die es
   begern."
59 See Schmid, "Hutsche Täufertum," 330–2.
60 *QGT, 2, Bayern, 1*: 49–50. (In A. Spittelmaier's version the kingdom of
   God is the second judgment rather than the sixth.) Eng. trans. in
   Donald F. Durnbaugh, ed., *Every Need Supplied. Mutual Aid and Christian Community in the Free Churches, 1525–1675* (Philadelphia: Temple
   University Press 1974), 25.
61 *QGT, 3, Glaubenszeugnisse, 1*: 22.
62 Packull, *Mysticism*, 130–8, 217–20; Gustav Bossert, Sr, "Augustin
   Bader von Augsburg, der Prophet und König, und seine Genossen
   nach den Prozessakten von 1530," *Archiv für Reformationsgeschichte* 11
   (1914): 31; also 48, 57, 61, 130–1.
63 Schmid, "Hutsche Täufertum," 338–9, 343.
64 L. Freisleben, confession of 15 November 1527; and Würzlburger,
   confession of 25 May 1528, in *QGT, 5, Bayern, 2*: 11, 34.
65 Packull, *Mysticism*, 142.
66 Ibid., 106–13.
67 *QGT, 3, Glaubenszeugnisse, 1*: 70.
68 Seebass, "Münsters Erbe," 1: 547–52, esp. 551.
69 John S. Oyer, *Lutheran Reformers Against Anabaptists: Luther, Melanchthon and Menius and the Anabaptists of Central Germany* (The Hague:
   Nijhoff 1964), 51–64, 75–83, 85–7, 92–5, 98–9; Eric Geldbach, "Toward

a More Ample Biography of the Hessian Anabaptist Leader Melchior Rinck," *Mennonite Quarterly Review* 48 (1974): 371–84.

70 Melchior Rinck, "Vermanung vnd warnung an alle so in der Obrigkeit sind," in Gerhard J. Neumann, ed., "A Newly Discovered Manuscript of Melchior Rinck," *Mennonite Quarterly Review* 35 (1961): 211–17, esp. 213. Regarding V.D.M.I.E. (verbum dei manet/maneat in eternum), see Jean Wirth, *Luther. Etude d'Histoire Religieuse* (Geneva: Droz 1981), 54–5; Tom Scott, "The 'Volksreformation' of Thomas Müntzer in Allstedt and Mühlhausen," *Journal of Ecclesiastical History* 34 (1983): 207.

71 *TQ Hessen*, 64–9.

72 Ibid., 69.

73 Plathans, confession of August 1533, in ibid., 65–6. The statement begins "Er hab auch kein mangel an her Milchers lere."

74 Gilg, confession of August 1533, in ibid., 69 ("Milcher Rink hat in getauft").

75 Junghen Lutz and Cuntz Hutter, confession of August 1533, in ibid., 69.

76 Paul Wappler, *Die Stellung Kursachsens und des Landgrafen Philipp von Hessen zur Täuferbewegung* (Münster: Aschendorff 1910), 168–76.

77 Casper Schneider's wife, confession of July 1533, in ibid., 173.

78 Margarethe, wife of Kessel Hannsen, confession of July 1533, in ibid., 173.

79 Peter Leyneweber, confession of July 1533, in ibid., 169.

80 Lentz Rudiger, confession of July 1533, in ibid., 171.

81 Hans J. Hillerbrand, "An Early Anabaptist Treatise on the Christian and the State," *Mennonite Quarterly Review* 32 (1958): 34–47; Walter Klaassen, "Eine Untersuchung der Verfasserschaft und des Historischen Hintergrundes der Täuferschrift 'Aufdeckung der Babylonischen Hurn …'," in *Evangelischer Glaube und Geschichte. Grete Mecenseffy zum 85. Geburtstag*, ed. Alfred Raddatz and Kurt Lüthi (Vienna: Evangelische Oberkirchenrat 1984), 113–29.

82 Hillerbrand, "Treatise," 37.

83 Ibid., 47.

84 Ibid., 39.

85 Ibid., 43.

86 Ibid., 41.

87 Ibid., 40.

88 Ibid., 44.

89 Ibid., 39.

90 Ibid.

91 Klaassen, "Untersuchung," 116–25.

92 James M. Stayer, *Anabaptists and the Sword* (Lawrence: Coronado, 2d ed. 1976), 170–2, 177–87.

93 Klaassen, "Untersuchung," 121–5.

94 Ibid., 116–17.

95 Hillerbrand, "Treatise," 36: "Vnd wie wol sich an ainem klainem
hȅuflin zum tail / oder gar in menschlicher schwachait / die gewaltigen krefft Gottes erzaigen / vnd yetz erscheinen / so feyrt doch die
bubisch Hur nicht / solche herrligkait (wie von anfang) auch wider zu-
besudeln vnd zubeflecken / durch vil verfuhrung vnnd irrthumb / so
mitlet von den Gotseligen aussgehn / Sy seind aber nit auss vns nach
der rede Johannis / I Johan. 2."

96 QGT, 9, Hubmaier: 475.

97 Seebass, "Müntzers Erbe," 1: 550. (I cannot trace his source, however.)

98 Wappler, Täuferbewegung, 234.

99 Thomas Brady, Turning Swiss: Cities and Empire, 1450–1550 (Cambridge: Cambridge University Press 1985), 126–7.

100 Friedwart Uhland, Täufertum und Obrigkeit in Augsburg im 16. Jahrhundert (Ph.D. diss. Tübingen 1972), 187–8.

101 Seebass, "Müntzer's Erbe," 2: 29.

102 Ibid., 2: 30.

103 Friedrich Roth, "Der Höhepunkt der wiedertäuferischen Bewegung
in Augsburg ...," Zeitschrift des Historischen Vereins für Schwaben und
Neuburg 28 (1901): 55: "sie soll die armen in bevelh haben, und wie
sie den armen jetzt thue, also wird man ir auch thun."

104 Uhland, Taüfertum, 187–94.

105 QGT, 3, Glaubenszeugnisse, 1: 137–8. See Otto Brunner, "Das 'ganze
Haus' und die alteuropäische 'Okonomik,'" in Neue Wege der Sozialgeschichte (Göttingen: Vandenhoeck 1956), 33–61.

CHAPTER SIX

1 Joseph Niesert, ed., Münsterische Urkundensammlung, 1: Urkunden zur
Geschichte der Münsterischen Wiedertäufer (Coesfeld: 1826), 160; corrected
in Carl Adolf Cornelius, ed., Berichte der Augenzeugen über das münsterische Wiedertäuferreich (Münster: Aschendorff 1983, repr. of 1853 ed.),
417. That this means there were no Christians for the fourteen
hundred years before 1533, when Bernhard Rothmann and Jan Matthijs of Haarlem revived Christianity in Münster and the Netherlands, is
clarified elsewhere in Rothmann's writings. Rothmann Schriften, 217,
291–2, 354; James M. Stayer, Anabaptists and the Sword (Lawrence: Coronado, 2d ed., 1976), 247. For a more elaborate statement of the
interpretation set forth in the first half of this chapter and its sources,
see James M. Stayer, "Was Dr. Kuehler's Conception of Early Dutch
Anabaptism Historically Sound? The Historical Discussion of Anabap-

tist Münster 450 Years Later," *Mennonite Quarterly Review* 60 (1986): 261–88.

2 See the contrasting treatments of Münster Anabaptism by Gerd Dethlefs and Robert Stupperich in *Die Wiedertäufer in Münster. Stadtmuseum Münster. Katalog der Eröffnungsausstellung …* (Münster: Aschendorff 1983), 19–36, 37–54.

3 Esp. *Die Täufer in Münster 1534/35* (Münster: Aschendorff 1973), and "Gab es eine friedliche Täufergemeinde in Münster 1534?," *Jahrbuch des Vereins für westfälische Kirchengeschichte* 55–56 (1963): 7–21 (Eng. trans. by Elizabeth Bender, "Was there a Peaceful Anabaptist Congregation in Münster in 1534?," *Mennonite Quarterly Review* 44 (1970): 357–70).

4 Calvin A. Pater, *Karlstadt as Father of the Baptist Movements: The Emergence of Lay Protestantism* (Toronto: University of Toronto Press 1984), 173–217.

5 Klaus Deppermann, *Melchior Hoffman. Soziale Unruhen und apokalyptische Visionen in Zeitalter der Reformation* (Göttingen: Vandenhoeck 1979), 57–75, 194–235, 286.

6 Obbe Philips, "Bekenntenisse," in *Bibliotheca Reformatoria Neerlandica*, 10 vols., ed. S. Cramer and F. Pijper (The Hague: Nijhoff 1903–14), 7: 121–38 (Eng. trans. in *Spiritual and Anabaptist Writers*, eds. George Huntston Williams and Angel M. Mergal (Philadelphia: Westminster 1957), 206–25.) Nicolaas Blesdijk, "Van den Oorspronck ende anvanck des sectes welck men wederdoper noomt," Universitätsbibliothek Basel, Jorislade X-4, described in S. Zijlstra, *Nicolaas Meyndertsz. van Blesdijk. Een bijdrage tot de geschiedenis van het Davidjorisme* (Assen: Van Gorcum 1983), 149–53.

7 Heinz Schilling, "Aufstandsbewegungen in der Stadtbürgerlichen Gesellschaft des Alten Reiches. Die Vorgeschichte des Münsteraner Täuferreiches, 1525–1534," in *Der Deutsche Bauernkrieg 1524–1526*, ed. H.-U. Wehler (Göttingen: 1975), 197–8, 213, 225, 230–3.

8 Taira Kuratsuka, "Gesamtgilde und Täufer: Der Radikalisierungsprozess in der Reformation Münsters: Von der reformatorischen Bewegung zum Täuferreich 1533/34," *Archiv für Reformationsgeschichte* 76 (1985), 234–8, 263–5.

9 Ibid., 238–9: "Eine so ausgeprägte Zuständigkeit des Volks eines Kirchspiels bei der Predigerwahl fand sich in dieser Zeit ausserhalb Münsters weder in den zwinglianischen Städten in Süddeutschland noch in den lutherischen Städten in Norddeutschland."

10 Schilling, "Aufstandsbewegungen," 206, 218–19; Günther Vogler, "Das Täuferreich zu Münster als Problem der Politik im Reich," *Mennonitische Geschichtsblätter* 42 (1985): 7–23.

11 Martin Brecht, "Die Theologie Bernhard Rothmanns," *Jahrbuch für*

Westfälische Kirchengeschichte 78 (1985): 49–82; Martin Brecht, "Die Ulmer Kirchenordnung von 1531, die Basler Reformationsordnung von 1529 und die Münsteraner Zuchtordnung von 1533," in *Niederlande und Nordwestdeutschland. Franz Petri zum 80. Geburtstag*, eds. Wilfried Ebbrecht and Heinz Schilling (Cologne: Bohlau 1983), 154–63.

12 Willem J. de Bakker, "De vroege theologie van Bernhard Rothmann. De gereformeerde achtergrond van het Munsterse Doperrijk," *Doopsgezinde Bijdragen* NR 3 (1977): 9–20.

13 Kuratsuka, "Gesamtgilde und Täufer," 240–8; Brecht, "Theologie Rothmanns," 64–5.

14 Confession of 25 July 1535, in Cornelius, *Berichte*, 370.

15 See Wieck's letter of 15 Nov. 1533, in Richard van Dülmen, ed., *Das Täuferreich zu Münster, 1534–1535* (Munich: Deutscher Taschenbuch Verlag 1974), 35–8. Here he repeatedly refers to Rothmann's followers as "Anabaptists," although adult baptisms had not yet begun in Münster.

16 Kuratsuka, "Gesamtgilde und Täufer," 246–54.

17 Frank J. Wray, "The 'Vermahnung' of 1542 and Rothmann's 'Bekenntnisse,'" *Archiv für Reformationsgeschichte* 47 (1956): 243–51.

18 Blesdijk, "Oorspronck," f. 16vo., 17ro.; Albert F. Mellink, "Das münsterische Täufertum und die Niederlande," *Jahrbuch für Westfälische Kirchengeschichte* 78 (1985): 14–15; the most comprehensive review of the beginnings of Jan Matthijs's prophetic career since the discovery of Blesdijk's "Orspronck" appears in Willem J. de Bakker, "Civic Reformer in Anabaptist Munster. Bernhard Rothmann 1495(?)-1535(?)," unpublished M.A. thesis, Queen's University (Ontario), 1987, 238–45.

19 Karl-Heinz Kirchhoff, "Die Endzeiterwartung der Täufergemeinde zu Münster 1534/35," *Jahrbuch für Westfalische Kirchengeschichte* 78 (1985): 24.

20 Brecht, "Theologie Rothmanns," 66: "Die Infizierung mit melchioritisch-täuferischen Vorstellungen in Münster erfolgte zuerst bei den Predigern und ihrer Theologie. Das geschah bereits Monate vor der endgültigen Ankunft der niederländischen Täufer und bereitete diese vor."

21 Kuratsuka, "Gesamtgilde und Täufer," 253–62.

22 Ibid., 261: "Das Wunder 'beweis' den Täufern überzeugend, dass gerade Münster die Stadt des Herrn und das Neue Jerusalem sei. Das 'Wunder' wurde auch ihnen zum Urerlebnis wie es das Wunder im Roten Meer für das Volk Israel wurde."

23 Kirchhoff, "Friedliche Täufergemeinde," provides the most satisfactory interpretation of 9–11 Feb. 1534.

24 Kirchhoff, "Endzeiterwartung," 31–7. Kirchhoff points out that it was not uncommon to see three suns in the sky and to interpret it as a

divine sign. To his examples we can add that of Jakob Hutter; see Robert Friedmann, "Jakob Hutter's Epistle concerning the Schism in Moravia in 1533," *Mennonite Quarterly Review* 38 (1964): 335.

25 See Othein Rammstedt, *Sekte und soziale Bewegung. Soziologische Analyse der Täufer in Münster* (Cologne and Opladen: Westdeutscher 1966), 62–3, 68–86.

26 Albert F. Mellink, *De Wederdopers in de Noordelijke Nederlanden, 1531–1544* (Groningen: Wolters 1954), 1–19.

27 Karl-Heinz Kirchhoff, "Die Täufer in Münsterland," *Westfälische Zeitschrift* 113 (1963): 23, 24f.

28 Gresbeck, in Cornelius, *Berichte*, 38, 51, 70.

29 W.J. Kühler, "Anabaptism in the Netherlands," in *The Anabaptists and Thomas Müntzer*, ed. Werner O. Packull and James M. Stayer (Dubuque: Kendall/Hunt 1980), 99–100.

30 Lammert G. Jansma, "De chiliastische beweging der Wederdopers (1530–1535)," *Doopsgezinde Bijdragen* NR 5 (1979): 41–55, esp. 53.

31 Zijlstra, *Blesdijk*, 155; Kühler, "Anabaptism," in Packull and Stayer, *Anabaptists*, 98–100.

32 Mellink, *Wederdopers*, 373.

33 For example, the execution without due process of the blacksmith Hubert Ruescher is discussed in Hermann von Kerssenbroch, *Anabaptistici furoris ...*, in *Die Geschichtsquellen des Bisthums Münster*, ed. Heinrich Detmer (Münster: Theissing, 1900), 5: 559–61.

34 Kirchhoff, "Endzeiterwartung," 39.

35 Jansma, "Chiliastische beweging," *passim*.

36 Kirchhoff, *Täufer in Münster*, 68–77.

37 H.-D. Plümper, *Die Gütergemeinschaft bei den Täufern des 16. Jahrhunderts* (Göppingen: Alfred Kümmerle 1972), 186.

38 James M. Stayer, "Vielweiberei als 'innerweltliche Askese.' Neue Eheauffassungen in der Reformationszeit," *Mennonitische Geschichtsblätter* 37 (1980): 24–41.

39 *Rothmann Schriften*, 441–2.

40 Kirchhoff, *Täufer in Münster*, 35–44, esp. 42: "... die Sozialstruktur der Täufer sich nicht wesentlich von eines zufälligen Ausschnitts aus der Gesamtbürgerschaft unterscheidet."

41 Ibid., 77.

42 This is the view of Kuratsuka, "Gesamtgilde und Täufer," 266–8.

43 Vogler, "Täuferreich."

44 James M. Stayer, "David Joris: A Prolegomenon to further Research," *Mennonite Quarterly Review* 49 (1985): 350–61.

45 John S. Oyer, "The Strasbourg Conferences of the Anabaptists," *Mennonite Quarterly Review* 58 (1984): 218–29.

46 Deppermann, *Hoffman*, 139–93.

47 Rammstedt, *Sekte*, 74–83, esp. 74: "Eine verfehlte Prophetie bewirkt nicht das Ende der chiliastischen Bewegung, aber die charismatische Herrschaft schlägt um in Institution und Dogma."
48 Richard van Dülmen, *Reformation als Revolution* (Munich: Deutscher Taschenbuch Verlag 1977), 307.
49 *Rothmann Schriften*, 184–5; Sebastian Franck, *Chronica, Zeytbuch und Geschychtbibel* (Strasbourg: 1536), f. 244.
50 Confession of Jan of Leyden, 25 July 1535, in Cornelius, *Berichte*, 374.
51 Niesert, *Urkundensammlung*, 161–2, 164.
52 Kirchhoff, *Täufer in Münster*, 24.
53 J. de Hullu, ed., *Bescheiden betreffende de Hervorming in Overijssel*, 1: *Deventer (1522–1546)* (Deventer: 1899), 153–4.
54 *Rothmann Schriften*, 51.
55 Gertrud from Münster, 18 March 1534, cited in Rammstedt, *Sekte*, 90.
56 Kerssenbroch, in Detmer, *Geschichtsquellen*, 556–8.
57 Gresbeck, in Cornelius, *Berichte*, 32: "Demnach hebben die propheten, predicanten und der gantze raet tho rade gegain, und wolden al guet gemein hebben." Seemingly this is contradicted by Knipperdollinck, confession of 21 Jan. 1536, in ibid., 410: "Er sagt, Johan Mathis, der Kuningk und predicanten haven gemeinschoft der guder ingefurt, und er nit." Certainly the council and burgomasters legitimated the abolition of property, even if the idea did originally come from the prophets and preachers.
58 Gresbeck, ibid.
59 Gresbeck, ibid., 33.
60 *Rothmann Schriften*, 256.
61 Gresbeck, in Cornelius, *Berichte*, 48–9.
62 Kerssenbroch, in Detmer, 558.
63 Kerssenbroch, in Detmer, 558; Kirchhoff, *Täufer in Münster*, 69; Gresbeck, in Cornelius, *Berichte*, 34.
64 Kerssenbroch, in Detmer, 541–2, 558; Gresbeck, in Cornelius, *Berichte*, 165.
65 Gresbeck, ibid., 34–5.
66 Gresbeck, ibid.
67 Kirchhoff, *Täufer in Münster*, 24.
68 Ibid., 68–77, esp. 77: "... auch in der Täufergemeinde, wo es nach Einführung der Gütergemeinschaft theoretisch keine Vermögensunterschiede gab, konnten die wolhhabenden Vertreter der früheren städtischen Führungsschicht in beträchtlicher Anzahl zu Rang, Ansehen und Einfluss gelangen."
69 Gresbeck, in Cornelius, *Berichte*, 149–50; Kerssenbroch, in Detmer, 690–5.

70 Kerssenbroch, in Detmer, 586: "si quis Deo sic dispensante ab hosti-
   bus transfossus aut alia quavis ratione obdormierit in Domino, bona
   illius relicta, ut sunt arma, vestes etc., nemo sua auctoritate capiet,
   sed ad Bernardum Knipperdollingum ensigerum deferentur, qui sen-
   ioribus ea offeret, ut illorum auctoritate veris haeredibus adiudicen-
   tur."

71 Gresbeck, in Cornelius, *Berichte*, 86–9, esp. 88: "So heft sick der kon-
   ningk ouck so kostlick gerust mit seinen dieners. Und dat iss al des
   Vaders wille gewest, dat hei sick so rusten sol, wante der konigh
   sachte, hei wer dem fleisch afgestorven und hedde dair gein homoit
   mede, und dede dat Gode tho eheren ... Mehr der gemein man en
   konde nicht wieder krigen von seinem gelt ofte von seinem silver
   oder golt, aver der konigh und die rede droegent und heddent under
   handen. Dieser konigh und predicanten plagen dat volck tho seggen,
   dat sie nicht na dem fleisch und na der welt solden leven, und in den
   menschen sol anders nicht sein dan der geist ..."

72 Ibid., 172–3.

73 Ibid., 69.

74 Ibid., 96–7; Kerssenbroch, in Detmer, 638–9.

75 Kirchhoff, *Täufer in Münster*, 68–77.

76 Gresbeck, in Cornelius, *Berichte*, 97–8.

77 Kirchhoff, *Täufer in Münster*, 4: "Bischof Franz liess später dazu er-
   klären, die Beute sei nicht gross gewesen ... Das in Münster vorhan-
   dene Geld hätten die Täufer für ihre Werbungen im Ausland ver-
   braucht." In the end the Bishop was able to touch only 13–16% of the
   value of the confiscated houses because of the high burden of previous debt weighing upon them. (Ibid., 7–8).

78 Gresbeck, in Cornelius, *Berichte*, 140–1, 175–6.

79 Ibid., 174.

80 See Rammstedt, *Sekte*, 83–6.

81 *Rothmann Schriften*, 256.

82 Karl Kautsky, *Communism in Central Europe in the Time of the Reformation* (New York: Russell & Russell 1959), 76, finds "it hardly possible
   to suppress the wish that, like Münster, Tabor had fallen in the bril-
   liancy of its communistic youth, and had not languished in the
   wretchedness of bourgeois senility."

CHAPTER SEVEN

1 Frantisek Hrubý, "Die Wiedertäufer in Mähren," *Archiv für Reformationsgeschichte* 30 (1933): 7–23. See 41–4 on the special conditions in
   Moravia, in contrast to Bohemia.

2 Jarold K. Zeman, *The Anabaptists and the Czech Brethren in Moravia, 1526–1628* (The Hague: Mouton 1969), 130–2.

3 Ibid., 175–85.

4 *QGT, 2, Bayern, 1*: 96–9: "Es kan aber ein jeder gerings verstands gar leichtlich merken, das dise sunderliche sect und bruderschaft allein zu aufrur und empörung fürgenumen ..." The mandate in question focused on the disruptive effects of the Anabaptist commitment to community of goods.

5 See Werner O. Packull, *Mysticism and the Early South German-Austrian Anabaptist Movement, 1525–1531* (Scottdale: Herald 1977), 99–106.

6 A.J.F. Zieglschmid, ed., *Die älteste Chronik der Hutterischen Brüder* (Ithaca: Cayuga 1943), 49–52; trans. *The Chronicle of the Hutterian Brethren*, 2 vols. (Rifton, N.Y.: Plough 1987), 1: 47–49.

7 *QGT, 9, Hubmaier*: 487.

8 *QGT, 3, Glaubenszeugnisse, 1*: 123.

9 Packull, *Mysticism*, 80–1.

10 *QGT, 9, Hubmaier*: 475.

11 Ibid., 178.

12 Zieglschmid, *Älteste Chronik*, 50–1; *Chronicle*, 1: 48–9; see James M. Stayer, "Hans Hut's Doctrine of the Sword: An Attempted Solution," *Mennonite Quarterly Review* 39 (1965): 181–91.

13 Torsten Bergsten, *Balthasar Hubmaier. Seine Stellung zu Reformation und Täufertum, 1521–1528* (Kassel: Oncken 1961), 476–8.

14 Robert Friedmann, "The Doctrine of the Two Worlds," in *The Recovery of the Anabaptist Vision*, ed. Guy F. Hershberger (Scottdale: Herald 1958), 105–18.

15 Zieglschmid, *Älteste Chronik*, 52–4, 86; *Chronicle*, 1: 49–51, 80; the influence of the Schleitheim Articles was strong in Nikolsburg within months after they were written. Hubmaier's last Nikolsburg book, *Von dem Schwert*, published in June 1527, was an anti-Schleitheim statement.

16 Zieglschmid, *Älteste Chronik*, 53; *Chronicle*, 1: 50, awkwardly translates "die so sich Gemainschaffter nennen" as "those who called themselves a community."

17 Zeman, *Anabaptists*, 191–3.

18 Zieglschmid, *Älteste Chronik*, 86–7; *Chronicle*, 1: 80–1.

19 Zeman, *Anabaptists*, 300–4.

20 Ibid., 224–9; Zieglschmid, *Älteste Chronik*, 85–6; *Chronicle*, 1: 79–80.

21 Carl Adolf Cornelius, *Geschichte des Münsterischen Aufruhrs*, 2 vols. (Leipzig: Weigel 1855–60), 2: 257.

22 Ibid., 258.

23 Zieglschmid, *Älteste Chronik*, 86; *Chronicle*, 1: 80.

24 Zieglschmid, *Älteste Chronik*, 98; *Chronicle*, 1: 91; see James M. Stayer, "Wilhelm Reublin: A Picaresque Journey through Early Anabaptism,"

in *Profiles of Radical Reformers*, ed. Hans-Jürgen Goertz (Scottdale: Herald 1982), 107–17.

25 Zieglschmid, *Älteste Chronik*, 105–13; *Chronicle*, 1: 98–105.

26 *Chronicle*, 1: 49, n. 4.

27 John A. Hostetler, *Hutterite Society* (Baltimore: Johns Hopkins 1974), 20.

28 Excerpts from Ascherham chronicle, in Christoph Andrea Fischer, *Der Hutterischen Widertauffer Taubenkobel* (Ingolstadt: 1607), 55–6.

29 Ibid., 56–7.

30 Hostetler, *Hutterite Society*, 35, n. 2.

31 Zieglschmid, *Älteste Chronik*, 435–6; trans. Hostetler, *Hutterite Society*, 34–5.

32 Christoph Andrea Fischer, *Der Hutterischen Widertauffer Taubenkobel* (Ingolstadt: 1607).

33 Hrubý, "Wiedertäufer," 74–5, 128–9; the source is a Polish nobleman, Andreas Rey of Naglowitz, writing about the Hutterites in 1612.

34 Christoph Andrea Fischer, *Viervndfunfftzig Erhebliche Vrsachen Warumb die Widertauffer nicht sein im Land zu leyden* (Ingolstadt: Angermeyer 1607), 53–4.

35 Ibid., 33–4; Robert Friedmann, "Divorce from Unbelievers," *Mennonite Encyclopedia*, 2: 75–6.

36 Paul K. Conkin, *Two Paths to Utopia. The Hutterites and the Llano Colony* (Lincoln: University of Nebraska Press 1964), 22: "To Riedemann, who reflected the prevalent attitude of his day, marriage was a matter of male solicitude and female obedience, as ordained by God. It did not involve any subjective, hedonistic, sentimental or romantic elements. In the golden period in Moravia, Hutterite marriages excluded all emotion, courtship and celebration." See Fischer, *Viervndfufftzig Vrsachen*, 52–3; Hrubý, "Wiedertäufer," 73–4.

37 Ibid., 17; Hans-Dieter Plümper, *Die Gütergemeinschaft bei den Täufern des 16. Jahrhunderts* (Göppingen: Alfred Kümmerle 1972), 101, citing Victor Peters with approval.

38 Peter Riedemann, *Account of our Religion, Doctrine and Faith* (Rifton, N.Y.: Plough 1970), 80–1.

39 Hostetler, *Hutterite Society*, 33–41.

40 Fischer, *Viervndfufftzig Vrsachen*, 57.

41 Zieglschmid, *Älteste Chronik*, 722; *Chronicle*, 1: 646.

42 Zieglschmid, *Älteste Chronik*, 211–12; *Chronicle*, 1: 199.

43 Zieglschmid, *Älteste Chronik*, 212–23; *Chronicle*, 1: 199–209.

44 Edward Surtz and J.H. Hexter, eds., *Complete Works of St. Thomas More*, 15 vols.: 4: Utopia (New Haven and London: Yale 1965), 140–1.

45 Hans Jedelshauser, *Zwelff wichtige vnd starke Vrsachen Hansen Jedelshausers ... warumb er ... von den Wiedertauffern ... sei abgetreten* (Ingolstadt: Wolffgang Eder 1587), 9–11.

46 Ibid., 6.
47 Fischer, *Viervndfunfftzig Vrsachen*, 10–11, 38, 65, 94.
48 Ibid., 79, 109.
49 Zeman, *Anabaptists*, 284–5.
50 L. Neubaur, "Mährische Brüder in Elbing," *Zeitschrift für Kirchenge-schichte* 33 (1912): 450.
51 Hrubý, "Wiedertäufer," 63–70.
52 Plümper, *Gütergemeinschaft*, 96–7, 207.
53 Claus-Peter Clasen, *Anabaptism. A Social History, 1525–1618. Switzerland, Austria, Moravia, and South and Central Germany* (Ithaca and London: Cornell University Press 1972), 15–29.
54 Peter James Klassen, *The Economics of Anabaptism, 1525–1560* (The Hague: Mouton 1964), 64.
55 Fischer, *Viervndfufftzig Vrsachen*, 82.
56 Clasen, *Anabaptism*, 371, 373.
57 Fischer, *Viervndfunfftzig Vrsachen*, 80–3; Christoph Erhard, *Gründliche kurtz verfaste Historia. Von Münsterischen Widertauffern: vnd wie die Hutterischen Brüder ... in vilen ähnlich, gleichformig vnd mit zustimmet sein* (Munich: Adam Berg 1589), fol. 45ro-46vo.
58 Erhard, *Historia*, fol. 33ro, ^{vo}.
59 Claus-Peter Clasen, *Die Wiedertäufer im Herzogtum Württemberg und in benachbarten Herrschaften* (Stuttgart: Kohlhammer 1965), 177–85.
60 Claus-Peter Clasen, *The Anabaptists in South and Central Germany, Switzerland and Austria. Their Names, Occupations, Places of Residence and Dates of Conversion, 1525–1618* ([Goshen, Indiana]: Mennonite Quarterly Review 1978), 10–11; Clasen, *Anabaptism*, 214.
61 Fischer, *Viervndfufftzig Vrsachen*, 113.
62 Hrubý, "Wiedertäufer," 75–8.
63 Hostetler, *Hutterite Society*, 54–6; Fischer, *Viervndfufftzig Vrsachen*, 71–3.
64 Fischer, *Viervndfufftzig Vrsachen*, 108.
65 Ibid., 64–5.
66 Ibid., 37–40.
67 Ibid., 100–1. Fischer complains of pro-Anabaptist lords, who "ein gantz Widertaufferischen Magen haben, denn dass haben sie von ihnen gesogen."
68 Ibid., 39; see Hostetler, *Hutterite Society*, 62, n. 2.
69 Robert Friedmann, "Gemeindeordnungen," *Mennonite Encyclopedia*, 2: 454–5.
70 Hrubý, "Wiedertäufer," 52–63; see the general treatments of Hutterite economics in Plümper, *Gütergemeinschaft*, 109–29; Klassen, *Economics*, 90–7.
71 Hrubý, "Wiedertäufer," 72: "Die Wiedertäufer entstammten zum grössten Teile aus dem Handwerkerstand der Städte des südlichen

und westlichen Deutschlands, oder aus der Schweiz und Tirol, selten aber aus der Landbevölkerung."

72 Clasen, *Anabaptists … Names*, 21–6.

73 Clasen, *Anabaptism*, 341.

74 Claus-Peter Clasen, "Anabaptist Leaders: Their Numbers and Background. Switzerland, Austria, South and Central Germany, 1525–1618," *Mennonite Quarterly Review* 49 (1975): 122–64.

75 Hans Amon, Leonhard Lanzenstiel, Peter Riedemann, Hans Kräl and Klaus Braidl, but not Peter Walpot.

76 Leonhard Dax, priest; Onofrius Griesinger, clerk of mines.

77 Jedelshauser, *Zwelff Vrsachen*, 9: "Hånsel Kråll ein Bawr von Kitzpichel."

78 Zieglschmid, *Älteste Chronik*, 368–78; *Chronicle*, 1: 340–8.

79 Zieglschmid, *Älteste Chronik*, 384; *Chronicle*, 1: 353.

80 Riedemann, *Account*, 126–7.

81 Hrubý, "Wiedertäufer," 71–2; Hostetler, *Hutterite Society*, 41–2.

82 See Walter Klaassen, *Michael Gaismair, Revolutionary and Reformer* (Leyden: Brill 1978), 73–102, 131–6.

83 See Thomas A. Brady, *Turning Swiss: Cities and Empire, 1450–1550* (Cambridge: Cambridge University Press 1985), 34–42.

84 Jedelshauser, *Zwelff Vrsachen*, 12.

85 Erhard, *Historia*, fol. 11vo.

86 Robert Friedmann, "The Oldest Church Discipline of the Anabaptists," *Mennonite Quarterly Review* 29 (1955): 162–6, corrected in *Mennonite Quarterly Review* 32 (1958): 236–7; see Zieglschmid, *Älteste Chronik*, 83–5; *Chronicle*, 1: 77–9; John H. Yoder, ed., *The Legacy of Michael Sattler* (Scottdale: Herald 1973), 44–5, 53.

87 John Horsch, *The Hutterian Brethren, 1528–1931* (Goshen: Mennonite Historical Society 1931), 24; trans. of Zieglschmid, *Älteste Chronik*, 436.

88 *QGT, 3, Glaubenszeugnisse*, 1: 244–7.

89 Zieglschmid, *Älteste Chronik*, 289 [my trans.]; see *Chronicle*, 1: 265–75.

90 My trans., see Riedemann, *Account*, 90.

91 The text of the third article of Walpot's *Artikelbuch*, entitled "Von der waren gelassenheit und christlichen gmainschafft der güeter," is in *QGT, 12, Glaubenszeugnisse*, 2: 175–238; there is an English trans. by Kathleen E. Hasenburg, "A Notable Hutterite Document: Concerning True Surrender and Christian Community of Goods," *Mennonite Quarterly Review* 21 (1957): 22–62. I have used my own translations.

92 *QGT, 3, Glaubenszeugnisse*, 1: 247; *QGT, 12, Glaubenszeugnisse*, 2: 175, 184.

93 "Ein lieb underrichtung Ulrichen Stadlers … der sünd halben und des ausschluss … auch gemeinschaft der zeitlichen güeter," *QGT, 3, Glaubenszeugnisse*, 1: 226.

94　*QGT, 12, Glaubenszeugnisse,* 2: 190, 195.

95　Ibid., 220.

96　Ibid., 223.

97　Ibid., 231–2, 237.

98　Packull, *Mysticism,* 106–13.

99　Jedelshauser, *Zwelff Vrsachen,* 11–12.

100　My trans., Zieglschmid, *Älteste Chronik,* 287: "... das sind geistlich Arme, die der himlischen güeter zu gwarten sindt, Vnd sälig gepreist werden. Die aber im gegentail steen, Werden Vnsälig sein." *Chronicle,* 1: 267: "... he is one of the spiritually poor. He may expect heavenly riches and will be called blessed. But unhappy are those who do the opposite."

101　Robert Friedmann, "Stadler, Ulrich," *Mennonite Encyclopedia,* 4: 607–8.

102　*QGT, 3, Glaubenszeugnisse,* 1: 225.

103　Ibid., 224–5.

104　Ibid., 225.

105　*QGT, 12, Glaubenszeugnisse,* 2: 176–7.

106　Ibid., 199–200.

107　Ibid., 225.

108　Ibid., 198.

109　Ibid., 185, 188–9, 191.

110　Ibid., 181–2.

111　Ibid., 189. Walpot goes on to interpret Matt. 19:26 as referring not to the grace by which God admits the rich man to the Kingdom, but to the grace by which God enables him to renounce his property.

112　Ibid., 201–3, 234–5.

113　Ibid., 224–5.

114　Ibid., 228.

115　Clasen, *Anabaptism,* 42; Clasen, *Wiedertäufer in Württemberg,* 68.

116　Leonard Gross, *The Golden Years of the Hutterites* (Scottdale: Herald 1980), 164–93.

117　Hostetler, *Hutterite Society,* 23.

118　Zieglschmid, *Älteste Chronik,* 180; *Chronicle,* 1: 167–8.

119　Clasen, *Anabaptism,* 296–7.

120　Conkin, *Two Paths,* 25.

121　Hostetler, *Hutterite Society,* 61–72; Conkin, *Two Paths,* 31–5.

122　Hostetler, *Hutterite Society,* 307.

123　Hostetler, *Hutterite Society,* 72–9, 91–118; Conkin, *Two Paths,* 35–48.

EPILOGUE

1　A.J.F. Zieglschmid, ed., *Die älteste Chronik der Hutterischen Brüder* (Ithaca: Cayuga 1943), 890–7; trans. *The Chronicle of the Hutterian Brethren,* 2 vols. (Rifton, N.Y.: Plough 1987), 1: 792–8.

2 N. Van der Zijpp, "Fonds voor Buitenlandsche Nooden," *Mennonite Encyclopedia*, 2: 344–6; J.G. de Hoop Scheffer, "Vriendschapsbetrekkingen tusschen de Doopsgezinden hier te lande en die in Pennsylvanie," *Doopsgezinde Bijdragen* 3 (1869): 1–26; A. Van Gulik, "De mislukte kolonisatie te Wageningen," *Doopsgezinde Bijdragen* 45 (1905): 112–68; vol. 46 (1906): 93–138; A. Van Gulik, "Uit de geschiedenis van de overkomst der vervolgde Zwitschers in 1710 en 1711," *Doopsgezinde Bijdragen* 48 (1908): 85–105; vol. 49 (1909): 127–55; W.J. Kühler, "Dutch Mennonite Relief Work in the Seventeenth and Eighteenth Centuries," *Mennonite Quarterly Review* 17 (1943): 87–94.

3 QGTS, 2, *Ostschweiz*: 228.

4 QGT, 4, *Baden-Pfalz*: 193.

5 John C. Wenger, ed., *The Complete Writings of Menno Simons c. 1496–1561* (Scottdale: Herald 1956), 558–60.

6 Michael Mullett, *Radical Religious Movements in Early Modern Europe* (London: Allen and Unwin 1980), 38–9.

7 W.J. Kühler, *Geschiedenis van de Doopsgezinden in Nederland*, 3 vols. (Haarlem: Willink 1932–50), 2: 9.

Index